WIFE MOTHER DRUNK

AN INTERGENERATIONAL MEMOIR
OF LOSS AND LOVE

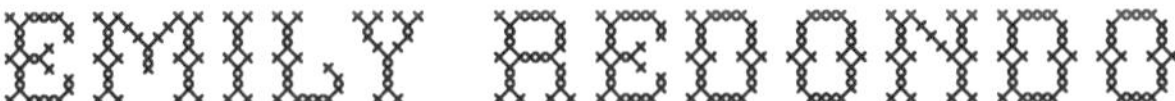

RISE
BOOKS

RISE
BOOKS

Cover design, jacket design, and illustrations by David Wojciechowski
Interior design by Neuwirth & Associates

Library of Congress Cataloging-in-Publication Data
Available on Request

ISBN 978-1-959524-07-6 (hardcover)
ISBN 978-1-959524-16-8 (eBook)

Printed in the United States of America
First Edition
10 9 8 7 6 5 4 3 2 1

For the woman hiding in plain sight, I see you.

For my children, Shelby, Rebecca, Stella, and Spenser,
I love you as is. No matter what.

"There is something in me maybe someday to be written;
now it is folded, and folded, and folded, like a note in school."

—SHARON OLDS

WIFE MOTHER DRUNK

INTRODUCTION

February 2011

"And how much would you say you were drinking, on average?" the nurse standing across from me asked as she leaned against the counter, looking at her clipboard. God, I hated that question. It was worse than being asked what the first day of my last period was, as if I had ever kept track even on my best days. A morning starting with an intake interview was not the best day.

"I don't know exactly. A lot," I said flatly.

For close to an hour, I sat in a sterile exam room, getting asked in fifteen ways about the alcohol problem that brought me to the inpatient rehab in February of 2011. Each question—what *type,* how *often,* how *long,* with or without a side of *pills* or *powder*—was a hammer to my head, pounding me like a railroad spike, beaten down enough to get run over. That's how I felt. *No one's going to pull me out of this,* I thought as I rehashed my secret drinking life out loud. It was like confessing my worst earthly sins to a priest. And I'm not even Catholic.

"Do you have any treatment goals you'd like me to add to my notes on your behalf?"

Come on, lady. I wanted my life back. I wanted those doctors and nurses to give me back my years of sobriety and erase the horror stories that replaced them.

"No, I can't think of any right now." It was almost over. Then something caught her eye.

"What's that?" she asked, pointing to a bag on the floor next to me.

"It's a breast pump," I said. She looked confused.

"For you?" she asked, giving a little point toward my chest. I hated admitting it. The nurse wasn't stupid, and neither was I as we looked at each other doing the math. No one gets to my level of drinking in a matter of days. It had been going on for months. Snip-it's of scenes from my relapse trickled into view behind my eyes, and the pain was excruciating. *I can't do this, it's too much,* I kept thinking. There was no pain reliever, no alcohol to numb me.

"We aren't set up for that here," she said.

"Oh, I didn't know," I told her, fighting back the avalanche of emotions. "Sorry. I have a nine-week-old baby at home, and I don't want my milk to dry up." She said nothing when I cried, "Please? I want to nurse him when I get home."

But I couldn't get more words to come out. I sat there hunched over, wiping snot off my nose with my sleeve—the first person to show up at the facility as a nursing mother. By a miracle, the breast pump stayed.

The first thing I noticed about my room assignment was the silence. All the other "clients" were off in classrooms or groups, and I stood there in a maternity top and a sloppy ponytail, feeling worthless. While my belongings were being searched for forbidden contraband like hairspray or dignity, I sat down on the edge of my assigned twin bed and started to wonder what my newborn, my toddler, my preschooler, my daughter in elementary school, and my overworked husband were doing in that precise moment. How were they doing? Better yet, how were they doing without me?

What I would have given to be with Spenser, to see him, touch him. A few weeks before, I was doing just that—holding him close on the couch one afternoon. I lifted him with his full little tummy after nursing him and watched his tiny back arch in a stretch the way his three sisters had done before him. I pulled him in nose to nose with me so I could smell his sweet baby's breath. I was caught in the perfect moment when I took that deep breath near his lips. I smelled a faint smell of wine, and my heart stopped dead. My life froze.

If I could have sunk down and vanished into that couch down to the ground below me, I would have. But I sat there in a moment I couldn't escape as I stared at him. What got into me? Who the hell was I? I begged to the silence that surrounded me to let me disappear into a cloud of nonexistence so those who loved me would never have crossed my path.

"Luggage," a man said with a knock, then walked away. I decided to use the pump before my afternoon schedule began. The rule stated I couldn't close my door, so I hid on the floor behind my bed and hooked up tubes with cups and funnels like a mad scientist. As soon as I flipped the switch on my 2008-model breast pump, I knew I was screwed. The machine was too loud.

One thing about rehab is people look for drama as a distraction. We can't help it. It's almost like a pre-programmed coping skill where we sniff out anything to talk and gossip about because, God forbid, we have to talk about ourselves. So I wasn't all that surprised when random voices called out from my doorway.

"The fuck?" said a 20-something male voice at my door. I ignored it.

"Are you, like, diabetic or something?" someone else asked a minute later, trying to start a conversation with the back of my head.

"Don't worry about it, keep walking, please," I said, getting more paranoid about the people in the hallway.

"She's the wine mom," someone muttered right before I switched the breast pump off. I wanted to whip my head around to see who said it but decided flashing myself to a stranger wasn't the best idea. To me, those words implied giddy day drinking from an actual glass, a circle of friends who planned playdates and always brought a bottle of vino while the kids played outside. It pissed me off. The insinuation that wine was too pretty and innocent to be taken seriously made me cringe. *Guess they're in for a surprise,* I thought. I drank wine like a drug addict, fast and alone, and it was never social or fun.

Now this. I sat there on that dirty carpet, holding my warm bottles of liquid gold. Was the hole I dug for myself too deep to even see light at the top anymore? I'd gone missing. No one knew me at all anymore.

I buttoned my bra and adjusted my shirt before I walked into the small bathroom connected to my new bedroom. A surreal emotion crossed over me as I watched the milk meant for Spenser swirl down the drain. I looked at myself in the mirror with familiar disgust. Both sides of the reflection hated each other. It was the collision of my two lives.

On one side was the stay-at-home mother and wife doing just fine after a cross-country move that separated me from family and friends. You could catch me tootling around in my minivan with a pretty smile, struggling with typical insecurities that came with the pressure of raising four young kids. We went to parks and played with sidewalk chalk. We grew a garden and played hide-and-seek. We had dance parties in dress-up clothes after dinner. I asked the same questions every mother did: Am I doing this right? Do the kids feel loved enough? Are they getting what they need?

But my other life was a private hell as an alcoholic so sneaky that even Pete, my husband, never saw me drink. Taking chugs of wine at 4 am from hidden bottles stashed all over the house to make it through the night, shoving it into my diaper bag at the grocery store the next morning, trying to sober up around dinner time when Pete came home from work then passing out after reading bedtime stories only to wake up and do it all over again.

That's what wine did for me right before it almost killed me.

Was it asking too much to want a do-over? Four times a day, I hooked myself up to the breast pump only to toss out the purest milk I ever produced for the baby I barely knew. I clung to the hope of one day nursing him. But those maternal hormones swerved aimlessly, driving me into fits of uncontrollable sobbing and me longing for the missing parts of my heart, to hold, to smell, to see. It reminded me of what I couldn't have. The sounds of my daughters' voices, the pattering of feet. I yearned to feel my tiny son pressed against my chest. I never knew grief like that.

I laid in bed at night replaying the last good-bye with my husband when we embraced before he left me there and drove back home. I wanted him to feel me saying, *I'm sorry I ruined your life. I'm sorry I did it again. I'm so sorry I ruined our kids.* And when we let go to say our "I love you's," what I really wanted to say was, *I will fix all of this. I will get better, and when I come back, I will be me again.* But I said everything on the inside, which made me feel even more like the outsider I was so used to being.

How did I become someone so unbearable in my skin that the simple act of closing my eyes to try and sleep bolted me up every night in terror? What the hell happened? The reality of my life felt like a nonstop freight train running over me, and as insane as it sounds, I wanted alcohol to save me and buffer all the pain.

All of it had to stop. I had to go home sober and get it right this time. Work harder. Get organized. Make a schedule. Make some friends. Do the steps. Clean the car. Find a church. Start a scrapbook. My entire existence depended on my decisions over the weeks to come.

But it's hard to stay sober, no matter how much I love my kids, if I still hate myself.

CHAPTER ONE

1976–1990

The smoke alarm goes off, and I am screaming across our living room as my parents shout to each other above the noise. I run to a bedroom for safety, turning into a siren myself with a blood-curdling wail as if someone is dying. Maybe me. I am two years old, and my first memory is fragmented with details of the sun shining through the windows and the temperature inside our small house in Detroit.

The first map pin in my life.

Was that the start of it? Did I crack from the sound of a smoke alarm and its aftermath? Could such an insignificant moment set off a tripwire in my little head to start me on a different path? I wondered why I remembered it so clearly, if there was more to it because this is what we do. Rather, what some of us are forced to do when we pick up a pair of imaginary binoculars and look backward toward a land we knew as childhood. Certain memories stand out right away while others gradually come into focus, sneaking into view. *Oh yeah, I forgot about that,* I think. I don't remember a lot; some I can't forget. Nostalgic, often hilarious and heartwarming, but that wasn't the point for me being there, two again, not this time.

I was searching for clues. I'd gone back to Childhood for a hundred reasons, but this time, I intentionally squinted harder and poked deeper, convinced there had to be something I missed to explain what happened. I had to figure it out but didn't know what I'd find.

Slam!

It was the way the front door closed that kept me from running to greet my dad. It was 1979, we were living in Minneapolis, and he'd come home every day close to 6 pm carrying his briefcase. If I heard a casual click in the latch, I'd scurry over for a hug, then follow him to my parent's bedroom so I could help put a wooden shoe tree into each of his leather dress shoes. It was my special honor, but not that night.

"I'm home," he called out, and maybe it was how his voice sounded that caused me to pause and watch him walk by. My father didn't say or do anything overtly alarming as my mother began to put dinner on the table, and yet he'd brought home a quiet unease too big for my vocabulary. I didn't know what it was.

My brother, Peter, three years older than me, walked into the kitchen and squeezed by the washer and dryer to give me a jab in the back. He and I were siblings, rarely friends. Our brother-sister combo, with his teasing and my tattling, sat across from Mom and Dad, and I was nervous.

Be good, I thought, while my dad slid a slice of meatloaf on my plate. A giggle accidentally escaped me when I looked over at Peter's perfect mashed potato volcano. I knew it was a mistake and nervously glanced at my parents who turned to look at his plate.

"Peter, it's not playtime," my mom said. "Just eat." But when he made one little jab at the mound and melted margarine oozed out, we thought it was funny and stifled our laughs. One slipped out, probably mine, and my father exploded.

"Listen to your mother!" my dad shouted. The boom of his voice startled me, causing firecrackers to go off my chest. I froze.

"Dan, it's fine," my mom said softly, but he ignored her, instead watching every move my brother made as Peter tried to eat. I didn't want to move. I sat suspended, anxiously waiting for the next boom to go off.

"*HEY!* Sit up straight," he shouted at Peter. "Shut your lips. And learn to chew with your mouth closed."

Not a minute later, it was, *you hold a fork like this.* He used a condescending voice, my dad emphasizing the way he held his utensil out in front of my brother's face. "It's not a shovel. Try using your brain."

All I could do was stare down at my plate, watching fat tears fall like bombs onto green peas scattered around my plate. I cried like I always did, trying to swallow my sniffles to be quiet so my dad wouldn't look in my direction.

"God *DAMMIT,* stop your crying," my dad said to me with a wham of his hand on the table. I did my best. *Hide and seek,* and bent my head down lower, eyes closed, hoping to disappear. I was four, embarrassed for being such a crybaby.

Stop it, I scolded myself. *Be a good girl.* I knew it was all my fault. The outburst started with *my* laugh, not my eight-year-old brother, Peter, and his craftsmanship for mashed potato volcanoes. The thick quiet hung over the kitchen table. I heard forks clink against Corningware plates and my mother's voice, soft again. When I looked up from my lap, the three of them were eating like nothing had happened. I didn't understand it. This beautiful mother—the one who knew how to fix, make, bake or sew anything in the world—patched us back together as if nothing had occurred. Invisible needle and thread, I watched her ask my dad if he'd like a second serving and then pick up her beer and take a sip.

"Daddy?" I said later that evening while he sat in the converted garage we called the TV room. In my Tinkerbell nightgown, my hair wet from a bath, I held out a hairbrush in my hand. "Will you brush my hair for me?"

My dad sat in his recliner in front of the television, unwinding with another beer and a box of crackers.

"Ok," he said, and I crawled onto his lap as he counted along to each gentle stroke through my tangles. "One hundred strokes for your pretty hair."

The man from the dinner table was gone. This was my nice dad, sitting in "Dad's Chair," an old recliner held together by brown-striped upholstery with a broken arm that hung outward because that was my spot, and the chair remembered to save me a space. We watched *The Dukes of Hazzard* until my bedtime with his arm wrapped around me, a perfect fit. He shushed me when I started to chatter, but I still got the message. He loved me, after all.

But look. Every day wasn't filled with dysfunctional blow-ups. Mostly, they'd come and go throughout the week in the privacy of our house. I loved my daddy. The unpredictability was part of our routine, balanced by the ordinary life of a family of four in a middle-class neighborhood outside Minneapolis. The best part of living in Minnesota was all the extended family in close proximity. My dad's folks lived nearby at their high-rise apartment across town. It had an indoor pool, which Peter convinced me had piranhas living by the drain in the deep end. We would gather with aunts and uncles from my mom's side, where I tagged along with a pack of cousins always up to something. It was all boys except for Jenny, who was older than me, like Peter and another cousin, Henry, were. My idol and undesignated boss of the show, Jenny, once saved me from getting kidnapped on a bike ride in the woods near my house. "The kid or the bike," some burly teenager said when a couple of them stopped us. It'd be hard for her to explain coming home without one of those, but Jenny was tough and shouted, "Neither!" We took off as fast as her feet could pedal, and somehow, I managed not to fall off the bicycle's banana seat. It was an act of heroism, but heroic acts were common in our genealogy. We had no idea we were part of a pattern. The generations in our family history where soldiers were the real heroes, since the American Revolution. Our lineage was marked with men who fought in the War of 1812, the Civil War, World Wars, and included the names of our dads, James and Daniel, in Vietnam.

It was a bore listening to family history. Enduring my grandma's long car drives at a 20-mph pace while she pointed out farms and houses along winding back roads on an endless afternoon. A later generation built a railroad, then another, where my grandfathers worked on the train. I found it dull and didn't care when I was young.

What gets missed in our talks about inheritable traits? Are there connections beyond eye color that tie us to our ancestors? We already know about genetic predispositions for alcohol addiction. I heard whispers and rumors relating to trauma and felt it stirring from the unspoken horrors of the pain held inside of us and the poverty we experienced.

Intergenerational trauma and addiction run throughout my family tree, flocked with the unspoken code to suffer in silence. Women and mothers tended farms and raised children while the husbands and men picked up their guns and left to fight a war they didn't start. The ones who made it home hardly spoke a word about the nightmares of combat. There wasn't talk about financial stress or family tragedy. What happened to all of their stuffed and silent misfortunes?

My great-grandma, Stella, kept quiet when her husband would disappear from the farm on a drinking bender. She never said a word, a custom passed on from proud Irish women and reinforced by a culture telling us not to acknowledge the terrible things that occurred. It passed along to her daughter, my Grandma Fern. She married a young man named Rona from a nearby farm during the start of World War II. Rona came from a big German family, hardworking parents with eight kids and a familiarity with hard times and booze. Together, my grandma and grandpa had eight children of their own, one of them being my mother, who married the same type of man as the women who came before her.

Is it any surprise that my father comes from a similar background? Both of my parents, then both of their parents stacking together, made one hell of a club sandwich. And I was underneath it. Histories of men and women affected by poverty, politics, farming, and war tapped out a pattern across time like a Morse code my little ears couldn't yet hear. The message was we didn't talk about uncomfortable things. Keep it to yourself, work hard, and eat your vegetables. Nobody spoke about problems of depression, alcoholism, suicide, abuse, and all the pent-up rage. They didn't know how, except for a whisper here and there. Silence can be heavy, and it adds to the pressure inside of a person trying to hold it all in. We say a lot with our mouths shut, but combined with all the unspoken words of my dead ancestors, my bloodline was destined for blow-ups. By the time I came along and added my little twig to the family tree, it was only a matter of time until the tinder exploded.

I adored my mother. She was the most beautiful woman in the world, except for my Aunt Sharon, her sister. But my mom had an agitation under her skin that calmed most nights when she drank. She harbored a nervousness that she'd one day name "worry." But I'd only ever known it as trouble. Was it my dad? Maybe the weather? I never knew what made her cry. Whispers on the phone about me? Peter and I constantly beating on each other? There was something in her smile that wasn't right sometimes. I always wanted her to tell me, but I was just a kid and likely didn't need to know. But between the two of my parents, there was a big space for a little girl to feel a constant threat of danger.

In family dysfunctions and my imaginative afternoons playing Star Wars or "house" with my best friend, Eric, who begrudgingly agreed to marry me, my parents sat Peter and me down one day for the unexpected news that my mom was pregnant. Boy, did they have some nerve. Trying to turn the announcement into a positive experience for me was a flop, and I wanted to wake up one morning and hear the whole "baby in mom's tummy" thing was a huge mistake. Then later, to find out it was another smelly brother? What on earth had they done? It'd be two against one for the rest of my life. And it made me angry, then sad. For six years, I'd been the youngest, the baby of the family.

What's going to happen to me? I wondered. If this baby stole my spot, then what would become of me? I couldn't even bring myself to visit the hospital to see the newborn invader. And maybe that's where I began to glitch. Adam was born in June. And if that wasn't enough of an adjustment, one month later, we moved to Texas. Everything happened so fast—the pregnancy, the baby, the move. Can a person slip through the cracks? Because suddenly, baby Adam wasn't the space invader; it was me. A missing person in my own family, an assistant-mother, and temperamental annoyance. I couldn't comprehend what was happening until I got there, but what seven-year-old would? I didn't understand how far away I'd be from my cousins and that it meant I'd only see them one time in the next couple of years. I'd never climb my favorite tree beside the house, build snow forts in the front yard, or boss around my reluctant playhouse spouse, Eric. None of it sunk in until I was a thousand miles away without a single say about it. And no way to go back.

I was lost on a different planet named Plano, Texas, what used to be a tiny town in farmland. But a hike in taxes and some reappraisals pushed the farmers out. By the time we showed up in 1982, Plano's population was full of professionals climbing the corporate ladder, eager to get rich and raise a family of high achievers like themselves in a safe, award-winning community. I wanted to go home.

When I searched the faces of my parents and Peter, it bothered me how they seemed fine. Because I knew I was not.

"You're so quiet. Are you nervous?" my mother asked on our way to register me for second grade. I was usually so talkative but didn't have the words for how I felt.

"I don't want a new school. I don't have any friends, Mom," was what came out.

"It's going to be *fiiine*, Emily. You always have lots of friends," she said for encouragement, but it felt wrong. I was never a popular kid, and the thought of having to meet new friends sounded terrifying.

Everything about Jackson Elementary was different the minute we walked in the door. I grimaced at the sight of the school secretary with her big, poufy hair and the thick, black liner around her eyes. Her lips were all gooey with a bright red gloss that smudged across one of her teeth.

"Good mornin', how can I help y'all?" she asked in a high voice. She talked weird.

"Hi, I'm Mary Ellen, and I'd like to register my daughter for school here. We're new to the area," my mom said in a professional tone that impressed me.

Down by my feet sat Adam in his baby carrier, so while the ladies carried on in conversation and my mom filled out paperwork, I crouched down in front of my new brother.

"A-boo-boo-ba-ba-ga-ga," I said to get his attention. By complete accident, the little creature was growing on me. It turns out he was adorable with his bald head, itty-bitty feet and pudgy hands. I stuck out a finger to see if he'd grab hold of it, and sure enough, he made a little fist around my pinkie.

"Emily, back up a bit, okay? Give him some room," my mom said, so I went and sat in a chair against the nearby wall.

"Oh mah gawwsh, a baaaby!" squealed the secretary, Mrs. Marshall, in her gaudy Southern accent. I rolled my eyes and listened to chit-chat about everything "baby," from outfits to sleep patterns. Even breastfeeding. *Hey, talk about me for a second?* I thought. All the excitement must have been a real thrill for my brother because he decided at that very moment to take the biggest poop of his seven-week life.

"I am so sorry," my mom said. Not half as sorry I was, until I heard the word "constipation" come out of her mouth. "Is there a place I can change him?" she asked, embarrassed, then motioned for me to grab the diaper bag for supplies. I wanted that morning like old times with my mom when we'd run errands and stop off at Dairy Queen for a Dilly bar on special occasions.

When we got back in the car, I let out a heavy sigh.

"Do you feel better about the whole school thing?" my mom asked me, and I wanted to scream, *Are you crazy?* But I just nodded. I didn't know a thing about how I felt.

We used to talk all the time, but now it felt like work to get a minute of her to myself. I didn't feel important to her anymore, and if I was, she didn't have the time to show it.

It's hard to figure out how to fit into a new place. It's almost impossible to ask questions when you're afraid of saying something stupid to highlight that you're an outsider. No one gives the new kid a handbook of do's and don'ts for avoiding unknown social catastrophes, but there I was in my hand-me-down t-shirts and homemade dresses with my tube socks pulled up to my knees.

I come from pioneers, something that should have given me some Irish guts for an adventure. My third great-grandparents, William and Eliza, decided to head west in a covered wagon pulled by oxen all the way to Pike's Peak in Colorado before deciding to turn back and settle on land once considered inhabitable in Nebraska. That's quite a bold move for a couple of farmers, especially by 1850s standards. Eliza always held my interest, and I loved her middle name. It was Jane, like mine.

One afternoon, when she was 25 years old, living out on the prairie, Eliza was home alone with her new baby when a group of native Omaha women walked into the cabin. They picked up her daughter, passing her to one another for a look as Eliza stood by quietly, frozen in fear. She watched as the women walked around the small indoor space, looking through her cupboards. Then, they handed back the infant, took one loaf of bread, and left quietly with no future trouble between them. I guess that's one way to meet the new neighbors.

Without a single thought of it, I'd gone on my own pioneer

adventure. My dad and me in the car with Sparky the cat howling in the back seat headed south down Interstate 35 on a thousand-mile journey to this strange place we'd never been. Our family left behind the richness of our little slice of history and settled in a town with no history of us at all.

Our move seemed too much for me. What lessons were passed down to my mother, letting her adjust so well, but had inexplicably skipped over me? By the looks of things, she adapted to our new world just fine, meeting the neighbors and exchanging phone numbers for future play dates with babies. I was out there flailing in the dust.

On my new street, all the houses were the same size and shape, with varying shades of light-brown bricks. Every yard had one lonely little tree that provided a shifting 3-foot patch of shade from the 100-degree summer heat. Kids my age cared about things I knew nothing about, like clothing brands, who was richer, and how big your house was. Suddenly, it mattered what you weighed, what college you liked, and who was in your friend group. All I knew was I left my Minneapolis neighborhood with quaint houses and massive trees for a suburb where everything was new and a little too perfect. Well, not that perfect.

My dad's drinking and hair-trigger temper still listed high on my concerns, but again, it wasn't discussed in the open. I didn't know what was wrong other than me. Was Plano the perfect setup for a girl like me to crack for good? Or was I already primed before we moved and would have snapped either way? The tug on the string that told me I was an outsider got stronger the more I tried to follow the new rules to fit in. I did the one thing I learned seemed to work the best. I kept my mouth shut about all of it. *Get through it.*

"Emily, can you run outside and watch Adam for a minute?" It was my mom, breaking me out of my television trance. She'd been sitting outside with a flock of other women, watching their little ducklings ride big wheels and tricycles up and down the sidewalk together.

At eleven years old, stuffing my face with food in the house for an hour or two while watching *Little House on the Prairie* was a daily ritual. I snuck sleeves of saltines, not wanting to think. I lived in a vacuum, like an invisible breath sucked up the happy days of how it used to be and blew a silent suffering that followed us from Minnesota down our chimney.

"Yeah, sure," I said, sitting up and watching a snowstorm of cracker crumbs fall onto the burnt orange shag carpet. Out in the kitchen, my mother fumbled around in the bottom cabinet next to the sink. I knew what she was doing before I saw the giant green jug in her hands. I kept walking, unbothered by the daily routine, when her afternoon wine started flowing. My mother's drinking never looked like my father's. I walked outside and looked in the mailbox, only to find a miracle. A birthday party invitation addressed to me! Sunbeams shot out of my eyes at the sight of my handwritten name and the fact somebody in my class, who was so pretty and popular, knew it and had written it down.

"Don't worry, Em. You're going to have fun," my mom said as we drove to Kammy's sleepover.

I was so nervous, second-guessing if the invitation was an accident, and there were too many girls and too much camaraderie for me. I was shy, and my sunbeams were fading. Even the pizza party was a bust when I ended up last in the kitchen, and Kammy's mom quietly said, "Two is plenty, dear, we'll be having cake." Other girls had more than two slices, and I knew why she said it. I wanted to go home, but it was late, and I doubted anyone would pick me up. We opened presents, played games, a Ouija board came out briefly, but the sight of it scared the shit out of everyone.

And then "Light as a feather, stiff as a board" was enthusiastically introduced.

"Can I try?" I asked after everyone else had a turn at trying to float off the ground using only the fingertips of friends. It looked like it worked. Maybe I'd give it a shot.

"I don't know if you can do it," said Jill, whose homeroom desk was next to mine at school.

"Yeah. You might be too big," someone pronounced, followed by a flurry of giggles like I was standing in Munchkin Land. *Who said that?* Oh, the shame I felt when the pretty witches confirmed I was the fattest girl at the party and thought it was funny.

What is it that tips the scale, where certain moments become childhood trauma for some kids, but others chalk it up as crappy moments and turn out okay? It's pressure—keeping secrets with yourself that even you don't understand. Since no one around me talked about feelings, I never learned what they were or how to deal with them. What's normal? Did other people have them? Imagine it. No friends to confide in, no adult to consult, no books on the shelf, and no computer.

We have academic and medical careers dedicated to children and how trauma impacts their development, but there isn't much written about the kids who fall in the middle, who are smashed between problems that are disguised as normal life. Our trauma isn't obvious enough to alert teachers, parents, neighbors or other grownups, so no one gets involved. It's why there's this lack of research—our skills are crafted to fool you. To be seen in families with a dysfunctional system was a constant dangerous threat.

"Kids are resilient." Then a sigh of relief. "She'll grow out of it." That's always the goal. But when Kammy and the girls from the party never talked to me again, I didn't grow out of it because I didn't know how. I settled there, getting lucky with a smile and a conversation or two. I learned most of what I knew about life on my own, true or false, by what I experienced rather than what someone coached or advised me during personal conversations.

When girls rejected me, I was the reject. When kids made fun of me, well, I was a joke.

"Hey guys, look! It's the wall clinger," I heard a boy's voice say in the seventh-grade hallway.

I didn't realize the shout-out was for me until I noticed myself sliding half my body along the walls with my head down. Jeremy, the jock who said it, had a locker next to mine.

"She's doing it again!" someone jeered for a crowd to laugh if I accidentally swiped against the painted concrete for an entire school year.

If I ever questioned whether the universe was punishing me, puberty cleared that up quickly at Haggard Middle School. I suddenly understood that people weren't looking with kind eyes at the pretty little girl anymore; they were looking with disapproval at some freak. It's jarring to watch it unfold and see nice words spoken in my direction diminish in number. I was still myself on the inside, outwardly feeling like an embarrassment. It's easy to have friends in Plano when you're thin and pretty with rich parents, but if you are the shy, awkward fat girl with big glasses and a home perm, you're screwed.

My social calendar was wide open on the weekends to tag or drag along with my parents for one of Adam's soccer games.

"Mom? Mom!" I called for her attention one Saturday. "Did you pack a drink in the cooler for me?"

The back of my thighs had melted into my lawn chair from my shadeless spot on the sidelines. I had no intention of peeling them off as I adjusted my posture, sweat drops trickling down my temples.

"Sorry, honey, the juice boxes are for the kids. It's our week," she said. "Maybe there'll be a leftover."

I cupped my hands across my forehead and squinted across the field. My father stood with other proud dads wearing the team's t-shirt and a handsome smile. He hollered encouraging advice to Adam from the sidelines on a sport he never played. My dad was living the dream at that very moment, and I watched with curiosity as a cluster of little boys ran back and forth, kicking at each other. When the game ended, my mom met Adam with open arms and handed out ice-cold drinks alongside my dad. They looked so happy as I finally got up, peeling the back of my thighs off the lawn chair to walk over and congratulate my little brother on a good game. Was I jealous? If so, I didn't know it, not yet, because I rooted for Adam along with everybody else. I didn't hate my little brother; I hated the way my parents loved him.

What did it matter anyway? The magical moment was over by the time we pulled back into the driveway.

"Hey, Phlegm-ily," Peter taunted me that afternoon in the kitchen. I turned around and shoved his taller, 16-year-old stature as hard as I could in his chest. He laughed and began singing in a Depeche Mode style *fat, fat, fat butt phlegm, phlegm-ily,* enraging me.

"Hey, ugly stupid jerkface," I said, "Shut up!" Then he knuckle-punched me in the arm.

"Ouch!" I yelled, "Come *on.*" His hit was too hard. "Mommm!" I whined, but she ignored us. We kept badgering each other in the kitchen with petty insults that usually sent me running for the lockable door of our shared bathroom to avoid a beatdown. Inadvertently, our racket interrupted my dad's television show in the adjoining family room until he sprang out of his recliner and headed straight toward us. My eyes widened. Peter and I were used to the unexpected eruptions of my father by now, but where I still instinctively reacted with fear, Peter had grown cold.

"Dammit, you two!" my dad bellowed on his approach. I started to back away. He stood right in front of Peter with his chest out like he wanted to fight, but Peter called his bluff and didn't move.

"What's your problem?" he snapped to my father. I shuddered at his audacity, thinking *Peter, shut up, what are you doing?* My feet were bolted to the ground.

"I'm sick of your shit, that's what!" My dad stepped forward as he yelled. Peter looked at him with blank eyes.

"Yeah, okay," my brother said flippantly, then tried to walk away. My dad wasn't having it, and a thousand prickly pins scattered under my skin at the sight. I stepped backward, looking for my escape, when I saw my dad grab Peter's arm, and Peter yank out of his grip and walk away.

"Get back here!" my dad shouted at him, but Peter didn't listen.

My mind raced like a fire, feeling the familiar burn of guilt over the shove I gave Peter in the first place. *Where is Mom?* I wondered, following their shouting match as it continued toward the back of the house.

The commotion spun me in circles until suddenly, I was bursting out the front door, *where's my mom?* I found her in the yard chatting with a neighbor, a plastic wine glass in hand, with Adam.

"Mom!" I shouted. "We need you." She sprang to her feet immediately. Instead of waiting for her, I raced toward my parent's bathroom. When I bolted around the corner, I saw Peter crouched over, trying to force himself backward, but my dad had his hand gripping Peter's head, trying to shove it into the toilet bowl. I let out a scream.

"Stop it!" I screeched before my mom rushed past me. "Leave him alone!" I kept crying out something, but I cannot recall what it was, only that I needed to be there and couldn't leave Peter until it was settled. But my sobbing, coming from the doorway, became a bother.

"Emily, leave! Get out of here," I was told.

Peter angrily stormed out and drove off to spend the night out with friends while the rest of us ate dinner, pretending to be a normal family. The guilt overwhelmed me. Again, I blamed myself. I could have stopped it or never started it. What got into me? I should have known better and kept my mouth shut when Peter pissed me off. I should have said the right thing at the right time to keep my dad from blowing up. Some things haunt us for the rest of our lives.

I stayed in my room most of the time after that.

"What's going on?" my mom asked me one day after school in 9th grade. Her hand reached out and stroked my hair while I hid my face in the blankets on my bed. I couldn't find words for what had become of me.

"Nothing. Everything. Dad," I mumbled to the wall, staring at a piece of bubble gum I forgot I stuck near the bedframe. "He hates us, doesn't he, Mom? Maybe I hate him too."

"Emily, don't say that. Your dad doesn't hate you; he loves you," she said, but I knew it was a lie. "Hey, what if we start going to church? Try something new, just the three of us, for a change," she suggested, meaning me, Adam, and herself. Peter had moved to Austin for his freshman year at the University of Texas. We gave it a try.

Somehow, the rows of metal folding chairs felt more comfortable than the typical warmth of wooden church pews. The Methodists were kind and welcoming enough, so we went back each week. I even started going to the youth group, loving the fact no one there knew I was a loser at school. I could be anything I wanted to be, coming out of my shell as a happy girl who fit in and had friends. I kept life inside my house to myself.

A young couple, Debbie and Terry, volunteered with our group, and their happy marriage mesmerized me. When Debbie expressed her opinion or disagreed with Terry, he didn't turn into an angry jerk. They didn't fight. They talked, even laughing and holding hands together later. I never remembered seeing my parents hold hands.

"Do you think you could help me with a service project for school?" I asked Debbie over the phone, but I already knew she would. She'd almost become my second mother over the last year.

"Of course!" This meant she'd be coming over to my house, a detail I neglected to think about until the week the work was due. She stopped over after dinnertime on a Wednesday, which was risky considering the constant ticking of the homemade bomb in the shape of my father.

As we spread out papers and poster board in the dining room and during some casual chitchat, I let something slip about my life in that house.

"It's not the greatest," was all I said, but she laughed and didn't believe me.

"Oh, Emily, what problems could you possibly have?" she asked me in a lighthearted way, which was the worst thing to hear from the one person on the planet I trusted. I only dipped my toe into the ocean of truth, and already I felt the coldness of doubt, the fear of being corrected or looking stupid, the questioning of my reality. I paused.

But who could blame her for being clueless? I was 15 years old and an expert on how to live a double life. As long as things looked fine to the outside world, the fact I was dying on the inside could stay undercover. I set it up that way, unknowingly drowning myself. I needed air.

"I think my dad's an alcoholic," I blurted out softly. I don't know why I said it. I'd never said that word before. As her expression turned into confusion, I wanted to suck the words back into my mouth.

"Really? Wait, how much does he drink every night?" she asked, and I didn't know how to measure something like that. I pictured the kitchen trash can and its nightly build-up of beer cans, then guessed at the number in my head.

"Well, he stops at a bar or drinks in the car driving home after work, but here at the house, around eight beers a night," I said, unsure if that met the qualifications for a problem or not until I read the cues on Debbie's face. I knew it wasn't good.

She looked uncomfortable the rest of the evening.

"I'm sorry," I kept telling my mom a couple of days later after Debbie called her.

"Emily, you have nothing to be sorry about," she said, but I saw she was upset, and I knew I had done something wrong. She made an excuse for the two of us to sneak out in the evening for a support group called Al-Anon and Alateen, where we sat in separate meetings. For the first time, I was in a room of teenagers with parents like my dad, and I listened to a kid tell a story about hiding under his bed from his drunk and pissed-off father. I don't know how he did it—it was such a tragically awful scene to talk about—but he told it in a way that had everyone in the room laughing hysterically. Even I almost let out a snicker. If I hadn't been so insecure and terrified of being noticed, I might have actually enjoyed the hour when I didn't feel so different from everybody else.

The contrast of walking to the car with sore cheeks from all the smiling compared to my mother walking next to me with red, swollen eyes and wads of snotty Kleenex in her hand from crying created a burden of shame that hid inside my chest. The place where I was finding connection with a bunch of misfits was the same place breaking my mother's heart, like a birth and a death all in one space.

My dad unofficially designated me his enemy the day he found out about what I told Debbie and where my mom and I went on our weeknight outings.

"Either she snaps out of this, or she's leaving!" he bellowed from my parent's bedroom.

"Come on, Dan, where would she go?" my mom said back.

"Send her to a relative! Hell, send her to boarding school for all I care!"

In a house our size with hollow doors, Adam and I heard the fighting, never saying a word to each other about them. I sat in my bedroom listening to my dad blame my mother and me for all the misery in his life. He boomed that he'd give to me exactly what I'd given him, "jack shit." Still, I pretended my dad would wake up the next morning and be different like he was in that armchair back in Minnesota brushing my hair. Maybe this time, he'd even apologize and mean it. He'd love my mother and give up the booze. He'd choose us. I even imagined my mom coming in and telling me everything would be okay and that she would finally be happy. I waited, but none of that happened.

By 15, I was already asking myself *what happened to my family? Why can't I get it right for once? Where did I go wrong?* I hated how I still wanted the same fairy tale of a happy family. It was the same dream every woman on my family tree seemed to want, but for some reason, I messed things up. Forget all the effort of trying to figure out the unspoken rules and be good all the time, I'd just settle for proof I was lovable. That I wasn't alone.

Six months later, our house was still a war zone, with my dad unable to put a cap on his drinking. My mom stopped me in the kitchen on a Friday afternoon.

"Hang on, I need to talk to you," she said with seriousness in her voice.

"Now what?" I said with an eyeroll.

"I have something to tell you about myself," she started to say. "And I'm not sure you're going to like what you hear." I stood there waiting.

"Emily, your dad's not the only alcoholic in this family, I'm . . ." But I cut her off, refusing to let her say the worst words any mother could say to their child.

"What?!" Feeling all the blood go up to my face. "Are you KIDDING?" I shouted in an awful panic. *She's lying,* I thought.

"I'm an alcoholic, too," she said through a sob, reaching her hand out for me to hold. My mom wanted to love me through the emotional apocalypse, but I wanted none of it. I shook my head to shake off the words and wanted to run away from all of it. I wished I had somewhere to be with friends I didn't have.

"Emily, wait," she pleaded, wanting to talk more, but it was too late. I stormed out the back door.

It made little sense; alcoholics were mean and loud and unpredictable, but my mother never spewed hatred in my face in a drunken rage or humiliated me in public. She was generous, kind, and timid.

When I looked back, my memories deceived me. The entire perspective changes when you remove the elephant from the room. I overlooked my mom—the same affliction I felt she'd done to me. The truth came through so clearly that I felt dumb to have missed the constant gallon jugs of wine and daily morning headaches. Broken wine glasses across the kitchen floor because she drank too much. The times I thought she wasn't listening to me like she was somewhere else because she was drunk. Her glazed look late at night because she was drunk. The calmness on stressful days at home because she had wine to numb her nerves.

The human brain can only stuff itself with so much before it all overflows and infiltrates areas that trigger a response, seemingly out of nowhere. I ran out of methods to survive. And I was overflowing.

I wanted to start over with everything, so I began every nightly prayer with an apology for bothering Him. Because if, by some chance, God saw me lying in my bed surrounded by such a mess, then He already knew I didn't look like those other kids at church. I felt unworthy of a private conversation, like I had cut in line in front of the good kids, who didn't have unanswered prayers. But me? I'd been bad from the beginning.

What if God was already disappointed in me?

"What did you just say?" my dad asked, glaring at me from across the table.

Right away, my brain flooded with confusion. I was a little girl again, stomach churning. *Did I say something? What did I say?* I might have mumbled something, but I couldn't recall what it was. Friday nights were notorious for my father coming home late, half-cocked and ready for a fight so he could storm out and head to his favorite bar.

"Nothing," I said, trying not to look at him.

"You got a problem with me?" he snapped loudly. I just shook my head and stole a glance at my mom.

"Can I leave the table?" I whispered pleadingly to her. "Can I eat in the dining room? Just for tonight?" She shook her head, not really as an answer, but as a warning to convey, *lower your voice, Emily. You will set him off, please!* I was desperate. So was she.

"No." The answer came from my dad. "You think you're too good for us?"

For the next thirty minutes, we sat hostage to the escalation of anger that eventually sprang him up from the table in a screaming fury. He was mad if we said something and mad if we didn't. Any attempt by my mom to calm him down only made things worse. Dishes banged while he shouted insults to us about how hard he works and how miserable we make his life when he comes home. Chairs and drawers slammed and crashed like background percussion, and I just sat there with my head bowed in a silent cry while it all went to hell. Like old times.

"I hope you're happy." His parting words before the back door slammed left us whiplashed from the cyclone.

I went straight down the hall to the bathroom, locked the door, and stood there. Then, without a thought, I stuck two fingers down my throat and gagged myself over the toilet. Nothing happened. I bent over and did it again, gagging repeatedly from my fingers reaching down my throat until I started throwing up everything that happened at dinner and then some. When I stood back up with a pounding head and watery eyes, I was empty. Gone were the emotion-attached memories I couldn't understand. Gone was my father's anger, my mother's silence, and the generations of unacknowledged tragic pain I didn't understand but somehow felt. My throat burned from the bitterness. But the relief I felt afterward—that hollowness and peace—became the answer I'd been searching for.

Everyone's got secrets. And I had mine.

x

Back in Minnesota, only two blocks away from our house, where I'd drag my feet and whatever doll I happened to have with me, I'd stare longingly out the front window, watching my mother drive away for the day. The minute she was out of sight, my babysitter, Nancy, opened a door just off the kitchen, and a feeling of yuck would fill my stomach.

"Okay, Emily, here you go. I'll call you when it's time for lunch," she'd say, and like a good girl, I walked down the stairs every time to a dimly lit basement, where a matching old couch and recliner, a television, and a corner bathroom I never used became my playroom for the next eight hours. At lunchtime, a light beamed down from the top of the stairs, and Nancy's voice called me to come eat.

"Emily? Come on up. I made you a grilled cheese sandwich." And I rushed up the stairs, pausing at the top while my eyes adjusted to the sunlight. She had a daughter my age who occasionally ate lunch with me, and I always wondered why I wasn't allowed to play with her. I chewed slowly, or at least tried to, but eventually ended up back down in the basement with *Tom and Jerry* cartoons.

It was so boring that even now, I can still feel the slowness of time and how it startled me like a surge of electricity when I'd see someone else was suddenly down there—an older boy, maybe late teens. I kept my eyes glued on the television when he walked in front of my show, unzipping his jeans on his way to the bathroom to shower. When that door reopened, a billow of steam would waft out with the bright light behind it. He walked toward me with his hand on the tuck of the towel at his waist, and my stomach got really sick inside. I gripped my hands together, pushed myself back into the couch until I felt almost frozen, and then poof. The memory stops. What remains is a blank spot, like a film cut concretely, and every time, my recall ends the same way.

I would pick apart that memory, toying with the red string that might connect me to my later madness to wonder, *Was I molested?* That zone of adulthood insanity, in institution after institution, where I obsessed over things my childhood brain blocked out, wanted facts and proof. Sometimes, it still does, although I've grown to trust the child who instinctively knew not to tell her mother anything about my days at Nancy's house. We know why. Still, was a babysitter's basement only a remnant of string or something already unraveling? I didn't know, but it was always there, on a shelf in my mind. And it's possible that my mother's drinking problem was on that shelf, too.

CHAPTER TWO

1991–1992

"Okay, what's going on with Emily?" the doctor asked, flipping through the papers I filled out in the waiting room. He wasn't sure who to address, me or my mother. I smiled politely from the exam table, suggesting I was perfectly fine.

"I caught her throwing up the other day. She's losing weight," my mom said, disturbed and worried like it pained her to say it out loud. She sat in a chair across from me on the brink of tears. "She doesn't look well, not to me."

"I see. How long has this been going on?"

It wasn't supposed to go this way. The secret was never meant to come out; it was supposed to be mine, just for me. But I blew it by forgetting to lock the bathroom door. My mother caught me, and the poor woman went directly into despair. To salvage the mess, I listened to the doctor give a brief lecture on ways I was damaging my internal organs while he drew my blood. Like a good pupil, I nodded along with a look of concern, promising to wise up and quit being so foolish. I offered a lie of hope to the mother I loved, but I never intended to stop.

How could I tell them that what I was doing actually made me feel better? That the blood-shot eyes, fatigue, even the dried cracks in the corners of my mouth were all worth it? The world out there was nicer now. This was hope, not a crisis; leave me alone. No doubt I was naïve about a thousand things going on around me, but one fact was clear—people see you when you're thin. You're capable of being pretty when you're thin. Thin meant you were likable. And God, I wanted you to like me.

Even my dad showed occasional signs of promise.

"We're still going this weekend, right?" I asked my dad nervously. Our relationship developed into a tenuous game of Hot Potato where we tossed each other verbal grenades and then waited to see what happened next.

"Yep!" he said that Monday, but by Friday he made plans to go fishing on *our* Saturday.

"We'll go when I get back," he promised me. I didn't know how my feelings still got hurt anymore.

He walked in Saturday evening while I sat waiting at the kitchen table, and our eyes met under the florescent kitchen lights. He was wasted. Denial can be so powerful we ignore what's right in front of our face.

"Can we still go?" I asked him even though my mom was shaking her head in the background. "We can at least look around for a little while."

At the dealership, an unlucky salesman got swept up in the grandiosity of my drunk father, overinflating his voice, his pride, and his pocketbook. I tagged along, uncomfortably watching the show of him pretending to be the big man on campus. To do otherwise would be tossing out a grenade and risking a public explosion. Inside the lobby, I sat alone for an hour until my dad emerged from an office with a proud grin on his face and headed out the front door.

"What happened?" I asked him as we got back in his truck.

"I bought you a car; what do you think happened?" my dad asked, pulling out onto the street. *Grab a grenade, pull the pin. Toss. Boom.*

"Dad!" I said, too loud for the proximity, but I couldn't afford the car the salesman convinced my father I needed. "I didn't want that one. I told you I don't have enough money for the payments, we didn't even talk." Another *BOOM!* because I said too much. He was shouting at me and driving down the highway like an intoxicated maniac, so I immediately started crying and apologizing. The sound of my voice infuriated him more, and in the middle of a *sorry*, I looked at the traffic in front of us.

"I don't think you should be driving," came out of my mouth followed by the realization I said something utterly forbidden. He swerved over and slammed on the brakes in the middle of the road near a concrete median separating six lanes of traffic.

"Get out," he told me, and I looked out my passenger window at all of the cars whizzing by. He wanted to put me in my place and scare me. *Screw it*, I thought to myself. If he wanted to play games, I'd play. I opened my door and jumped out to the sound of whooshing vehicles and honking horns.

I made my way a mile or two back to the dealership, where a few salesmen still lingered after hours. I called my mom from an office phone, then sat and waited outside on the steps for her to come get me.

It was actually a nice night. The stark contrast between my dad and the men in loosened neckties standing behind me like watchdogs overwhelmed me with so many feelings. Part of me wanted to turn around and tell those men not to worry. My dad wasn't coming back for me.

Somewhere that night, he was shutting down a bar with strangers, and long after I'd fallen asleep, he crept back home to sleep it all off like he did every single time. Later I wondered, when he walked to his bedroom, did he pause by my door to see if I made it back home? Did he think about me at all?

I'd be hard-pressed to find a teenage girl who didn't argue with their parents, but we didn't fit the standard family model. We'd never heard stories or bought books explaining how alcoholics lead double lives. I knew nothing about addiction; I just saw two versions of my parents. But addiction to alcohol is a fluid sickness. It seeps in slowly, coming up through the floor cracks and sneaking out of nail holes that hung pictures of us on the walls. It wasn't just the ones who were drinking. We all got soaked. We all lived double lives.

Families like mine have unspoken rules: *don't talk, don't trust, and don't feel,* but the oversimplifications, while helpful, left out how exhaustingly complicated it could be. My guard was always up. I was always pushing down anxious energy, deciphering cryptic messages and passive mannerisms, keeping a close eye on every mood. In truth, I had no concept or understanding I was participating in "The Cycle." It was just me against *him. Both of them. It.* I was fighting some elusive enemy that kept ruining the family portrait I painted in my head. Never did I tie a string between my parent's alcohol addiction and myself. No connection existed beyond the thought of, "I'm never going to be like that," and I meant it. It's only now, decades later, that a shred of understanding is offered as to why someone like me, living inside a bomb factory, started drinking.

"Just try a sip," said a voice from the front seat, handing me a red plastic cup.

There I was, my junior year of high school, squeezed against the window in the back seat of a car next to my friend, Tracy, and two friends from her school across town. I swallowed down the grape taste of something called Purple Passion, most likely found in a gas station refrigerator bottom shelf somewhere next to Mad Dog 20/20.

It was 1991 and when Pearl Jam's new song started playing through the speakers full blast, I smiled because I thought it was a sign.

"I—I'm still alive," I sang along, exactly how I felt when a weight lifted off me and a tingling sensation trickled up my neck and into my ears. *This is the buzz I heard about.*

It was fun driving around and going back to someone's house later to hang out, but I didn't know the group and couldn't add to the stories they told and laughed over. I still thought they were funny. The entire night would have been forgotten if it weren't for the alcohol, for how it made me feel. Because, like every alcoholic's story told before me, I liked the effect. What I didn't like was coming home at the end of that night. In the strange space between my two worlds, a knotted feeling pulled me in opposite directions. I'd joined the drinking club. But the bowels of an alcoholic home were nothing like my lighthearted night with friends. I thought the feeling in my gut was a sign I was different from my parents. I didn't know it was my own knot, attaching me to the beginning of the same rope choking us all.

To drink was to live, as far as a high school social life was concerned. I even made a few friends out of the deal when word went around one Friday night someone's parents had gone out of town. It's why my house was packed with people who didn't know me, but by the night's end, I was sucking face with Matt, our student body president. He even put his hand up my shirt and touched my bra. A major first for me. When we stared into each other's eyes, I was convinced we were transmitting love messages about being together 4EVR.

"I have to go, but you're awesome," he whispered at the end of the night.

Monday morning, I walked into school, starring in a teenage romcom playing in my head. Finally, *the cool crowd.* But as I walked the crowded hallways between classes and saw the same kids who were in my house spilling schnapps on the carpet, they wouldn't look at me. Worse was seeing the girls. We talked so easily like friends that night, and how coldly they stared right through me, like I wasn't even there. Matt was no different. I watched him avoid me until the last second then glance in my direction, only a quick head nod in passing. I was erased, by them all, like some sort of mistake. It was a bad ending reminiscent of Kammy's birthday party all over again. I never looked at him, at any of them, again.

In my run of bad luck, I got fired from my job at a pizza place. Better said, I was told to resign immediately by my manager when twenty bucks went missing from the same register he opened when he took a pretty girl to lunch. I was so appalled by the accusation that I might have called his wife if I had the phone number. It all turned into a nice opportunity for a fresh summer job before my senior year.

I decided to work at an outdoor day camp with kids doing outdoor games and crafts, a little fishing, and singing cheesy camp songs. I found out on my first day that the other twelve counselors were college kids, meaning a safe escape from high school faces for a couple of months.

"Do you have a boyfriend?" asked one of my new friends, Amanda, after work one day. We sat with two other girls on a blanket at the park while a few of the guys tossed around a football close by.

"Ha! No," I said with a little eye roll.

"Seriously? I don't believe you," she said.

"I've never had a boyfriend. Never even been on a real date," I told them.

"Are you fucking joking? Guys around here must be insane," Dani chimed in, and it put a smile on my face.

"Chad's totally into you, I can tell," said Amanda with a devilish look, and my heart skipped a beat. "So you better be prepared for a first date." She had a teasing voice that made us laugh.

She was right.

"Hey, Emily, do you have plans this weekend?" Chad asked after camp.

"Not really," I told him, feeling awkward suddenly.

"Okay, so Saturday. Can I buy you dinner?"

No one had ever asked me on an official date. Chad was a cute guy, with blonde hair and a nice tan, but not someone I'd particularly choose, were there more options. I knew nothing about dating, romance, the process or the timelines.

"Wow, you look really pretty tonight," he said across the restaurant table.

"You're lying, but thanks," I said, brushing off the compliment because it felt uncomfortable. But also, nice. My idea of a love story was *The Little Mermaid* and *Footloose,* a tell-tale sign of why I froze when he reached across the table and gently caressed my forearm before holding my hand. No one had ever touched me like that.

I think he really likes me, I began to believe. That night ignited the possibility that there was something lovable about me. It felt sophisticated and mysterious to date someone older, and as the weeks went on, I thought we were falling in love. Maybe things were different on his end, and he got razzed for having a girlfriend still in high school. Maybe his friends made fun of him for dating a virgin all summer long, and that's why we started talking about sex right before he went back to school. But it wasn't because of love, not when boyfriend and girlfriend meant pool parties, drinking, petty fights and making out to second or third base. When summer was over, Chad went back to college for his sophomore year, and I went back to high school as a senior, still together but in separate directions.

Then, in early September, Chad came home for a weekend visit and without a warning or discussion, we took the plunge. Or did we?

Wait a second, I said to myself, driving home that night. *Was that . . . sex? Did I just have sex?* Because honestly, I wasn't sure. It happened so fast. He put it in, he took it out, and it was over. I thought there must be more to it. My curfew was midnight, the reason I raced out of his parents' apartment so fast, but there wasn't much to say about the experience. It felt more like a dot of punctuation at the end of a long sentence. It's probably why we never talked about it.

He called me later that night, and I could tell from his voice he was smiling. We kept it short.

"I love you," he said, causing me to inhale sharply and wiggle my toes because I wanted to scream with excitement, *Hooray!*

"I love you, too," I said, and I meant it. We both let out a sigh of relief before we said goodbye and hung up.

But age makes a difference when it's 17 and 20. Weekend visits slowed down as college campus came to life, but I told him, "That's fine! No problem," and laughed it off like no big deal. The heat of summer cooled into fall when a worry took up residence in my mind. By late October, or was it early November, I wasn't laughing anymore.

I drove home during off-campus lunch after making a quick stop. In the hallway bathroom, while no one was home, I stared down at a pee stick with double red lines, but my brain could not believe it. *No. This can't be right. This isn't me. Do it again.* The second test from the box, studying the instructions, the agony of waiting. Another positive test, thinking, *I'm a good person, a good student, this doesn't fit me.*

Suddenly, my body felt so hot, and my vision lost focus, and I slunk down to the cold bathroom floor. I sat there, afraid to open the door and let the truth out, listening to my ears ring and watching my future life pass by until poof. Nothing.

I can't be late for English today, was my next thought. I'd never been tardy to a class, not even once. I sat at a red light, trying to snap myself back. *I am pregnant,* I thought, but I couldn't quite get the information to move over out of the way. *I am pregnant?* When I sat down to take the English test, I stared in a fog at the paper, watching words blur into black-and-white clouds of nonsense. *Pull it together, or you'll fail.*

Everyone around me needed to know I was fine, a good person. And good people were good students, and good students made good grades. I took a couple of deep breaths to muster up 45 minutes' worth of focus. I took the test in a familiar fog reserved for girls like me who roamed high school hallways—the swallowed-up ones with pretty smiles.

Seventeen was supposed to be the age of fresh anticipation where our future was finally ready to leap out of grade books and into young adulthood. Girls like me looked the part by being polite and quietly attractive, blending in nicely with the background. Bad things were happening in our lives, but not bad "enough" to end up on anyone's radar in a school with 2,400 students. How unfortunate to be so well-disguised that we didn't even recognize the same pain on one another's face. Maybe if our circumstances were obvious—dead parents, a severed leg—someone would have seen us, but we hide things for reasons.

Chad didn't want a pregnant girlfriend. That's why he gave me the money. I kept the pregnancy a secret. I couldn't bring myself to tell my mother because, in my eyes, it was another burden for her to withstand, another heartbreak, another sad story about the daughter she loved so much.

My mother was never shy to mention her intelligence and accolades. She was the 17-year-old senior in high school I may have hated, the popular class president who joined all the clubs and graduated 2nd in her class. My grandma Fern had already graduated by that age. She lived at home to help on the family farm and taught grade school part-time. To compare myself to those women and come up remarkably short devastated me well beyond the limits of my understanding. It felt as though I'd cast a permanent mark of shame on all the women who'd outdone me now and in the generations before me in my family.

I remembered reading somewhere about Fern's great-grandmother. She moved the entire family farm to another state from the utter disgrace of her unwed daughter getting pregnant because the risk of judgment was too high. It translated now to mean everyone would hate me. Would they publicly shame me? Shun me out of town? My head swam with childish-sounding questions that pulled at a primal need for survival and made things like rejection or abandonment feel life-threatening. The young were not created to survive on their own.

I asked God to send a car to crash into me on the way to my appointment, but it didn't happen. I tried to barter with Him to let me cut off my hand instead, but no. As soon as my sneakers reached the sidewalk leading to the building, picketers shouted at me and shoved blown-up pictures of fetuses cut into pieces in front of me. I noticed they were doing it "in the name of our savior, Jesus Christ" and to save what was growing inside me. I heard the name and for a second I thought, *I know him, we were just talking.*

"Murderer!" The shouts rang out from the crowd. It took a minute to register they meant me, that I was the murderer.

"Do you want to go to hell?" a woman near me by the sidewalk asked, leaning toward me. She looked like a witch. *Why would you say that?* I thought as I rushed inside the doors.

Right and wrong, winners and losers; it was the easy way to split a crowd and ignore how complicated it was to be human. For the vast majority of God-loving Texans that year, abortion meant you were nothing more than stupid trash and a selfish sinner. Case closed. They didn't have to see a different perspective, blessed, I guess. There was no need for them to consider less divisive lines where what's right for them may not be right for me, or what looks simple for them may be impossible for me. I wasn't there to argue or upset anyone, and whatever lie they believed about me was their doing, not mine. They offered me nothing more than a reminder that only unborn lives were worth saving. From the lobby, I glanced back over my shoulder at a scene forever stuck in my head. Maybe I didn't know why they were there at all.

"You'll need to undress and put these on," a nurse told me when I walked into the sterile room and started to sit on the exam table. "I'll be back in a few minutes." Then she walked out and closed the door behind her.

Taking my clothes off felt strange. I didn't want anyone to see me naked or look at my body, not even a doctor. I'd never had a basic pelvic exam, and the thought of someone staring at my vagina scared me. *I don't want to be here, dammit,* but I propped myself up on the table and stayed. I wished I had more money for the extra cost of anesthesia so I could wake up and it would all be over.

"Scoot your bottom down more, please," the doctor said before a touch landed on one of my bare legs. I flinched. A nurse held my hand for comfort, then used her soft voice to tell me what was happening "down there." I kept my eyes on hers when the sound of a machine startled me and squeezed her hand when I felt a foreign pain inside of me.

The procedure was over in minutes.

"Do you have someone you can talk to when you get home?" asked a nurse later, walking me out a back exit to avoid the crowd.

"Me? Oh, yes," I said. "Thank you." I turned to sit on a cement block at the edge of a shaded parking space as we said goodbye, then she closed the metal door. I tried to wrap my head around what happened, thinking *when did it go so wrong? What happened to me?* I didn't know what to do at that moment with my time. It was too late to go back to school and too early to go back to my house. I thought I should cry, but I couldn't. I wanted to pray and talk to God, but now I was too afraid He'd be angry with me. It was an awful thing to judge myself with the same callousness as those strangers and feel my faith dissolve in front of me. There wasn't enough room left over in my head for another traumatizing experience, not without a finger pointing me out as the cause of death, as if I didn't know. I went home and walked in the door with homework due the next day.

Something horrible happens, and we want our idea of normal to come back. Returning to my everyday life, I pictured what occurred as staying thirty miles away where I left it, and each day that followed took me another mile further from it, as if time and distance could erase the past. Chad was my boyfriend, my house was a war zone, high school graduation was six months away. But I couldn't ignore the new emptiness I had for a companion. It was a quiet, impenetrable space with both a flatness and ferocity, like a weightless steel room. No one could see inside. My artificial social life remained with a little group of friends and random drinking on the weekends, where I got drunk for other reasons, the way outsiders often do. Chad visited me from college, but we didn't last. I'd had an abortion, and he got angry when I wanted to talk about it.

"Why bring this up again? You always act like it's this huge thing, Emily. Like you're trying to make me feel sad or something. It sucks that it happened, but it worked out. What the fuck do you want? Seriously, you sound so negative. Why do we need to talk about this?" It was the last time I brought it up, and the first time I realized how lucky Chad was. I should have ended it there, but my lack of courage prevented me from breaking it off with him completely. Eventually, I could no longer pretend I didn't hate the sight of him. The constant accusations looked pathetically shallow when I started to pull myself away, and I grew to despise his jealous outbursts with an equally silent hostility. By the time we went to prom together, it was over.

My voiceless state of existence was supposed to be an act of self-preservation. When someone young and naïve is drowning, our instinct kicks in. We do what we know, and what we know is what we see every day. Let's hope it's enough. Naturally, I turned inward and had a hard time believing that love was ever kind or patient. I didn't know what was true, but I kept hearing those ladies' voices in my head. I may have killed a baby, but they destroyed my faith in God. I guess we're all a bunch of sinners in the end.

CHAPTER THREE

Fall 1993–1994

"I guess this is goodbye," I said, standing in my tiny dorm room on the massive campus of Texas A&M University in the fall of 1993. Sounds of heavy footsteps of parents and their daughters lugging boxes up the stairway and nervously chatting wafted into my room through the gap under my closed door.

"Just for now," my mom said to comfort me. I wasn't ready for her to leave. I had so much more to say.

"I'm going to miss you," I told her, leaving out how scared and lonely I already felt. When she told me I could call her anytime, I knew she meant it. She stood right in front of me with her hands on my shoulders and looked straight into my eyes, but I felt a cry beginning to burn behind my nose, so I looked away. She was the strong one, not me. And I wanted to be more like her.

My mother leaving that day was the equivalent of losing half of myself. Were we bonded, enmeshed, codependent? I don't know, and a proper word didn't matter because, at that very moment, more important things were on my mind. I worried how she'd do without me at home, and I worried about Adam, too, who was next in line for my dad's angry outbursts without me there to shield him. And where the hell do I go for my student ID?

I hate to admit it, but I thought a high school diploma and a change in geography would end the chapter of my childhood, and I'd magically show up on the starting line for my actual life. We graduated into young adults on an equal playing field now, right? That was the idea: a fresh start. It's strange, then, for some of us to realize we'd spent years fixated on wanting to leave, only to wind up taking it all with us when we did.

Did I actually pull off a miracle and put it all behind me? For a while, I thought I did. My first week of school, I met a few girls who became my circle of friends. Monica and her twin sister, Teresa, along with two other girls, Sadie and Bella. I thought four friendships meant I was set for life. Although, when I could have chosen any crowd to gravitate toward, I hung around people like the ones who burned me in high school, likely because it was easy. We do what we know and settle for what's familiar. It's tolerance, and that's exactly what I practiced in the new circles of strangers I knew so well but didn't know at all. I went along with it, just happy to be on the scene, never considering I might be happier elsewhere around a different crowd.

"Hey! There's a huge party tonight, Brandon's going. He wants to know if we'll be there," Sadie informed me with a wink on a Friday morning in late September. We walked together for a minute on our way back to the dorms, putting a plan together for later that night. We'd all meet up at my dorm. Sadie would bring the alcohol, like usual.

To call it an "identity crisis" would give the impression I saw a problem with my new and wild ways. Parties, drinking, boys, all of it was incredibly fun at that moment, to the point of almost forgetting I had another life underneath all the excitement. I never mentioned an eating disorder to my new best friends despite how often I threw up in community bathrooms. I didn't want to get into the story of why my parents were getting a divorce after 24 years of marriage or the fact my family was broke and theirs wasn't. Why tell them I had sex on dates more than they ever did when the point was to make friends, not lose them? Who wants to talk about killjoys and financial aid? Let's trade clothes instead.

I had a job that semester, unlike my close friends, and was working as a model at an agency in Dallas. To them, it sounded glamorous, but to me, it was money for college and raging insecurities. All I could think about when I put my key in the ignition later that morning was whether or not I looked fat.

"Beautiful, just beautiful," Claire, my boss, said when I finally stood in her office after the three-hour drive. Her hair was pulled back in a tight bun tied with a scarf as she looked me over like I was center stage at a cattle auction. *Blue eyes, long brown hair, tall, 19 years old. Do I have any bidders?* Something about her appearance reminded me of old money, the kind reserved for people who've never been without it. My clothes felt wrong. I should have worn a short skirt. Curled my hair a little. Different shoes. Anything other than the denim shift dress I wore with a pair of flats.

"How are classes going, Emily?" she asked me.

"Pretty good so far, I think," I said. "Chemistry is going to kill me." It sounded fake. Why can't we just tell people we're nervous? Or shy?

"Yes, yes," Claire said with a nod "Have you heard of the 'Freshman Fifteen?' We need to watch out for that, okay?" And right as she said it, I felt the blood rush out of my face. *Jesus Christ, it's true. I'm getting fat,* I thought. The mental checklist of Diet Coke, the bag of pretzels, Tic Tacs, and gum that day seemed fine until I remembered the taco run at 2 am. *What was I thinking??*

"She looks fine to me," her assistant chimed in, but Claire decided to mention the option of plus-size modeling anyway. I watched the assistant shake her head slowly as if to disagree, and when Claire's eye caught the gesture, she informed me of upcoming work available.

Why did she have to make it so miserable?

Claire could have invited me into her office and simply said, "Great news, there's a job coming up that's perfect for you," and told me how once or twice a month, I'd fly to cities in Mexico for Winston car races, assuming I could travel with my schedule, and I would have said, "Wow, yes!" It paid the bills, which was the whole point, and my self-esteem wouldn't have splattered across the floor. Instead, I walked elegantly toward the exit and gracefully doused the room with my gratitude. I thought I owed it to them like I was a charity case.

On my way out the door, three other girls sat in the front lobby, waiting their turn at auction. Females can size each other up in less than ten seconds, and that's exactly what we did. Tallest, thinnest, best hair, all-American, edgy, runway, those types of things. It's always someone's turn.

Beauty. Something changes when we outgrow the innocence of our mothers being the most beautiful women in the world. For a lot of women, it's our first abusive relationship. The beginning stages of praise and attention, even the subtle stares we pretend not to notice, romancing us into believing that we've got potential. A shot, not at just being pretty but of being exceptionally pretty. Perfect. Flawless. Just the idea and I was swooning.

I wanted beauty, and I wanted it to love me the most, like a million other college girls sitting in their dorm rooms flipping through a stack of fashion magazines. How you looked was the key to getting the guy. Best guy for the prettiest house and the perfect life. But then it turns, our love affair with beauty, the way it does with all abusers. The ugly truth was as soon as we got behind closed doors, the beatings began. Bashing ourselves with insults for the tiniest imperfection, we stared at our bodies obsessively. The eyes, our thighs, a pimple on our skin. The width around a waist, a pudge below the navel, skin around the elbow, the cellulite got bashed for hours with glossy ads and on-screen alterations lecturing that we are flawed individuals. I stuck around because I still believed in fairy tales and the perfect shade of pink. And it beat me up for years.

Who wouldn't want to come unglued after a day like that? I wasn't going back to campus for a six-mile run or a pottery class to blow off steam, and the thought of anything beyond my friends, alcohol and boys didn't stand a chance to ever register as a better idea. I was going to a keg party.

"So many guys!" Monica shouted over her shoulder when we walked into the crowded keg party with her sister and Sadie that night. I nodded enthusiastically wearing my favorite little t-shirt tucked into a tight pair of boot-cut jeans as I held her hand into the middle of the mayhem. A push from my left, then right, when a line of girls shoved past me, and I lost her in a sea of sweaty coeds.

"Mind if I buy you a drink?" some guy said and the humor caught my attention. Drinks were free. He handed me a red cup of cold beer, and with each sip, I could not care less about the details of my sweaty appearance or the stress of my day. Pesky thoughts about calories buzzed across my mind like a fly I couldn't swat, but I'd deal with the annoyance later. Somewhere in our flirty conversation, he said his name was Ben, a sophomore from Houston. Ten minutes later, we kissed. Not some romantic display of affection, but a beer-breathy face mash with my hair sticking to the sides of his face until my friends came looking for me. It was great.

"Jesus, Emily," was all Monica said before the burst of laughter escaped me, and those four best friends of mine joined in. Ben stared at me, his eyes captivated by my mixture of innocence and recklessness. He promised to call the next day, and he did. In fact, Ben took me to dinners and walked me to class. He turned out to be such a nice guy I wondered if maybe my luck had changed yet again. Until one day out of the blue, he decided not to call me anymore.

Can you be dumped if you aren't officially boyfriend and girlfriend? Nineteen years old, and you'd think I was still in ninth grade, biting my fingernails by the phone. The void unearthed questions I wished I could ask, like *What went wrong? Was it you, or me, or something else? Did you meet someone new? Did something happen to you?*

No one gets an answer. We never get to find out, so the assumption is always that the problem was us. Boys lose their interest, and we lose our minds.

When the phone finally rang, it was my mom. I pressed the receiver against my ear, listening.

"I finally filed for divorce today," she said, barely getting the words out. "It was so hard. So sad to me." And part of me understood. As we talked, I remembered pictures of my mom and dad, young lovers in a different life, with the whole world ahead of them. Big family gatherings with aunts and uncles and all of my cousins, where did it go? My mother grieved more than the end of her marriage. That ended long ago. She grieved the collapse of a family and, also, of who they used to be, Dan and Mary Ellen. She'd never know that man again, and he'd never know her. There had been so many endings, but now, it was over.

Already heartbroken, I felt the heaviness of it all. I was lost on a map, going through the motions of a college freshman in her prime, but something wasn't working. My tight-knit friendships kept making new friends with ease, and I hid my embarrassment for not knowing how. My envy triggered worries I'd be left out, replaced. It felt like my old life was creeping in when my exams were finally over, and I drove home at the end of fall, ready for winter relief and a hug from my mother.

On Christmas morning, my brothers and I converged half-asleep into the kitchen like little kids over to the family room where the tree stood. I plugged in the lights and then sat on the carpet in the same spot I'd taken since I was seven years old. Mom made a pot of coffee, and when it was ready, we took turns opening our modest presents while holiday music quietly played from a boom box in the background. The scene in front of me ran like a finely rehearsed play, where a change in the script seemed to go unnoticed, but not to me. I missed my dad.

I pictured every year before—how much he loved to watch us get the things we'd put on Santa's list, how good it made me feel to see him get new things. He rarely ever did. I always gave him socks; it was our thing. Where did that all go? What happened to the years when my dad pulled out his huge Swiss Army knife to rescue our toys from their impossible packaging? I shook the thoughts from my head.

The idea of him alone in a barely furnished apartment hurt my heart.

"I feel so bad for Dad," I finally said, then immediately felt my face begin to burn. I didn't want to cry, but I did. "He must be miserable. I mean, it's Christmas."

The room grew stiff. My brothers went silent.

"I think we all feel bad about it," said my mom. She choked up, telling us the few things he took with him, and I assumed it was his prideful anger that kept him from taking more. He didn't want to look like he needed it. I didn't want my mom to feel responsible like any of this was her fault. All my sadness and thoughts about our family not being together and what my dad was doing at that moment crashed against images of my bullish father looking so weak and alone and all the awful words I screamed at him in the past. The weight of the morning, the complexities of divorce, surprised me. I never thought it would be so hard.

How do you prepare for something you're assured will never happen? Mommy and Daddy love each other. Mommy and Daddy love *you.* The messages embedded in the early stages of our brains don't magically separate because of a court document signed by a judge. I think no one who's experienced or saw the deterioration of a marriage wishes for unhappy parents to stay together for old times' sake. What we yearn for is to go back to a capsule of time, to freeze a moment and wrap it up with familiar smells and sounds, to carry it with us so we can believe we were right.

That the world is safe and everything works out in the end.

What's more nostalgic than Christmas morning to conjure up memories of that childhood? I sat like a child, smelling baked ham and homemade rolls wafting out from the kitchen and watching college football playing on the TV. It wouldn't be a true Christmas, though, without some type of drama. From the kitchen, I heard my mom scream.

"Goddammit!" she exclaimed. "Son of a bitch." I ran over, thinking she burned herself when her chow dog blew past me in a streak of puffy black fur. "The ham! She's got the ham," my mother cried out, everyone running around the house and out the back door in pursuit of a little ham stolen right off the counter. I held off on the backyard chase. Yogi the dog could be scary, and my brothers were fun to watch. Eventually, the hunk of meat was plopped back on the counter, covered in grass and dog hair with a big chunk missing.

For a moment, my mom stared at it with a sad, defeated look on her face while Peter, Adam, and I stifled our laughs behind her. How could she *not* think that was funny?

"What if we just cut that part off?" my mom asked, planning to rinse off the ham in the sink.

"Jesus, Mom!" Peter groaned, and then, like a chorus, the laughter came.

We ordered takeout. What made the night magnificent was the simplicity of it all. No anger or hostility, no faulting someone, no tiptoeing in fear. Nothing was ruined at all that day. We had unknowingly accomplished a foreign feat for our family. We found our own way through a shitty situation. A Christmas miracle, indeed.

January came with a new semester, and it felt like the fresh start I wanted. With a new attitude, I kept my goals simple. *Let's settle down a bit, maybe a boyfriend. Go to class, be on time, pay attention. Don't be so, you know, bulimic.*

I didn't plan to go out that Wednesday. Someone invited me, she lived in my dorm, and I said, "Sure." Not until I was there, at a local sports bar to meet up with a couple of her friends, did I remember precisely how much I hated trying to fit in with girls I didn't know. The second they told me their names, I forgot them.

"I'm Emily," I said, sticking out my hand for a shake, but

conversations had already started. I headed off to look for a bathroom. While I mingled through the crowd for a path, someone tapped me on the shoulder. I turned around.

"Who, me?" I said, pointing to my chest. The place was so loud from everyone yelling to talk over the band. The guy nodded with a smirk; his confident brown eyes locked onto mine. I smiled back at him, assuming he needed directions to the bathroom or I was standing in his way. Instead, he leaned down to my ear and told me his name was Jeff. He'd seen me before and I was beautiful. Again, I thought, *who, me?*

He mentioned a party later that night. I walked off to the bathroom then to find my friend, intrigued.

"You know who that is, right?" said Jennifer after I pointed him out from across the room. Jeff's little entourage should have tipped me off. He played varsity on the football team.

"No shit?" I said with a giggle and took a sip from one of the fresh beer bottles a stranger bought for us. *The guy must have confused me with someone else.*

Maybe it was the beer or seeing Ben with someone new when I walked by him. Whatever was in the air on that cold Wednesday night, I decided to go to Jeff's little party. Jen came along but left early, and I felt miserably out of place, pinned to the wall by my insecurities. What the hell was I doing there? The other girls seemed so fancy, so much older and in standing near them, I knew these were not people who hung around with little freshmen wearing dirty Keds with no socks. I was headed to the door to leave when I saw Jeff. He walked over with his face lit up and a smile just for me. *Okay, maybe I do fit in.*

"Let's go somewhere quieter to talk," he said. I nodded with a smile, thinking *this guy actually likes me.* He held my hand, and I almost died. That bubbly feeling of excitement mixing with romance fluttered inside me when he led me into a dark room that smelled like musky cologne and sweat and textbooks. A light was coming through the cracks around a window's closed blinds as my eyes adjusted.

"Are you having a good time?" he asked me, but I didn't know how to talk to someone like Jeff. I asked him if he liked football, then laughed at myself, and *thank God he has a sense of humor* because he laughed, too. We talked our way through light conversation until his hand began to play with my hair. My heart almost exploded. I needed water, a stick of gum, a mint for the anxious slow-motion moves he was making. And when we finally kissed, ohhh . . . I started planning our wedding in my head.

The sudden knock on the door startled me, even after Jeff whispered, "Ignore them." Two males quietly walked in the room, and I wondered if I was in their room. *I should go.* I didn't understand why they were there or why Jeff didn't tell them to leave. What time was it? The sudden lock of the deadbolt was like a warning shot straight into my brain. *What the hell is going on?*

"I'm gonna head out; it's late," I said to Jeff and tried to stand up.

"Nah, I think you should stay," he said, holding on to my arm. The way he said it, I wasn't flattered.

"Please," I said. I don't know why.

"Just be cool," said one of the strangers, wearing a baseball hat. Those words set me off. *This can't be real,* I thought, this isn't happening, but I knew it was. That moment, a fraction of a second, was the detonation button that changed everything. Because someone grabbed my other arm, and I felt a push on my back. I lost my balance and did a face-plant into the mattress.

I thought I knew what to do in that type of situation. I thought I was smart enough to predict when something awful was going to happen. Or if I did end up being attacked, I'd have the ability to fight with invincible strength. We've seen the articles and read the pamphlets that scared us. But not until I felt hands yanking off my clothes and my underwear did I believe it might be me, and then it was a terror like no other.

No didn't work. Other things, *I'm sorry,* like I was being punished for something I did wrong. *Get off me! Stop! No, I need to leave* swirled somewhere in my memory, but nothing happened.

To breathe, to endure, to escape—all of it collided in the abstract of time. I cannot gauge it properly. Rape is nothing like the neatly typed word you just read. Rape is vulgar and dirty and cruel. You can hear it and smell it. It stuck to me as my hands fumbled for my clothes, pulling them over me fast and gently before bolting out the door. I was not myself. I know I walked to my dorm and climbed four flights of stairs to my room. I know I stood in a shower. There wasn't enough soap to scrub myself down the drain.

Sunlight was coming in the window where I curled in a ball in my bed, lying there to fester over all the ways it was my fault. *I'm so stupid,* I said repeatedly. *You fucking idiot.*

Details showed up like a slideshow every time I closed my eyes, split-second nightmares where I forced my eyelids open to make them stop. My brain kept it that way, as if politely handing me time to pause and take a breath.

I woke up in the early afternoon feeling needles between my legs and lead in my chest. It took me a second to register the source. The clock by my bed said twenty minutes until my next class. The thing . . . from last night. It became a heavy, disfigured blackness. I labeled it nothing and gave it no words, but everything that made up my insides knew it was there. My feet, weighted down by its size, swung to the edge of the bed and met the ground, coaxing me out of my flowery sheets.

Get up. Get dressed, put your makeup on, get moving. No one needs to know. It's your fault anyway. And you're failing chemistry.

This is silence. At face value, it looks a lot like a shame. My vain attempt to save a little reputation. No one wants their name in embarrassing gossip. Rape was automatically put in a category with both males and females making assumptions about a woman's character. *What was she wearing? She probably led him on. Was she drunk?*

That guy? No way he did it, he can get any girl he wants. Just thinking about what others might say kept me awake at night. My silence felt like the only way to protect myself.

But what's really at stake is the reputation and image of men and our age-old belief that they'll protect and provide. To speak up or even whisper out loud in the middle of nowhere about the atrocities they did to someone like me required a willingness to call out an entire system of beliefs of historical—even biblical—proportions. And you think I'm going report a campus rape by a student athlete and two other males at Texas A&M University? I couldn't even tell a best friend because they, too, grew up with the same ideas floating in their head, and my story wasn't enough to change their mind.

Hell, the truth didn't even change my mind; it was too much.

And the system that kept me quiet ran through the blood in my veins. I come from women surrounded by men who fought in wars, hardworking farmers, and middle-class salesmen like my dad. It was our job to make men's lives easier, and if you were a woman who didn't agree, well, good luck finding friends. I never thought much about it, probably because I liked the idea of a man taking care of me and paying bills. I wanted to play "house" for a living.

Jeff probably saw that from across the room.

That's why he tapped me on the shoulder in the first place. I had the look. Someone who blended in but was a bit of an outsider, my weakness. I looked like the voiceless. He was looking for someone without a voice.

While I looked perfectly presentable on the outside—going to class, socializing and casually dating—under my surface, the blackness raged inside. I felt so full of it that I tried to shove it down with food and puke it out of me or drink it away with alcohol. It was better to feel nothing than to feel miserable, so I sought constant emptiness, purging several times a day in random campus toilets or sinks or plastic bags. Or I'd try to starve myself until the desperation for emptiness turned into a problem I couldn't control.

"Hi, Mom, I need to tell you something," I said over the phone one night while my roommate was gone. She said *okay* in the way a mother does when she's freaking out on the inside, wondering, *what the hell did she do now?*

"I tried really, really hard, but grades are going to come out, and I want you to know I flunked Chemistry. Like 'F' flunked it," I said.

"Well, at least you did well in your other classes, Emily," she said for comfort.

"I just couldn't figure it out, Mom, even with the tutoring. Maybe it's a sign I shouldn't be a nurse, I don't know." But then I changed the subject. That was my big news, along with the depression and migraine headaches that kept sending me to the emergency room. And that was enough.

I wonder how many young women made the same omission over long-distance phone calls to their mothers. Statistics for sexual assault on campuses confirm that what happened to me was undoubtedly shocking but also shockingly common. I wasn't scared of what my mom would say. I was afraid to face the horrific and shameful crime I was a part of.

What I really wanted was for someone to rescue me. It was the only answer I could come up with to solve such an explosion of trouble. Even though it seemed so irrational, I wanted a knight to come and save me, to love and protect me from everything awful inside and outside of me. Come carry me out of this mess of a life with his sword drawn to ward off all the assholes and whisk me away to the happy ending. I clung to the dream of a fairy-tale ending, but I also recoiled from it.

I was like the dog at the shelter who pined for an owner, but the second someone opened the cage, she snarled her teeth and crouched in the corner, ready to tear you apart. Don't fucking get too close; I might snap.

"Emily, you have to take care of *yourself*," my mom told me before we ended the conversation, and I told her I was, or that *I will, I promise.* Of course, I wanted to tell her about the rape. I secretly hoped she'd get in her car and run up the stairs of my dorm to crawl into my bottom bunk to run her fingers through my hair and rub my head. Sing me "Hush, Little Baby" until I fell asleep like we did when I was younger.

But at some point, the girl who told her mother every corny detail of her little life learned that sometimes we suffer by ourselves. The way our parents taught us to.

CHAPTER FOUR

1994

"I think I'm starting to like you," I told Ryan after a few dates. Those words almost needed to be surgically removed from my tongue to get them to come out, and then afterward, they hung frozen between us, waiting for his reaction.

God, I loved the way he stood there in his boots and Stetson hat in front of me just outside my dorm, and the way it took us so long to say goodbye because we didn't want the night to end. He was two years older than me, a senior from a little town in Utah who grew up on a family farm and wore an infectious smile on his face. It took me three dates to warm up to the guy and I think he'd say the same about me. We were from circles that rarely mixed. He was a country boy, and me? I'm not sure.

After I said it, I wanted to kick him the way a little sister would just so he knew I could fight or put my hand softly at the back of his neck and gently kiss his lips. It's those mixed brain signals that seep out and expose the damage of my life's events. Behind my smile swirled a nerve-jangling inner chaos that pulled me in a thousand directions. You want to protect your future self without having a crystal ball to see into the future. My feelings for Ryan scared me with the same impending dread as watching a horror movie. And I love horror movies. Here was a nice guy doing nice things for me, and it didn't add up. It was the kind of good that made a girl like me into a mental maniac trying to guess her own death. Where was he hiding the pickaxe? Was there a butcher knife under his seat? Would he try to kill me in my dreams?

Because our pasts come with us, those old relationships and bitter breakups, the lovers and the leavers, the screaming and violence, it's all in there. Even fragrant fresh love can't completely cover up the smell of the crap we walked through. We still try. But no one wants to notice, and certainly no one wants to talk about it.

When it turned out that Ryan liked me in the same way, the rest of the world seemed to dim ever so slightly when we were apart. It was as though we were meant to be together. When I was 20 years old, Ryan proposed before his graduation, and I said yes without giving it a second thought. I didn't care about transferring schools or leaving my family and friends when he accepted a job back in Utah 1,000 miles away.

"Come with me," he said, with our fingers intertwined. "You'll love it there." Ryan's eyes were beaming at the luckiest girl in the world.

All that sounds like radical change for a couple of college kids. It sounds a little stupid and naïve until a bigger picture comes into view. The prospect of a brand-new life sounded easier than the one I was living. It's exhausting trying to block out tumultuous events. I needed the hero I saw in Ryan, and he held me with the safe and rescuing arms of a loving man.

The appeal of independence, the concept of creating my own life with a career to support myself, it all dropped with a *thunk* to the bottom of the same deep well where my grandmothers threw their fleeting plans and possibilities. It was so normal to come to a complete stop and then orbit your life around a man that we didn't even notice what was left behind when we switched course. Almost every woman I grew up around did it, so why wouldn't I? My mother moved to Germany in her twenties to be with my dad during

Vietnam. My aunt Kathy did the same thing, marrying my uncle Jim after the Vietnam draft. Their mother, Fern, left family in rural Minnesota for California to be near her new husband, Rona, when he was drafted during WWII.

The list goes on. I wasn't radical at all.

It's not a debate over right or wrong choices because, in my eyes, there was only one choice—get married and live happily ever after. But a year later as I sat in the student union as a married woman at the local state university I read the same paragraph in my textbook ten times, losing my place repeatedly. I looked up to stare out a nearby window because I couldn't focus. *I think I made a mistake* was the secret thought I fought to keep under my surface, rationalizing it as adjusting to marriage, a new city, a new school, no family, no friends.

Grow up, I thought to myself as tears percolated high enough to fall down my cheek. The wet streaks embarrassed me. *What the hell is wrong with me? This is the exact happy ending I wanted.* The frustration inside me started to grow because this was everything I asked for, and still, I felt an undefined inadequacy. Right before I left the building, I called Ryan's office from a pay phone to see if he could come home early.

"Aw, Sweetie," he said. "You know I would. Steve's boss is in town. I gotta stay late," he talked in hushed tones like he wasn't allowed to use the phone for anything other than cold calls.

"No, it's fine. You've just been working late every night. I hardly see you, so I thought I'd ask. I've got a lot to do anyway." I was worried he felt guilty. Did he feel guilty?

I treated myself to an ice cream shake on my way home, then headed straight for my bathroom when I got there to puke it all up in the toilet. Afterward, I picked clothes up off the floor and used a sock to dust off the top of our nightstands and dresser, perfectly arranging sentimental knick-knacks and photos across the top. What next? *I'll start a load of laundry, then make a grocery list,* I thought, because the stagnant feel of the empty apartment smothered me.

When I eventually gave in and went through kitchen cabinets, searching for snacks to temporarily fill the hole inside of me, I knew I was stuck. And I hated that this was my daily routine again. I thought for sure marriage and the move would cure me, and when it didn't turn out perfect, I knew exactly who to blame.

Dear God, please send help was the hail-Mary prayer that reached no one since I stuffed it down my throat with a bowl of Cap'n Crunch and a peanut butter sandwich. For a good five minutes, I sat on the couch in front of the television I never turned on because a good wife doesn't actually watch daytime TV while her husband is working hard to provide for the family. But she also doesn't get up and head for the bathroom and force herself to purge on the off chance it brings her a sense of relief. I'd have to be crazy to start a discussion about my secret afternoon activities with Ryan when he walked in the door. He wanted a happy wife who had dinner ready and the place picked up, so that was exactly what I gave him.

Besides, he knew about my eating disorder before we got engaged, and he knew the problem didn't disappear after we exchanged our vows.

"I'll sit with you after meals," he'd say lovingly. "We can go for walks or something," but what was meant to be supportive felt like his unwanted parental obligation. I got the feeling the offering ranked up there with a diarrhea diaper blowout or endlessly waiting for a toddler to finish a hot dog. He looked disappointed, so I dug in my heels, thinking, *I can do this all by myself,* unaware of how much I needed him to be happy with me so that I could be happy with me.

That Friday night, we went to an outdoor concert with a few friends Ryan knew from high school. When I glimpsed him laughing at the carefree way I danced around to a Dave Matthews song, I stopped and held his face for a kiss, saying, "I have never been this happy in my whole entire life." And at that precise moment, I meant it. He smiled at me with that country boy grin I fell in love with and said, "Em, you're the best thing to ever happen to me." The familiar way his arms wrapped around my waist confirmed our love was real. The smell of his flannel shirt whispered that Ryan was still Ryan, and I was still me. We made the right choice. It was only in moments of stillness when I stepped back and looked around that I realized how lonely it felt to surround myself with friends that weren't mine in a place meant for him.

I was a long way from home, and I wanted to go back. But to what or to where I didn't know.

I was in that state of mind making dinner one night before Ryan got home from the office. I don't know what emotion rumbled around inside of me, only that I didn't like it. I stood at the counter cutting up vegetables for a healthy dinner I hoped wouldn't end up in the toilet this time, my thoughts drifting in and out when I looked at the knife in my hand differently. I slid the sharp blade across my right forearm, then I did it two more times in horizontal swipes and watched the blood come. A feeling of intense pain followed by relief bubbled up from deep inside of me. I set down the knife and walked calmly into the bathroom to clean the dripping blood off in private, even though the apartment was empty.

This pain is better, I thought from somewhere in the recesses of my sick brain. And it was. I could see it, touch it, watch it, and feel it pass through me. There was a beginning and an end; it made sense, and the best part was the internal numbness at the end. I felt too much but now I felt nothing. I was hurt; I could heal. I was alive.

When I went back to the kitchen to cook, I thought about the strange thing I just did with a tinge of forbidden excitement, like back in '79 when I found my mom's copy of "Our Bodies, Ourselves" with black and white illustrations of vaginas or when I had a coughing fit after my first puff of a cigarette. I didn't care if it was taboo. I was already planning to do it again.

My newfound secret overshadowed the fact I found another way to hurt myself during the happiest time of my life.

Anyone in their right mind would have freaked themselves out the next morning when they woke up looking like they had an encounter with Freddy Krueger during the night. But this wasn't *Nightmare on Elm Street,* the horror movie I watched in junior high that scared me so much I had to sleep on my parent's bedroom floor for days. Truthfully, I ignored the slashes and acted like I didn't even see them. Covered them up so Ryan didn't notice before he left for the office and I needed to get to class.

You wonder how I could split myself into two people like that, where one was the happy new wife and the other was caving in on herself, but secrets and hiding the ugly parts were easy for me. I watched my mother bustle around the house after my dad crushed her heart in a screaming rant, just as she had learned how to carry on so well by watching her mom hide her own struggles. My grandma Fern still didn't talk about her pain. Each time I quietly pulled a knife from the kitchen drawer and quickly slid it across my arm, I didn't think I was hurting anyone. It was a harmless little secret, tucked tenderly under my sleeves like a private collection of my pain in a secret room. I hid it for weeks.

One afternoon, I walked into work at the archives department, down in the bowels of the university library.

"Hi, ladies," I said as my Mormon coworkers side-eyed me like a sinner for bringing caffeinated coffee dangerously close to their souls and government documents. Sheepish Kendall looked up through her long eyelashes and raised her hand to greet me with a whispery hello.

For the next several hours, I sorted through boring stacks of papers spread out on the table in front of me, removing staples and paper clips, reading through typed correspondence in case something looked important enough to flag. Sometimes, I'd pretend I was about to discover something scandalous, like a hidden affair, but I never got that lucky. Since I wasn't interested in library science or

Utah politics, this was one of those paycheck jobs, not nearly as respected as Ryan's job, making cold calls all day for a securities firm. Every so often, I'd join in on the casual conversations happening at the tables in front of me.

"Who brought those muffin things on the counter? Are they homemade? Because they're delish," I asked, knowing it would be a hot topic.

"Oh, I whipped them up yesterday with some ingredients I happened to have. Some orange zest, a little cinnamon, Granny Smiths, and then the usual ingredients, you know," a woman, Margaret, said. And no, I didn't know.

"We should all bake a sweet treat and bring it next week!" was someone's bright idea for a send-off before Thanksgiving break. The way everyone's voice amped up in excitement was comparable to titillating foreplay.

You can tell the same story five ways depending on who's listening, and my audience of five always got an edited version of my life when I spoke, like when they asked me if I liked to bake.

"Are you kidding? I love it," I said, "especially this time of year. I could bake all day." Because if you're going to lie, you might as well go all the way.

"Well, you know what they say," said Kendall, "the way to a man's heart is through his stomach." I knew at that point something was seriously wrong.

To find words to explain the utter demolishment of myself wasn't just impossible, it was unbearable. I was a run-of-the-mill, middle-class suburban girl who naturally gravitated toward the dream of becoming a good wife and a good mom with a nice little house. How many women grew up wanting the same thing? And why is that? Our lives as young wives were made with the fantasy of past generations, except now that it's real and I'm here, I don't like it. Could I admit it out loud? Never. My great-grandmothers would cross their arms and shake their heads at me from the grave. Stella, in her younger years, might laugh and tell me to get used to it. My own mom might say it's always been this way.

This wasn't a woman who made it through years of medical school and then realized she hated being a surgeon. If that were the case, I'd switch careers. What was happening was the slow and scary realization that my role of a proper wife brought me no joy. This *thing* I'd been daydreaming about from the time I watched my mother zip around the house with the vacuum cleaner had slapped me across the cheek for having my head in the clouds. What did I expect? Leaving my home and starting my own family wasn't a decision but a legacy I'd attached to my identity. And beyond my predestined, ideal design was a vast expanse of nothing, not even a way to change my mind. This is who I was.

So my reality wasn't that I was a young woman who made a poor decision to get married so young; it was that I was an overall flawed human being. But who has time to think about such awful things when it's snowing outside and you're baking?

"Holy smokes, what's going on in here?" Ryan asked me when he walked into the kitchen. It looked like a bomb filled with flour went off all over the counters and linoleum floor. We looked at each other and laughed.

"What does it look like? I'm baking," I said with a smile.

Stone Temple Pilots blasted from the stereo while I whisked a chocolaty batter together. I read every step of the recipe like my life depended on it since this would be the measure of my greatness tomorrow at work.

"It's not a competition," Ryan reminded me as he swooped his finger in for a lick of frosting. Like hell, it wasn't. Nobody could resist the deliciousness of a Texas sheet cake.

The cold weather outside helped to get me into the holiday spirit, and it also helped me find excuses to hide my bare skin from my husband. Cutting became my new secret obsession, and it fooled Ryan into believing I was getting better. My eating disorder died down, but my new sick secret quickly became a problem, and it didn't take long before I took scissors and knives to my underarms, my ankles, and the back of my legs.

Ryan opened the oven door as I carefully slid in the pan and set the timer for 35 minutes. I started cleaning up at the sink, running hot water over dirty mixing bowls and wooden spoons. The dish soap smelled like apples, little bubbles drifting over my hands and onto my shirt sleeves. I didn't notice Ryan standing there when I absentmindedly pushed up my sleeves.

"Oh my God, Emily! What happened?" Ryan's voice startled me. I didn't know what to say as I yanked my sleeves back down.

"It's nothing. Don't worry about it," I said, but he already knew; the evidence was far too stark to deny what happened. Even a good boy like Ryan could see these injuries weren't an accident.

"Why would you do this to yourself?" he asked me, and somewhere in his voice, I heard anger. When I turned off the faucet and tried to walk away, I glimpsed his face out of the corner of my eye and saw pain in it. *I hate myself,* I thought. Because I didn't have room for the guilt and I didn't have words to explain, so in a split-second reaction, I got mad.

"I don't want to talk about it," I said. "And you never have time to listen to me anyway." It was my way of ending the conversation, of protecting the one thing saving me, saving us both from the truth.

Silence says a lot sometimes, and that night Ryan said plenty without ever uttering a word. We didn't go to bed angry but in a state of indifference, which was much worse. In the morning, we did our usual routine and politely passed each other in the hallway until eventually we locked eyes and stood still.

"I love you," I said.

"I love you, too. We'll figure this out," he said. And I believed him.

On campus, I froze my ass off, walking to a midterm, carrying my dessert like it was more precious than a newborn baby. When the cake squares finally made it to the countertop where seven other lovely indulgences sat, I arranged the pieces perfectly before I took my seat. *Act casual, let them be shocked,* I thought, hiding my devilish grin. I knew I won. Not like it was a competition of course. We were all *friends.*

"Not bad, Emily," I heard over my shoulder. *Not bad? Are you fucking kidding me?*

"Oh, yum, very moist," came later when someone took a square of my cake. I hated that word. Moist is not a compliment.

"These are to DIE for," was the first comment to cause me to turn in my chair. My self-esteem desperately needed that kind of compliment until I realized Kendall was holding a bar that had pretzels in it. Pretzels? Was there a conspiracy with those Mormons?

We all took samples home with us, and the truth was those women could bake circles around me. I loved every morsel I ate. If only I could have switched out my eyeballs for a new set and seen it as a win for us all instead of a failure on my part. Instead, what my eyes focused on was inadequacy, just another example of not quite being good enough to belong.

That Thursday, Ryan and I drove out to his parents' house to spend Thanksgiving. If our car had been driving toward my mother's house, we'd be wearing jeans. I'd have a bag of chips and my favorite dip sitting by my feet, along with the current green bean casserole that sat on my lap, and I'd be excited to lie around all day in my socks. After we ate, maybe I'd drift off into a turkey slumber, but not this year.

"Happy Thanksgiving!" Ryan's parents chimed simultaneously when we arrived. I returned the greeting and gave one-armed hugs, wearing a long jumper that hugged my figure with a long-sleeve cotton shirt underneath, my hair hanging in big, chunky curls.

"Here, Emily, bring that to the kitchen," Ryan's brother-in-law, Randy, said, so I followed him toward the warm smells of melted butter, pumpkin pie and spices that wrapped around me like a blanket. *Now what?* I wondered, looking for Ryan so I'd know what to do.

Tom, his dad, poured a bottle of wine into spotless glasses. I took a sip and sat down in front of a tray displaying an assortment of cheese and crackers. *Relax, Emily,* I told myself, though I desperately wanted an excuse to go outside and play. On a past visit to the farm, I liked to help Tom and Ryan out in the fields. I learned to siphon the irrigation pipes, walking along the ditches carrying on small conversations about agriculture and different crops, mostly sugar beets. I even drove the tractor once. I was so enamored with farming I couldn't wait to tell Ryan's dad about the kitten we adopted—a white one I affectionately named Sugar.

During dinner, the meal felt formal and went down my throat as perfectly as the polite conversations around the table.

"Emily, we heard you've been spending some time with Rachel and her sister. That sounds nice," my mother-in-law Beth said. She was referring to the governor's granddaughters who we occasionally went with to the bars downtown on weekends. Earlier that month, Rachel's sister got us busted when she used my expired license, but we got off because of her last name.

I probably shouldn't mention that.

"Yep, they're very sweet," I said, not understanding why Beth had a look of importance on her face from mentioning her friends in high places. I wasn't impressed when Rachel's younger sister said her last name as often as she could. Was I supposed to feel special? Or maybe honored? Thank God the topic moved on to Randy's vet clinic. Ryan reached under the table to rest his hand on my leg, sending me a message that should have given me a comfortable reassurance in which to breathe and embrace this new other half of my family. Instead, my toes curled inside of my shoes. My hand began to shake when I picked up my glass of water, and when I ate my last bite of turkey, the air roped around me like a lasso pulling tight across my chest. I didn't belong there.

Like I said, our pasts come with us. It's more than tragic memories and bad relationships, or the harmful things we did to heal or to forget. The parts of our personal history we thought were dead and buried learn how to breathe underground. What if some of the things that messed us up are suddenly sitting beside us? Because by the time I realized I was in the wrong room with the wrong people, I was lost on how I got there.

That's exactly how I felt standing in Beth's dining room, watching the men depart from the table without even clearing their plates.

"Where are they going?" I asked Maggie, Ryan's sister. She shrugged her shoulders and told me, "Downstairs."

"The guys don't help us clean up?" I asked as I walked into the kitchen carrying dirty dishes from the table.

"Oh, no," Maggie chuckled, "and definitely not when football is on."

I stood there staring at the mess of dishes and uneaten food, feeling ripped off for having a vagina. *This is the wrong way*, I thought, but who could I tell? Should I break the rules and go downstairs, too? Beth was nothing but nice to me, yet I wanted to keep a distance as if she had a contagious disease. At the same time, I wanted to do everything right by her standards.

Surely Ryan wanted a wife who looked so content standing there cleaning an eight-hour mess that took 20 minutes to eat, with no male in sight, no slash marks across her body, no regurgitated food in the toilet.

I felt uncomfortably domestic, dishtowel in hand, trying to look good in my new role. My only escape was to sneak downstairs, where, thankfully, I received a warm welcome. Ryan snuggled in with me on the couch to watch the college football game, and the tension in my shoulders was just about to unclench when bam! A trigger went off inside me that I wasn't expecting when something on the television told my brain to remind my body about that other football player who raped me with his friends. And immediately, my skin began to sweat and cringe at the feel of someone touching me. I wanted every man in that room to disappear. At the same time, I wanted them to circle the fucking wagons to protect me and keep me safe. What a mess. I sprang up and stood there, rattled and full of guilt.

"I'm gonna go check on the ladies," I said, leaving out how I was a bad wife for ditching my duties in the first place. Back and forth I went because I couldn't figure out where I fit. It wasn't with the women or the men that day. Dammit, I wanted to go home. *All the way home*, but I didn't belong there anymore either. I didn't know where to go. For someone who only wanted a simple, settled life, I sure had a way of complicating things.

My dear sweet mother-in-law saw that day and the weeks surrounding it as a case of homesickness. I wanted to think the same way, and after getting a prescription for my first antidepressant, I thought my "adjustment" would improve.

Beth invited me for lunch downtown, and when I arrived, she hugged me in her sweater set and pants with her shoes matching perfectly with her purse. Everything she wore fit just right except for the awkward smile on her face.

"How are you doing?" she asked me from across the table for two planted in the middle of the Italian restaurant. Someone walking by us would have thought I was dying of cancer in a week from how she sounded and the pained look on her face. *Actually, I'm only going to a treatment hospital for a month or so, Beth.*

Throughout the conversation, I tiptoed around her question and dammit, I didn't know why I had to be so problematic when women like her could be so uncomplicated. She radiated a sort of Catholic good wife aura, like someone who was born knowing where every fork went in a place setting. And there I was, stumbling over my words like an idiot trying to sound normal. That bright-eyed girl with a bubbly smile and so much to say was nowhere to be found; I couldn't reach her. Finally, I just leaned in, slid up my sleeves, and laid my butchered arms out.

"This is how I'm doing," I said.

Beth gasped and covered her mouth in shock. I looked, too, to see it from her view, and just like her, the sight shocked me. Jesus Christ, had I gone completely mad? All the cuts added up at once were too much to look at, and I couldn't cover them fast enough to erase what I'd shown her.

"I . . . didn't know you were so unhappy," Beth said, tears in her eyes but something else, too.

I don't know what's wrong, I swear, I wanted to tell her. As I sat there, I started second-guessing my own emotions, not knowing if the sadness was real, if the love was real, or if everything about me and my life was one big lie.

"I'm sorry," I said, and I genuinely was. *What am I supposed to say?* I wondered and glanced up at her. My god, that subtle look of reproach not only caught my attention, it ripped the heart out of my chest. She got me good. Rejection at its worst because I wanted to love her like a mother, and she just showed me I wasn't good enough to be her daughter. I didn't blame her for wanting better for her son, which only went to feed the beast that told me I was a bad wife, not a sick one.

Two weeks later, with Ryan's love and support, I drove from Utah back to Texas to Presbyterian Hospital in Dallas with our cat Sugar as my copilot. Where would we be without the unconditional love we get from our pets? That fluffy fur ball became my ride or die after my mother arranged for me to go to a type of intensive psychiatric treatment for eating disorders, self-harm, and depression that wasn't available in Utah.

"I'll be thinking of you constantly," Ryan said, a desperate look in his eyes. "Call me every day, Em, I'll visit in a few weeks," he said under the carport in front of our apartment, then he handed me the cat carrier, like a concession prize for him not making the drive with me.

CHAPTER FIVE

1995

On my first day at Presbyterian Hospital's fifth-floor psych unit in Dallas, a girl my age walked by me with chopped-off hair and a short, bony frame. She stopped next to me and looked me over, pausing at the red slash marks down by my ankles showing below my jeans.

"So you do it, too," Neely said.

I stared back at her for a second before looking away.

"Yeah," I said, my eyes straight ahead. We glanced at each other. She smiled; I nodded before she walked off.

I stayed casually cool in my demeanor that day, but my mind was blown. I thought I was the only one. I never realized that someone else would be strange enough to think of intentionally sliding sharp objects across her skin. I didn't even have a word for the behavior. Easy, private online access to odd information didn't exist, and I'd never seen marks like mine on someone else. Relief set in with the realization that I wasn't alone, then it mixed with the uncomfortable awareness that I found this company in a nuthouse.

Another new girl started the same day with skin so orange I couldn't stop staring at her. We sat next to each other, and we awkwardly exchanged names. Emily, meet Mariah. Mariah, meet Emily.

"What the hell happened to you?" I asked in a half whisper.

"Carrots. I fell asleep," was all she said, not needing to explain she dozed off before she could puke. I gave a knowing nod.

Five of us sat on couches with mirrored glass windows behind us overlooking the expressway down below while we waited for instructions. The eating disorder unit took up half of the locked-down 5th floor as an 8 am–6 pm intensive outpatient program. We had a nurse's station, a large room for group activities and doors along hallways that opened into smaller classrooms. If I wanted to use the bathroom, a nurse accompanied me and flushed my toilet.

"Good morning!" said Gary, the only male, who also was the lead therapist. He walked in wearing a dark gray suit and a smile covered partially by his mustache that twinkled the wrinkled corners of his eyes. "Did all of you fill out your menus for the day?"

When I raised my hand as a confession, he handed me a long sheet of paper with personalized instructions regarding what I could and could not choose to eat off the hospital menu. In my case, I had to pick one main, two sides, one dessert, one drink. Or I could switch it up and pick one main, three sides and a drink, and that was just breakfast. An ordinarily simple task to complete in less than five minutes set a panic inside of me. I turned it into life and death decisions. I meticulously studied each option, making sure I circled the perfect answer, calculating which vegetable carried the most calories, which meat had more fat, which side came with larger portions and which foods I refused to eat. I wanted more time to check and balance. Too late.

An hour later, when I stared down at a plate of food for breakfast, I decided I hated this place. No way could I stomach all that. I thought I was being subtle when my fork separated a small portion of eggs off to the side. Then I took a chunk of a canned peach slice, smashed and slid it over from the rest of the fruit. *There,* I thought to myself, *I'll eat everything else.*

"What are you doing?" Neely asked me from across the round dining table. *What's her problem?*

"I'm eating," was all I said.

"Really? Then how come you separated your food like that?" she asked with one eyebrow raised. A swirl of her finger toward my plate, and now I had an enemy. She knew exactly what I was doing.

"Why are you so interested in my food when you haven't touched any of your own?" I shot back. The doctor swept in.

"No, no, no, girls. We aren't going to be confrontational here. This is about supportive feedback," she said, referring to peer accountability, a fancy term for calling someone out on their bullshit.

I hated knowing other girls watched me in the same suspicious way I watched them. It's hard to hide your crimes in a room full of criminals. I could tell right away that Olivia, the soft-spoken 17-year-old, was bulimic by the pace of her eating and the old nicks on her knuckles from jamming her hand against the edges of her teeth. Jan, a doctoral student older than the rest of us, was anorexic with her skeletal appearance. Neely? She was like me, somewhere in the middle screwing around with all of it, acting skinny more than sickly to trick strangers into thinking we were special. She and I clashed for two days until one afternoon in Process Group therapy when Mariah broke down talking about her parents.

Why did we have to do that crap? I went to that treatment program for an eating disorder. I wanted an educational day camp, not this. Teach me to eat like a normal person and quit cutting up my body so I can get on with my life, and that's it. Leave me out of emotional drama.

"Did he tell you he took away my car?" she asked Gary. "He sold it! Without telling me! So yeah, I'm pissed." Her Spanish accent flew out louder with every word.

"He's worried about you," Gary said.

"Oh, bullshit. If he was so worried, he'd pay a little attention to me when he was home instead of always sneaking around with a woman behind my mom's back," she said. *NO, I cannot.* Part of me wanted to reach out my hand for support, but I didn't know what I'd say. There was a "do not disturb the process" policy anyway, forcing me to sit there in my own discomfort. I wanted things to wrap up nicely in the next few minutes, like an ending to a TV drama, but the scene kept rolling.

I never heard about that part of treatment programs, those gruesome moments of watching someone else unravel right in front of you. Mariah continued to thrash like a child as she talked about the time in grade school when she caught her father out with another woman and how he expected her to keep that a secret. How dirty it made her feel. How betrayed she felt by her hero. How love turned to hate.

"Do you have any idea what that did to me?" she wailed through dripping snot. We just sat there watching her until a quiet voice next to me said something.

"I do. I know."

It was Neely. I didn't look at her, but the hot bitterness I felt toward her cooled into a gateway for compassion. All sorts of little dots across my mind lined up perfectly as I sat there listening to dialogue between Gary and the two girls. She wasn't heartless; she was guarded. Dammit, Neely was human, after all, and not the bad guy I needed her to be. She hit my nerves because she was just like me. If I liked Neely, then some part of me liked myself. And as much as I hated to admit it, I was starting to like her.

Food fixation and body obsession seemed easier to deal with than complicated relationships. I could touch it, pinch it, shrink it, flush it. Even quit it, right? The emotional mess inside me proved more difficult, primarily because I refused to allow anyone near it. I considered Gary a trustworthy candidate until he pulled me aside one day after morning check-ins.

"Emily, how many family members will be coming to Thursday's weekly family night?"

My head whipped around for a double take. "I'm sure your mother can make it; what about your dad?"

I felt eyes drilling into the side of my face.

"He won't come," was all I said.

"Did you ask him?"

"No. I don't need to. He won't come," I said with a look of defiance. We stared at each other until a loud commotion rang out from the hallway.

"We'll talk about this later," he said, then darted toward the source of the noise. Neely scurried over to me.

"Jan got busted," she whispered.

"Busted how?" I asked, leaning in with wide eyes, unable to contain my excitement for a little drama. Apparently, Jan had been pouring her supplemental protein drinks into the potted plants.

Right in front of me? Impressive, if not sickeningly sad.

Jan and I sat next to each other on a couch, hating every second of every sip of those drinks, but we never said a word about it. We didn't admit to each other out loud how we felt because we couldn't even be honest with ourselves. Something like that took guts beyond my capabilities. At best, I snuck a chewed-up cracker into a napkin here and there.

I tried to get mad at her. Instead, thoughts about being an outsider in that place shrank my thick skin that day. I suddenly found myself in a strange sisterhood, realizing that I not only cared about Neely, I cared about Jan, too. Everyone there, actually. It still drove me crazy the way Jan insisted on chomping her teeth together to chew a fucking bite of yogurt, but it didn't matter so much when I thought about the ways we were alike. Was it realistic to think I'd admit my envy that she outsmarted us all? Or that I wished I had thought of the same thing? Not really. But I saw how Jan was good, *too good.*

She came back the next morning with a feeding tube hanging out of her nose. That's how she'd eat those protein supplements for quite some time. It's no sweet victory when addiction wins. She fell quiet after that, in a way that reminded me of myself when I'd slip into a pissed-off state of silence. Watching her made me wonder if I was headed there again. We sat together at Process Group that afternoon where I'm sure we both prayed Gary didn't see either of us.

"Emily, let's talk about your dad," Gary said. *Shit, I knew it.* Time to skate across the topic.

"There's nothing to talk about. He's an alcoholic, and things weren't that great. But I've moved on. Life's good. Well, except for this part." I motioned in his direction with my hands. "I'm okay with it, really."

Why did I get the impression everyone thought I was lying? I didn't want this kind of spotlight, but I liked Gary, even in the awkward silence. We made fun of his quirks out of earshot, each one of them slowly earning a badge of respect from the part of me that suspected he was a bit of an outsider, too.

"Tell us more about that," he said with a grin that made him look like a wise ass. I let out a loud laugh and then thought about it. So much had happened since the days with my father that my mind had to move intruding images out of the way even to find him. I settled on the first thing I found.

"About why he doesn't want me in his life? Or about what it was like?" I asked him without waiting for an answer. "I haven't thought about this in so long, maybe it was a holiday or something, and my parents took us to the lake and brought the secondhand boat my dad had bought for fishing. I knew how to water ski from youth group trips and wanted to show them my stuff, ya know? But I kept falling. I went face-first into the water, then I'd watch the boat circle back around for me, and I told my dad that I needed a little more speed to get me out of the water and balanced. I mean, I was trying to be helpful." I paused, caught temporarily in a memory too big to find the right words. "Anyway, he got mad. Screamed at me about how he thought I knew what I was doing, and wouldn't you know it, I fell again. He whipped that boat around to yell at me some more and came close to running me over. Then he threw me the rope to do it again. Seriously, we did that about ten more times, and he was livid by the last one. I was fifteen? Fourteen? I didn't know the motor wasn't big enough for the job; I couldn't even start the damn thing. It was me, bobbing in my life jacket, and everything depended on what was about to happen. I was like, *if I can do it, he won't be so mad. If I can't, then we're all gonna pay.* I gave it everything," I told them, letting out a loud sigh, "But I crashed down into the water in two seconds. I wasn't in a big hurry to come up for air, either," I said, shaking my head.

"I looked up, and the boat was driving away. He left me. My dad was so mad that he took off and left me out in the lake."

After I spoke, the entire memory seemed to float in a dreamlike experience where the girl in the water was a separate version of me. "So what did you do?" Mariah's voice rocketed me back into the room.

"What?" I said, disoriented. "Oh. I swam back to shore." I suddenly felt self-conscious. *Did I tell them he was drunk? That he couldn't even steer the boat back on its trailer so we could leave?* I couldn't remember what I said, nor did it matter.

"Well, Emily," Gary began, then slowly said, "I believe you are the most superficial person I have ever met."

He sat back in his chair, saying nothing more, so I did the same thing. He wanted something, but all I felt was an embarrassing anger over the petty jab.

"That's a horribly sad thing to have happened, Emily," Gary finally explained. "Heartbreaking, really. And I'm looking at these other young ladies, and they're upset over it, for you, but you're not." I wanted out of that room right away, but he went on, saying, "It's like you were reading an article from a newspaper, keeping everything right above the surface."

With his hand, Gary gestured the image of a smooth, straight line. "That's what I mean by superficial."

Thanks for the clarification, I feel so much better, I thought to myself.

Did he know? Because I couldn't articulate how hard I tried to feel something. From the moment I started talking and through the stagnant silences, I dug into that resurfaced recollection. I tried my damnedest to drudge up some emotional connection because I wanted to be like the other girls, to reach in and get it all out of me. Scream, punch pillows, cry my eyes out. What the hell was wrong with me?

The outpatient groups carried on as usual as the weeks progressed, but on my own, I wasn't my best. Meals turned into an obsessive nightmare. Ten chews for each carrot. Three spoonfuls of applesauce, not four. Leave half the ranch in the packet, walk the long way to every scheduled activity to burn calories. If I broke even a tiny part of my rules, I failed the entire day. I ruined everything and immediately started plotting when and where to purge or starve or make up for my indiscretion. I couldn't stop the thoughts; I couldn't NOT do it. Something wasn't working. I knew it was me.

I failed to understand that my brain worked a lot like the eating disorder I wanted to fix. Whether I liked it or not, parts of me functioned on a filter—similar to my menu selections—where some were allowed, a few were partially allowed, and others rejected completely. The idea of it sounds great initially until you realize something else is running the controls. It's why some of us are hiders. I didn't choose to keep those closest to me in the dark. The truth was I had locked myself out, too, and I started to wonder whether anything was actually in there.

Maybe I was empty—it was the feeling I had chased for years.

What would they see if someone dug inside of me? I'd be nothing. Too empty, like Jan.

I doubted my ability to be someone significant and instead chose to work at being average. I ate with a little less angst. Accepted the idea of "more" and opened up to the possibility of being a little nicer in conversations with myself. I sucked at it. I exploded multiple times and had to rebuild. But then, one out of ten times, I paid the new stranger in my skin a compliment. She thought it felt nice and took another bite.

Weeks later, I invited Neely to come with me on a weekend trip to visit my friends at my former university. We'd become close friends, voluntary sisters, and I felt unencumbered around her.

When Monica, my best friend, opened the front door of her apartment, we screamed with excitement and embraced in a familiar hug. I quickly introduced her to Neely as we carried our overnight bags into the living room positioned between four bedroom doors. One by one, roommates came out to greet us, including Monica's sister. Less than two years had passed since I left, and throughout our conversation, the girls looked at me strangely. Something was different.

"So what's been happening?" I asked the roommates, ignoring my intuition and amping up a bubbly demeanor with a smack on my seated thighs. *Smile, be happy, get it together, Emily.*

"The usual, school, boyfriends, work. Erin is planning her wedding, Rachel is graduating in December, stuff like that," said Monica on their behalf. "What about you guys?" *I'm supposed to answer?* I felt a tension in the living space and let out a lighthearted laugh, shrugging as if to say *oh, you know, not much* . . . I stole a look at Neely. She seemed just fine. Monica waited for me to say something as her sister stared at the bright red lines healing across my arms. I knew right then that I lost my spot in the pack if I still had a spot at all. Or ever did.

I split in half that night, trying to figure out which side of me was me. *Was this who I used to be? Is this who I still am?* I wondered privately. I thought it was supposed to be simple—high school, then college. A psychiatric institution didn't exactly fit the plan. A panic kept swooping in, like a bunch of birds pecking at me. I assumed they knew something I didn't and talked about it behind my back with better people. I didn't know how to stick around in the face of all my doubts and insecurities, and I thought it was easier to keep it quietly tucked in behind a smile instead of trying to explain how it felt to be surrounded by old friends who had suddenly turned into grownups because it felt like I hadn't.

And if I opened my mouth to talk about it, who knows what would come pouring out. I didn't want to think about heartbreaks and horrible things. I'd feel too much if I mentioned Ryan's name. The fear sent me spiraling backward into believing that hiding the hardest parts was for the best.

"Hold on, you're married?" Neely had asked during a group meal at the facility with the other girls. When I told her yes, the sense of accomplishment I normally felt for finding the love of my life now embarrassed me like I was pulling out a crumbled piece of paper from my pocket that said "wife" on it.

"How the heck?" was another girl's way of asking to hear the fairytale story, so I gave them a shortened and glossy version of Ryan's and my whirlwind romance.

"Wow, he must really love you." It was Mariah who said what we all longed for—the idea that someone out there loves us unconditionally. As if any of us believed we were worth that amount of devotion. As if anyone at that table thought a good man could love us. Maybe that's why I felt like a fraud. That I was sitting there proved I wasn't such a phenomenal catch someone needed to stake claim on me at the young age of 21. Less obvious was that good and happy wives don't go to hospitals like the one we were in. And good men like Ryan didn't want one who did.

It had been almost a month before I saw him, and by that time, our phone conversations sounded more like a weekly weather report. Our reunion felt out of sync as if we were trying to find the rhythm with a new dance partner.

"How long until you think you're better?" Ryan asked me on the last night of his weekend visit. We'd spent the entire day trying to reclaim that happy couple we once were, and his question made me angry, so I didn't answer right away. It was a flood of emotions going in the wrong direction, or maybe it was me feeling conflicted for thinking the blame could be shared instead of carrying it all myself. Ryan's assumption was for me to repair not only my problems, but our marital ones, too.

Both Ryan and I initially thought if I quit cutting and acting like a food freak, everything would be perfect, and all our problems would go away. When we realized that wasn't the case, I knew I had failed in my role as a woman and a wife. Because it was my job to fix the problem, and I just didn't know how. Words caught in my throat like they were stuck to flypaper and not allowed to be said, not because of Ryan, but because the world might hear me and cut out my tongue. I was so tired of something being wrong with *me* according to unwritten laws about the American wife. I'd have to break the system; I'd get kicked out of the club. *Did you think of me when you took a job so far away from my life? Are you a good husband? Can you meet me halfway? Is your job and reputation more important than me?*

That night in our hotel room, I could hardly lie next to him. I wanted to break through the invisible wall between us and reach out to him. He'd reach back, meet me halfway while I cried my eyes out, and he'd hold me like he'd never let me go. We could tell each other *I love you, I need you, I'm sorry, I miss you,* and things would go back to being comfortable. Back to us. Love is supposed to win.

"I don't know how long it takes . . . to get better," I finally said, but I wanted to say so much more. I would have stayed up all night talking to the man who stole my heart, but that's not the way it happened. Everything felt fragile in a way I didn't want to touch, like when someone loses a loved one, and your words are chosen so carefully that you barely say anything. I feared scaring him off with too much honesty and couldn't bear to see another look of disappointment on his face.

Ryan held his tongue, too. We were chickens pecking out fragments of what needed to be said until, eventually, we just laid there in the dark, falling asleep on separate sides of the same bed with the world between us.

Barely adults, already out of time. We said goodbye the next morning when I dropped him off at the airport, standing on the curb next to a flow of travelers and the sound of shuttle buses rolling past in traffic. I stood afterward and watched him walk through the automatic doors until they closed behind him. *He didn't turn around; he didn't wave good-bye,* I thought to myself, remembering one night in college when he walked me to my dorm, and we said goodnight at the door after our date. I did the same thing, stood outside and watched him walk away, not wanting the night to end, ever. Ryan turned around ten times, both of us smiling with a little wave to each other, and as he started to get in his truck, he stuck his head out and shouted, "I LOVE YOU, EMILY!" at the top of his lungs. It was the first time he'd ever said it.

My meltdown came as I drove away, frantically rifling around all the floorboards in my car until I found something that would fix the way I felt. I didn't think about pulling over and calling someone. Coping skills and strategies never crossed my mind. Forget everything about mental illness or addiction because the tidal wave known only as pain knocked out the power of everything else. All that remained was a bright red glow, *Emergency*. I unbent the paperclip with one hand on the steering wheel and raked the sharp end across my arm, repeatedly, until the burning pain consumed me.

The horror show in my head transformed as it slid down into my throbbing arm. I saw a wound that bled and pulsed with pain, but this one I understood. I could take care of it. Fix it.

The throbbing subsided, but the pain of our relationship reverberated on. I could feel it coming, the knock at the door on an otherwise boring Monday morning. A man required a signature for the envelope from Utah serving me with divorce papers. It probably wasn't my best choice to call Ryan to let him know his letter arrived, and when I hung up the phone, the unbearable urge to inflict pain upon myself ran all the way up through my ears. I wanted to rip out the feelings and bleed them dry. Tear it all up into shreds and let the pain come once, then leave me alone forever. *But no,* I thought, *I can't do that anymore. I could, I shouldn't.* There was nowhere to run, and I was dying to escape.

The truth was I didn't get out much after leaving the treatment hospital. Group therapy and a part-time job as a grocery store cake decorator were about it. So, on a whim, I bought tickets to an Indigo Girls concert that fell on a Thursday when I had therapy. Loud, live music was exactly what I needed, and when the day arrived, I remembered what excitement felt like again.

Until my mother stopped me that morning.

"I'm sorry, Emily, but I called Gary about your plans for tonight. I'm concerned you aren't being honest with him, you know, about going to your group." *She called my therapist?*

"You called him behind my back?" I asked.

"No, not behind your back. I wanted his opinion. Anyway, he said you have to go to therapy. We'll do the concert another time."

"That's so stupid! Why does he care? It's not a big deal." But she insisted.

Later, I grabbed my keys and purse and took off barreling down the highway for his stupid office. I threw open the door when I arrived.

"I know you and my mom talked, but whatever. It's ridiculous I can't even miss one night," I announced when I walked into Gary's little office with a circle of chairs in the room. *There. I said it,* I thought. I sat down with an eye roll after he asked if I was angry.

"I'm fucking pissed!" I declared, with my arms folded until the rest of the girls arrived and took a seat.

"Emily," Gary began, even though I didn't want to hear any of it, "your mom has news, and she was afraid to tell you. That's the real reason you had to be here." I sat back in my chair. She and I were just talking, and she never mentioned that part.

"What happened?" I asked a little softer.

"Sugar died."

No softening the blow to my head as he said it because that's not Gary's style. More words from his mouth continued to ping against my ears about Adam finding my cat dead in the backyard. Poisoned by the neighbors. Buried by the rose bush next to the side of our house. I let the rage and grief tear a hole right through me so deep I forgot what or why I even started crying in the first place. I needed to get the hell out of that room, away from people staring at me, to run from all the things that kept leaving me.

Poor Adam was the only one home when I got there.

"Where did you put him?" I asked him when I burst through the back door. He looked scared or confused.

"Tell me where he is!" I screamed in hysterics, and Adam slowly understood what I meant, taking me out through the sliding glass door into the backyard to the spot with the freshly covered dirt. Then he stood there while I fell to the ground and sobbed.

I woke up early wondering if they took off Sugar's rainbow-colored collar, so I called my mom at work to hear that no, she hadn't. And I wanted it. So I hung up the phone and grabbed a shovel from the garage, then walked to the backyard and started digging. Not too far down, I found a hint of my dead friend's pretty white fur all covered in dirt. I held my breath and kept digging, part of me thinking there'd been a mistake, and he was still alive. And I didn't want to bury him back under that dirt after I found the collar and unhooked it, but I did. *I'm killing him all over again. I'm sorry.*

It's hard to predict what catalyst will cause a person to finally snap. Is it punch after punch after punch at the same point of weakness? Or is it the inability to recalibrate after the initial blast that causes the break? I wonder if we could stop, pause to let our minds catch up to what's happening around us. If I could think for a fucking second and slow down—but it feels like there's never time. The world keeps spitting its expectations out like little marbles, and there we go falling apart on them.

That's the problem with tragedies that don't look bad enough for a case study or a spot on the news. If I'm not an overachiever, either, then I flounder around with the invisible throng of women labeled "hypersensitive, immature, and dramatic about ordinary life." *You had a rough start. Who doesn't? Your marriage failed; get over it. It's a cat, stop overreacting.* I sat in the aftermath and thought the same things.

But one loss after another was too much to face all at once. When it finally sunk in Sugar was gone, it was all gone, the way a long embrace releases between two people as they turn to walk away, fingertips still touching, and then suddenly, nothing remains between them.

And I couldn't feel a thing.

CHAPTER SIX

1997

"Justin? Long time, no see, man," Peter said when Justin came over to the apartment I shared with my older brother. I admit, Pete was slightly surprised to see his friend back in my life.

"Yeah, well, you never know with this one," Justin said, affectionately giving me a little jab. Peter nodded and walked to the fridge for a couple of beers. It didn't bother me they were buddies. Justin was the type of guy who was friends with everyone.

Earlier that night, he and I were at dinner, reminiscing about the hot summer day when we met. He graduated from college when I was still in high school.

"Remember when you recorded that song?" I asked him. "It was 'True Colors.'" He sat across from me in a booth at Chili's, his good looks and dark brown eyes unable to distract me from the open sores of my divorce even as his face turned a sweet shade of red.

"Oh, God. Do you have to bring that up?" he groaned, remembering himself singing Cyndi Lauper on a cassette tape. It was a sweet thing to do, but he sounded awful.

There was comfort in a reconnection when I felt lost as a human. Justin was a much-needed break from the drama of divorce and its aftermath, like a warm glow of light. And even though there'd always been chemistry between us, I loved him the way I did in high school—like a best friend. While we carried on in conversation, happy memories boldly stepped out of the shadows for me to see I wasn't at the end of my rope. Life goes on. And we go with it.

Slowly, over time, change felt less and less like a boxing match where every start-over punched me in the gut. I'd catch myself feeling happy when nothing particular was going on, or I'd crawl into bed and forget to be sad.

On the night when Justin was over, I listened to the boys talk about sports like brothers and felt the absence of angst inside of me. My mind drifted outward toward a foreign idea that I could be alone and still be complete. It's a rush to think about that amount of independence, post-divorce, post-failure, post-insanity. But the crash came quickly staring across our living room floor to the spot where Peter and I unpacked two huge boxes sent from Ryan only a few months earlier.

"Jesus, Em, what the hell is in these?" Peter asked me, out of breath from carrying the heavier one up the flight of stairs for me. I gave a shrug.

"I don't even remember what I left out there," I said, thinking about some coats and winter clothes I kept in Utah.

It wasn't until we started unpacking the contents that we understood what Ryan had done. Along with the clothes were things like the sheets I used to sleep on every night, all the gifts I'd given Ryan, even refrigerator magnets from places we'd visited while we dated. Every framed picture of the two of us together, every trinket of memorabilia I'd saved from special little memories of us, any evidence that a love or marriage existed were dumped into a box for me to unload. And piles on top of piles of photographs—some of the two of us, some of just me, all of which made me want to vomit when I looked—were forming in stacks at our feet.

"Shit, Em," Peter finally said, and I didn't know what he meant by the tone of the word. Was it directed at me or at Ryan? I never asked.

"What are you going to do with all of this?" he asked. And the only thing I could think of was to put it all back. Box it up again.

"Let's put it in my room for now. My closet, I guess. I'll figure it out later," I told him, and we tossed it all back in. So what if something broke? It was me who felt fragile like the glue that held me back together hadn't had time to fully dry. Some things might break me if I looked at them again, especially the fact I'd just been erased.

Justin isn't like that, I told myself, looking over at him to steal a smile. Nothing was wrong with him, except the magical spark that was supposed to ignite between two people only happened on his side, not mine. He was *in* love while I simply loved, and we both knew it. When we went to bars or watched movies on the weekend and flirted with each other, we knew what we were doing ever since my summer before college. Now, the night might end with him dropping me off, but sometimes we stayed together in a space where the kind of love didn't matter, only that it existed between us.

One night, together in my apartment, I held his hand as we walked through the middle of that living room where an old ghost haunted me. Peter was already asleep when we tiptoed into my bedroom, past my closet. When I turned around at the edge of my bed to wrap my arms around Justin, I did it because I wanted to. It was freedom that I felt, instead of obligation. When his familiar lips melted softly onto mine, I was alive. *Life goes on.*

"I'll pull out," he told me when he didn't have a condom. "I promise," he assured me, straight into my eyes, and I trusted him. I could have said, "That's a terrible idea," but I didn't. I don't know what Justin was thinking when the crucial moment arrived, and his 6'4" body stayed pressed on top of me, but he didn't do the one thing he promised.

"Sorry," was all he said afterward as I stared at the side of my dresser.

"You're an asshole," I replied. A long, heavy sigh escaped me to say the rest. Within minutes, he fell asleep next to me.

He knew I wasn't happy. All these thoughts ran through my head, but I couldn't figure out the proper words to fit what I was thinking. Maybe that's what it means to be speechless, a voice stuck in a vacuum of figuring out what to say. Suddenly, I felt small, and my mouth, the one that had welcomed his kiss just moments before, was shut up tight, holding in all of my fear. What if I said, out loud to Justin, that he didn't give me a choice? That I couldn't move him off me or out of me? He knew I tried to push him off me, but he chose not to pull out, so why couldn't I say that? What scared me wasn't what Justin might think but what he might say. I didn't know a single line of defense against the old debate of one-sided voices that rang in my head. It felt like he had an army behind him, and I wasn't taught how to fight.

The pregnancy test was just a formality to something I already knew in my gut. For a second, sitting on the edge of the toilet with a white stick in my hands, I pretended I had some magical power over the outcome of the rest of my life. It was like watching strangers stand at the gas station counter with that look in their eyes as they scratched at a ticket to win the lottery. I peed for confirmation, then called Justin and broke the news.

"Oh, okay," he said so casually I thought I'd misunderstood.

"Did you hear what I just said? I'm fucking pregnant, Justin," I said with a panic in my voice.

"Yeah, wow," he responded, and I waited for him to freak out even a little. Give me a shocked tone of voice or at least a sign of surprise at the news. But when he said, "I guess we should move in together," my room started spinning.

"What? No! No way." I balked. "Wait, what are you talking about?" Because suddenly, it was like we were on different planets. "Move in together?" I tried to figure out how he got there so fast when I was still reeling over the sperm, egg, and implantation part. I wasn't even his girlfriend.

I told him to call me after work. Until then, I grabbed a roll of toilet paper for Kleenex and set off to cry for a while. What a strange spot to be in. It was maddening, really, to come so far only to find that the ground, once again, was cracking underneath me.

When I considered my options, I didn't picture the actual procedure of my previous abortion and think, *absolutely not.* What kept coming to the forefront of my mind was the vitriol on strangers' faces, looking at a teenager without a speck of compassion. For five years, I wondered if those same people sat silently on a nearby chair listening to the same sermon I did on a Sunday morning, and a sick feeling came over me thinking about witnessing that level of hostility again. Those people hid behind religion to justify their hatred, and I refused to participate. It was my choice, and that meant Justin and I had a lot to figure out.

"What about this one?" Justin asked, holding up a newborn yellow onesie with ducks on it as we wandered through a baby superstore on a Saturday afternoon. The sight of it caused an unstoppable smile on my face, imagining what it would be like to have my own little human one day soon. Up and down the aisles, we walked with overwhelmed looks on our faces like most couples shopping for answers. The distractions helped him ignore how I refused to hold his hand. I couldn't do it. I pretended we were a married couple and this was my future.

I imagined one day, we'd drive home with a kid in the back seat and another baby on the way, Justin in the driver's seat. I wanted to like what I saw, but I didn't.

"When we're done here, we need to start making a plan," I told him, buying a copy of *What to Expect When You're Expecting* and calling it a day. Later, I read that book like a bible and wrote down all the things we needed to do. I left a few messages on Justin's phone to call me when he had time.

Can it be both? Are women allowed to have regrets, and, at the same time, be given support and permission to experience the ups and downs of pregnancy without marriage? Am I allowed to embrace the wonder of motherhood and say no to the man who ejaculated inside of me without my permission? Because it felt like I was pregnant and handcuffed to something well beyond by own body. Consider it: I was expected to embrace the gift of a woman's maternal nature—me, the woman who'd been prepping for this moment since changing Betsy Wetsy's diapers in kindergarten—and I was expected to be judged, ashamed, and criticized for being in that condition in the first place. Brutal. No wonder some of us don't want a turn to talk. We'd rather survive. There weren't classrooms with single pregnant women in their 20s. I knew no one my age who'd gotten married yet. I was 23 years old and divorced, single and pregnant in Texas in 1998. Good luck finding a connection with those odds.

Moments of joy, like the hilarious sight of Peter sprinting through our apartment parking lot like a racecar driver with the 3-in-1 stroller we bought at Goodwill, reminded me how good it felt to laugh. Sometimes, he walked through the living room cradling and cooing at something ridiculous in his arms, like towels or junk mail, then tripped and sent it all flying across the room.

I was allowed, at least for a little while, to be happy, and boy, was I ever on the days I couldn't hear what had been said my entire lifetime—*you should be ashamed of yourself.*

People began to notice the weight, but no one was willing to ask the loaded question, "Are you pregnant?"

It wasn't like I called my relatives to squeal about the happy news. I never skipped through the doors at my workplace for everyone to congratulate me. But sometimes, I stared at my naked profile in the privacy of my bathroom mirror and forced a good look at the truth, willing myself to fight back tears and say, *okay, fine, I love myself. All right, it's a miracle.* Because I needed to love the way my skin was tenderly wrapping itself in a protective stretch around my baby.

Eventually, body obsessing and self-loathing became too exhausting when I had more important things on my mind like Justin avoiding my calls. When we finally talked, a frustrated flood of pent-up fears and unknowns ran out of my mouth.

"Why are you in such a bad mood?" he asked me.

"It's not a bad mood; I'm trying to be serious. I have no health insurance, Justin, because I'm considered a part-time employee and that means no benefits even though I work almost 40 hours a week. I'm already on a tight budget. How are we going to afford this? And what are we going to do after the baby's born? Daycare is insanely expensive. How many hours can I work? I'm going back to school; I haven't even graduated from college yet," I said.

"What do you have to buy?" he asked, missing my point. "Everything doesn't need to be a big production." This is where perspectives go in different directions. For me, the answers to my panicked questions determined the rest of my life, and I lived with the pregnancy every second, everywhere, every day. For Justin, it was basic duties, then hang up the phone, or get in the car and go home to his life.

I figured I was old enough at 23 to make motherhood work. But I concluded that by picturing a baby in blankets sleeping peacefully in my arms. I soothed myself with the thought that one day, I'd read a stack of picture books to a toddler before I kissed a freshly, effortlessly bathed face goodnight. *Yes, I can manage this,* I thought, ignoring all the hard parts like where I will live and how I would pay for a bed for that toddler. I depended on those daydreamy thoughts at night when all the lights were off in my room, and voices leaked out of my head and onto the pillow. *How could I have been so stupid?* My own voice berated me, insisting it was my fault we had sex without a condom. *What the hell was I thinking?* Because how dare a woman be interested in sex in the first place. *You got what you deserved, you little slut.* And everyone will know it. It's just a matter of time.

Change can be jarring but also ruthlessly slow. It feels impossible to make it to the other side. But every now and then, it can happen in an instant, and suddenly, it's impossible to go back to the place or person you once were. On the day I used my unpaid vacation time to cut work and stand in line at the Department of Health and Human Services for Medicaid, I fit in the category of people who change because it's the only option. I took my place behind a woman with an exhausted look on her face. We both knew it, without insurance, we're screwed. I knew the assumptions certain people made about my predicament. And despite my circumstances, I assumed the same when I arrived that morning. I don't know who taught me to think welfare was beneath me or that people are lazy, milking the government, getting a handout, however the stereotype is phrased. But these thoughts were embedded in me so deeply, I couldn't help but apply them to myself.

Looking around, I kept thinking, *I don't belong here.* The long line of us standing outside with our crinkled collection of required paperwork in our hands crept along so slowly, one by one, our faces fell in defeat, a look we shared with each other as we inched along. I watched three young kids who belonged to the woman next to me play in the grass by the sidewalk while her husband studied the long line ahead of him with a look of concern. A laugh jumped out of me when the toddler tumbled head over feet and landed squarely on his diaper-padded bum.

"He's so adorable," I said to the mother, and a smile lit up her face.

"He wears me *out*," she said before adding that he doesn't stop moving unless he's asleep, then we both turned toward the kids.

"Do you have any?" she asked me, and the question confused me.

"Excuse me?" I asked.

"Kids. Do you have any kids," she repeated.

"No," I told her. "I mean, yes. Well, no, not yet," I fumbled my words until I finally blurted out that I was pregnant. I felt 15 years old as I said it, thinking how unprepared and irresponsible I was compared to the woman standing next to me, just a few years older than I was. Motherhood came straight at me at that moment, headlights and horn blaring, and it struck me instantly.

The woman, Margaret, sped the time with easy conversations that seemed to brighten her day, too. I knew I believed in angels. Exceptional goodness existed in unlikely places, and I needed to open my eyes to it. But I also knew that ever-present vision, the dream I'd had since dolls in cradles, was over. There'd be nothing to resemble the picture in my mind of a loving husband holding my hand while we strolled with this child for an evening walk.

I was catapulted into another world, one that opened for me after the nausea passed. I was eager for a glimpse inside my growing abdomen and scheduled to see my doctor at the ob/gyn office. My first appointment with Dr. Johns resembled a counseling session because I turned into an emotional disaster. This wasn't the first time, considering the man took me under his wing after I told him about my abortion.

How was I supposed to know most obstetricians didn't accept Medicaid insurance?

"Aw hell, Em, don't cry yet," he said, then rolled his eyes like I was the biggest pain in his neck, which I probably was. He started muttering and got out of his chair, pacing until he pushed the button on the intercom.

"Linda?" Pause. "Linda!" he said louder.

"Yes, I'm here, what can I do for you, Dr. Johns?" a patient voice responded.

"I don't take Medicaid, do I?" A rhetorical question. "I've got Emily in here, and we're in a jam. Figure out what we need to do to cover her under this Medicaid stuff, will you? Because she's having a baby." That's how he saved my life that day. I cried anyway, but for different reasons.

How does someone properly thank another human for a thing like that? There was nothing I could give him he didn't already have, and I couldn't afford a proper gift. I fought with myself about feeling unworthy in the face of such enormous kindness, while just the other day, I considered myself too dignified for government insurance. What a terrible thing to admit, until I saw how my guilt and pride worked against me. If only I knew what to do next.

"Wait. Are you . . . pregnant?" asked my coworker, Darius, the next day at the front desk of the recreation center, his hands awkwardly pointing to my midsection.

"Where the hell have you been?" I asked, looking slightly offended, and he burst out laughing before shutting down his grin. He only worked weekends, so I cut him some slack for being oblivious.

"Sorry, my bad," he said, almost falling out of his chair. "I just can't believe Emily got knocked up."

I shook my head at the response, and I laughed. It was the way he talked to me, so genuine as though nothing about me as a person was different. I basked in how wonderfully comfortable it felt to be seen. There were no awkward pauses or stares, no thick air to swat at. It was a rarity I'd come to discover the next weekend when one of my favorite patrons came in.

"Mr. Joseph! Good to see you," I said to the nice old man who always greeted me with a smile that matched my own. "Where've you been? We missed you," I said.

Sometimes, he brought homemade cookies specially baked for me, and we'd talk about things like the weather, but now his face was flat. He refused to look at me and wouldn't answer me even after I said hello a second time. He walked right past the place I stood to greet him and never spoke to me again. Mr. Joseph decided to erase our friendship by eliminating my existence. The "silent treatment" was the passive type of cruelty that didn't just make me feel humiliated and ashamed; it made me feel invisible. I was six months pregnant, carrying a child, and considered by some nothing more than trash.

Unless someone's paying attention, it's hard to notice the subtle nature of being ostracized. Naturally, it hurt, and I drove home that night, blaming myself for the way people treated me. I wanted to be stronger, but I wasn't there yet, and when I walked into an empty apartment, I lost it. Peter was always out with his new girlfriend, leaving me with too much space to feel significant.

"I'm not going to make it," I said to my mom over the phone through unstoppable crying. She came and found me on the floor of my closet with swollen red eyes surrounded by wads of snotty Kleenex. The guilt. Why did I have to be the kid always in crisis? But as she spoke her words to comfort me, and I did my usual thing of half listening, I saw her face. We'd make it.

"You're moving back home," my mom told me. "It's not good to be alone right now," and she was right. A mother's instinct, formed in the shape of our history, circled the two of us with assurance. When my mom was a child, her father died, leaving Fern, my grandmother, a widow. In her time of need, it was Stella, a widow herself and Fern's mother, who said, "I'm moving in to help you," packed up her things and lived in their house.

First, we made a plan, something Justin and I seemed incapable of doing. By midafternoon, I knew when I'd move out, which room I'd move into when I'd see my obstetrician, and what we'd eat for dinner. My heart was full.

I was about to give up on talking to Justin when, one morning, he finally answered his phone before I went to work.

"I can't afford to keep putting this off," I said. "We need to work some things out, get it on paper."

"Like what?" he asked.

"Like will you pay for some of this? A crib, a car seat, medical stuff, diapers. It's a lot, Justin, and what if something goes wrong?"

I deluded myself into thinking he'd be willing to commit to half of something, anything.

"Oh my God, Emily. I don't know. I have bills, too."

"What does that mean?" I asked.

"It means everything isn't about you. I'll help when I can, but I'm in a relationship now. I have my own expenses," he said. "You wanted it this way."

"Oh really? What the hell is wrong with you? We're not sharing a pet fish, Justin. I don't get to *move on* like you do. And I'm not doing this *to you,* you're in this as much as I am. And you won't take my calls? Stop fucking around," I said.

"Calm down, damn," he said with a condescending laugh. "You sound crazy."

The comment collided with my hormones and blinded me for a minute. It's hard to come up with a cutthroat comeback under that kind of pressure, so I had to settle for the satisfaction that comes from slamming a telephone down onto its receiver.

The truth was Justin changed from the moment I didn't want to move in with him. This time, it wasn't me with daydreams of happily ever after. Justin, for a reason I never knew, wanted to crown himself the hero who rescued me from the crisis he created. I had only to follow along, but I changed the whole story by *not* changing. My feelings for him stayed the same. And when women in similar situations don't "agree" with what they're offered, it's called selfish or ungrateful or, in some parts of Texas, disobedient. That's a big no-no for women who used to be girls who wanted to be good. I should just shut up and be grateful, but I failed that part, too.

I watched our affection flip like a coin being tossed into the air over what we used to be, and land with a thud, face up on hostility.

Silence became my public armor while others used it as a weapon against me. When Justin quit talking to me, my only choice was to ask a lawyer for help. His own attorney ignored her, too, and each time he did, it cost me more money. Every phone call and typewritten letter she sent meant hours of my wages went wasted as he silently rejected my efforts. Within weeks, he refused to acknowledge he was the father. On behalf of Justin's brass-knuckled silence, he had his lawyer dispute paternity.

That was my state of affairs when results from a blood test taken at Dr. Johns's office suggested my baby might have Down's Syndrome. "Would you like to have further testing?

"There are risks," he said, referring to the needle that would plunge into my stomach and break through the placenta to suck up amniotic fluid for further analysis.

"I'm calling my mom. Put me down for an appointment," I said after hearing the pros and cons. I wanted to know if my baby had Down's. And I wanted to know quickly so I'd have the most time to read every book before I gave birth, not after.

But when the morning came, and my mom and I walked into the hospital, I wished I had other options. Irrational ones, like fast-forwarding to the part where it's all over, and I've got a baby in a bassinet. Or I wanted to rewind life and go back to high school when my mom and I drove to a church every year during Christmas for the Messiah sing-along because we thought we sounded that good. Except the minute we walked into the exam room, she wasn't my mother anymore. The woman next to me, Mary Ellen, was my significant other standing with my hand held tightly in hers.

"You're doing great," she lied when I saw a needle the length of my femur. Both of our heads whipped away from the sight to focus on the image on a screen.

"No movement, please," said the woman carrying out the procedure. I never have a problem holding still until someone tells me not to move. With every click across my lubed-up stomach, another angle of the human inside me emerged. We were awestruck, speechless, unable to blink out of fear we'd miss a fraction of a second of the sight.

"Do you want to know the sex of your baby?" Without hesitation I said, "Yes."

If I could have chosen one moment to relive out of all the ones I remembered until that second, I'd choose what happened when I heard her tell us, "It's a girl." It was as though the world cracked open and out from its center came the sound of my own mother's voice from my mouth.

"A girl?" We said it at the same time. I carried a baby girl, not a shameful mistake. *A she, her, daughter,* and she was *mine.* I was a *mother* with tears running down the sides of my face like a baptism personally delivered just for us. In an instant, everything changed, and I looked at my mother, knowing she felt it, too.

Little else mattered. Negative results eventually came four weeks later, but that afternoon, the smiles between my mother and me said it all. At home, she unfolded the living room hide-a-bed couch and made a lumpy bed for me to sag and watch television. We ate ice cream and talked endlessly about little girl things. Sitting still like that, I relaxed enough to feel a kick on my tight little tummy.

"Mom, give me your hand, quick!" I don't know why I whispered, but she reached out, and I held her hand still until the fluttery kick came again. We gasped and giggled in a whisper as though we might disturb her playtime. We sat like partners, equally enthralled with whoever was growing under my skin.

That's the sweet spot of pregnancy before the hips ache and the ankles start to swell. My younger brother Adam, still in high school, got a kick out of sticking his fingers on the tops of my swollen feet like they were Play-Doh. Hardy har har.

"Contraction!" he'd yell on nights my mom and I practiced breathing techniques for labor. He'd call out commands, and we'd do the drill, making childbirth preparation a family affair. If it got boring, Adam would mimic me, acting out his breathing and contractions, or sing in his opera voice and depending on my mood, I'd either laugh or want to strangle him.

Since my twin mattress felt too small, I cozied up most nights next to my mom in her bed. It reminded me of when I was a little girl sleeping next to Stella, my mother's grandma, in the house where my mother grew up. I imagined my unborn daughter sleeping with her grandma. Not enough time had passed for me to consider how my tragedies had led to the most magical moment of my life. But I knew I was happy, even if things were far from how I'd imagined them as a little girl in pigtails daydreaming of motherhood.

I went into labor around 1 am, but do we know we're in labor at the beginning? Did other moms have a flurry of questions that somehow never made it into pretty pregnancy books? Because I thought I wet the bed, an unsurprising "leak," but not labor. Only I kept wetting the bed a little bit at a time. *This is weird,* I thought, then gave my mom a nudge.

"Hey, Mom. I think something's happening," I whispered.

"Nothing's happening. Go back to sleep," she croaked into her pillow without a hint of urgency.

I hyper-fixated on every ache and gurgle in my body until my thoughts took a nosedive into nightmarish scenarios. I nudged my mom again until she fumbled for her glasses and turned on a light, then I told her what was happening.

"Is this my water breaking?" I asked, and she looked at me confused.

"I thought it was more like a gush or something," she told me, but clearly, she didn't know either. We were clueless, even after all our hours of meticulous preparation. At one point, the two of us studied something gross and disturbing on a piece of toilet paper like we were scientists, assessing if it was a mucus plug. After three hours and a quick learning curve on what a contraction feels like, we headed to the hospital.

Firstborns are notoriously slow. Fine. However, a woman who hasn't given birth can't comprehend how a contraction feels. I didn't understand the talk about the pain until I wanted to back out of the entire ordeal. I was inconsolable, rocking on a couch, when I blurted out, "What idiot has more than one of these?" And begged the nurse for an epidural.

"I put in the order," she confirmed. "We're just waiting now for your turn." I wasn't the only person in need of an anesthesiologist. Meanwhile, it was cool damp washcloths, my mother's selected mix of classical music CD, and breathing, lots of breathing.

Nineteen hours and a failed epidural later, I was holding my baby girl. The way a newborn feels in a mother's arms is the trap that makes us forget how we almost murdered someone in the process. It's a love like no other, and I shared my proudest accomplishment with my partner, my mother, while Adam and his friends cheered from the waiting room like a gang of wild teenagers, and Peter came by later to hold his new niece.

I named her Shelby Maren, her middle name the combination of my mother's name, Mary Ellen. Later, after everyone had gone back home, I sat in my hospital room alone with one small light shining down from behind the bed. I laid her down on my legs and unbundled the swaddled blanket to examine every perfect toe and speck of beauty about this 8-pound, 3-ounce human I made. Oh, did I cry. She was the only thing I'd ever done right.

Early the next morning, Dr. Johns came in to do his rounds and saw her sleeping in the hospital bassinet. He peeked at her, then scooped her up and cradled her in his big arms. The sight of them together made me cry again. Suddenly, I was terrified to go home, to be a mother, to not have this man taking care of us.

He saw me crying and looked back down at Shelby.

"You did good, Em, real good," he said. I nodded and sniffled while he kept talking. "I gotta tell you, there's something about this girl. I don't know what it is. But she's got something special. You remember that. This one here is going to do something big; I can feel it."

"Thanks. You're just the greatest, really," I said, feeling love and loss collide with my heart. I grabbed my disposable camera and snapped a quick picture of the two together, which later would turn out to be a crappy photograph, too dark and out of focus. The moment, though, was frozen in my memory. Had the photograph turned out, it would have missed too much. It's impossible to capture what it felt like to replace a shameful mistake with a new mother's pride, to feel the flow of life-altering change wash over me but this time come out clean, not stained. For something so pure and innocent to come from me meant that maybe I had those same things somewhere left in me. I was pure in this new life, so I closed the door on my old demons. If only I had locked it.

CHAPTER SEVEN

1999-2001

A mountain of assignments sat on my shoulders. I gripped the steering wheel, festering over everything I needed to get done before Monday. Two papers to write, a test to study for, homework assignments to catch up on, plus I had to work on Saturday night. The days of camping out at the library were long gone now that I had a busy one-year-old getting into everything.

It was my first semester back at school after Shelby was born. My mom watched her during night classes. Sometimes, I took her along with me, and she'd get passed around the class to be cuddled by peers with attention, once or twice being carried around sound asleep by a professor.

I enrolled her in the daycare where my mother worked after she turned a year old, a couple of days a week, but if she got sick with an ear infection or a cold or popped a fever, then I'd have to dash from campus, an hour away. It'd been that kind of week—getting a call, leaving class, bringing Shelby home, and putting everything on hold to take care of her. Being her mother was so natural. I yearned to have her near me, to nurture and love, and when she was sick, we'd snuggle together while I watched her sleep.

I missed two days of class that week, ignoring the workload stacking up in my last semester of a seven-year pursuit for a college degree. Beyond tired when I drove along the highway that night forty minutes from home, I thought about other moms out in the world and pictured lives in pretty houses with dinner on the table. They'd sit down with their husbands and two kids, say grace, and have casual sips of wine as they threw back their heads in laughter. All the maddening moments of exhaustion, ear infections, tantrums, and crying were worth a moment like that, right?

I need a drink, I thought. It's what normal moms said after a long and hectic week. They had a glass of wine in times like this, and as I kept driving, I understood why. It sounded so logical, and I hadn't thought about drinking since Shelby was born. I'm an adult. Why not? I pulled into a gas station where I bought myself a 4-pack of mini chardonnay wine bottles. I hid them in my bedroom when I got home, knowing I didn't want Shelby or my now-sober mom to know what I was doing.

After bath time, Shelby and I played the messy way she liked to do things. We dumped the blocks out, and then we put them back in. She threw every piece of Tupperware out of the cupboards, then climbed inside for a game of peek-a-boo with the cabinet door. We were equally entertained; I could watch her for hours, even in her sleep. Later, we snuggled and read books until I finally put her in her crib to pat her back and sing her a song.

Then I thought about that wine.

I was more than ready for it when I snuck into my room, right next to hers, the one I slept in as a little girl, and closed the door. I sat on my bed, in the same spot my old bed used to be when I'd hide from my dad, my mother, the fighting, the world, and dug out one little bottle of wine from between the wall and my mattress, unscrewed the top, and took a big sip. It felt scandalous. But as the liquid sank to my stomach, I let out a heavy sigh with the simultaneous satisfaction of both excitement and relief.

I stuffed a piece of gum in my mouth and chewed, then dug out some flowery scented lotion from my purse to put on my hands before walking down the hall into the living room where my mom sat watching television.

"Bet you're glad it's Friday," my mom said, glancing over in my direction as I stretched out on the couch.

"Oh, my God, you have no idea," I said while I opened a box of crackers and flipped the channel to *Antiques Roadshow.*

After a few minutes, I got anxious just sitting there, thinking I might want just one more sip, and I nonchalantly went back to my room and quietly closed the door. This time, I guzzled the rest of the remaining little bottle and then sat there for a minute on my bed. *This is not good,* I thought to myself. *It's not normal. Regular people don't hide their drinking. I bet this is how alcoholics do it. Shit, never say that again. I'm only doing this in here because I don't want to make my mom uncomfortable. It's not that big of a deal,* I rationalized.

When I was a teenager, I went to AA speaker meetings with my mother, once listening to an old man talk about turning from a cucumber to a pickle, and at the time, I thought that was the dumbest thing I'd ever heard. He said, "Pickles can't ever go back to being cucumbers." My grandma used to make pickles from cucumbers. Dusty jars lined old shelves in her creepy, dirt-floor cellar where Peter and my cousins used to tell stories of men who'd hanged themselves in there. Half the time, I dared not look at what might be floating inside the glass; I was afraid I'd see eyeballs staring back at me. With that, I twisted off a new wine top and sucked down the entire thing before heading back to the television and my mom.

It wasn't until my last two weeks of classes that that secret drinking showed its true colors, like a little red spot turning into a rash. I pretended it came out of nowhere when, in truth, I'd seen it from the start.

"I'm not going to be like this," I told the face in the mirror. I was a good person, a good mother, I got good grades, I worked hard.

Before the ceremony, I sent out announcements of my accomplishment, licking stamps on envelopes, including ones for the father and grandmother who I thought could barely stand me. I wasn't even sure if I could stand them. We'd hardly spoken in years after a final blow-up over the fact I didn't put my dad's name on my long-forgotten wedding invitations.

Countless nightmares of forgotten classes kept me from believing the day would actually arrive when I'd be handed a rolled-up diploma on a stage in my cap and gown, but I did it in May 2000 with my daughter watching somewhere in the audience. I graduated with honors with a bachelor's degree in psychology, of all things. Afterward, as masses of people congregated proudly for photographs, I searched for my mom and Shelby. Standing along a brick wall with a bouquet of flowers from the local grocery store in hand was my dad. He showed up unannounced with my grandma. To see him there was so shocking. It was as if I'd been transported back into a little girl lost in a crowd who finally sets eyes on her daddy. All we were—the emotional cacophony of clamor between love, betrayal, abandonment, and hate—rested quietly as instinctive smiles swept across our two faces. He was happy to see me and to be there. I was happy to see him and glad he came. All the rest didn't matter so much at the moment.

If only it were all that easy. If so, I can't imagine what my future would have looked like. Fresh starts and cleans slates were scarce. All the strings in my life wrapped tighter the more I tried to untangle them. Classes, work, motherhood, alcohol, loneliness, secrecy, and shame pulled to constrict me until I forgot what living felt like. I was spread out and spread thin. Some days, I wanted to cut loose from all of it and feel the emptiness of falling, not caring where I landed.

I arrived at that exact spot partially because I'd been given poor directions. What did it matter? For me, I was born without an internal compass, never knowing which way was North, perpetually lost from turning left instead of right. I had a degree now, an opportunity for a new start with Shelby and so much excitement I could taste it. I kept moving, unaware that I didn't know where we were going.

For some people, it leads to adventure. For others, it turns to disaster.

When I met Chris several months later on a blind date, that's where I was, spinning around in avoidance. I was the wild one, and he was stiff as his starched jeans. But sometimes, opposites attract, and for some ungodly, regretful reason, we began a whirlwind romance. When I say he was anal-retentive, I mean he was obsessed with everything from making sure his ironed t-shirt was tightly tucked into his jeans at all times to buffing out any fingerprint or dust particle that landed on his precious BMW. The guy almost had a heart attack when Shelby got in the back seat without washing her hands after ice cream.

We got married.

I told him in advance I was a free spirit and thought I was an alcoholic. He told me in advance he liked guns and right-wing politics. The one unspoken common ground we shared was the belief that the other person would change. He would loosen up and learn to have some fun, and I would become a more well-behaved, submissive trophy wife. Neither one occurred.

At dinner, Chris expected to be sitting across the table from a miniature adult who politely asked for *extra* broccoli while wiping the corners of her mouth after every perfectly chewed bite. He insisted she use her fork the right way; it's bad manners to eat with your hands.

"Sit still. Don't use your fingers. Chew with your lips closed. Hold your cup with both hands. No whining," were a few of his parental conversations. I sat there bewildered by the control freak, wanting to tell him to stuff it, but instead, I looked over at Shelby who was just trying to eat her dinner. Nothing came out of my mouth; I just sat there pretending it was only Chris adjusting to parenthood. He'd change, and besides, if I said something, he'd only get angry. I believed I was being a good wife, even while wishing I had a big, fat gulp of wine to wash down the scene in front of me. I missed the irony of it all—Shelby was me, I was my mother, Chris was my father.

Grad school made me feel selfish, or maybe that was Chris's doing. I couldn't ask him to pay for my education now that my marital and income status inadvertently knocked me out of previous funding options. It was *his* money, and it was my duty to be the wifey in my free time, not study under a pile of textbooks. I thought I was doing the right thing by dropping out and rearranging my priorities. Passive aggressive statements about my spending on home décor for his bland bachelor pad led me to believe I wasn't pulling enough weight, so I got a full-time job.

I guess it's hard work to mold some women down to armpieces, but the whole process drove me nuts. And it wasn't just me who was disillusioned with their new spouse.

"This isn't working the way I planned," Chris said with his back toward me as I walked across the living room one night.

"What isn't working?' I asked, thrown off by the sound of his voice because we hadn't talked in two days. We were in a fight after I admitted I thought it was stupid to pay a guide to drive him right up to a "trophy" moose, so all he had to do was pull the trigger.

Then he asked me about my drinking, so of course I lied.

"Us, this," he said, like a business deal had gone in the wrong direction, and he wanted his money back. I turned around and froze. At the moment, I wasn't sure if I wanted to beg him to give me another chance or kick him in the balls. I eventually did both in a sense. I can't remember what I said, except I was crying and yelling and begging all at the same time. He remained stoic and rehearsed even as I scooped up Shelby in her pajamas and her blankie and left in a mess in the dark for my mom's house. The next day, he had all the locks changed on the house.

His attorneys portrayed me as a single mom out for his money. If that were my intention, I would have aimed much higher than Chris, the engineer. When it was finally over, he boxed up my belongings and dumped them in my mom's front yard. Several things never arrived, like Shelby's princess bedroom furniture, which I'm sure the new bachelor needed. She and I met Chris at a fast-food restaurant one afternoon, where he told her goodbye.

"Sorry, it's not going to work out for me to be your dad," he said. He tried to hand me a personal check written out for a considerable amount of money, when it dawned on me how stupid and shallow Chris thought I was.

"Please," he said. "Take it." I shook my head "no" and shoved the sorry paper away from me.

"For what?" I asked him with rage in my eyes, to see if he had the guts to tell me it would make him feel less of the asshole he was, but he bolted. I drove off with her crying in confusion from her car seat.

"Hey, we're gonna be okay. Mommy's right here," I said, reaching my hand back to hers in the back seat. "I'm not going anywhere. What do you say we go get a Slurpee and play at the park, huh? It's a nice day outside," I said. She agreed. I turned into the convenience store, already knowing the plan. She got the red Slurpee, and as usual, it overflowed all over the cup. I scurried over to turn off the flow and grab a handful of napkins like it was no big deal because it wasn't.

On the way to the register, I snuck my hand out and grabbed a small wine without Shelby noticing. After we paid, I led her to the bathroom.

"Let's go potty because they won't have one at the park," I said to my three-year-old. "Tell me if you need help," I said from the stall next to hers, then I twisted off the cap to the wine and chugged, counting seven hard swallows as they sunk into my belly. Now, I was ready. Ready for the park, the talk, the lawyers, the lies, and another new life I had no idea how to live.

More accurately, though, I was never really ready for any of it.

"So, what brings you in today? What are you looking for?" Cal, the car salesman, asked me while we walked from the lobby to his little office with glass walls. I didn't have a dime to my name when Chris wanted back the SUV he bought for me, and I wouldn't have cared, except he traded in the car I already owned when he made the purchase, leaving me with nothing.

"Well, I got screwed in a divorce. How's that?" I said, sitting down in a chair. "And I should probably look for something extra affordable since I'm broke, but I want a truck, so maybe we could start there."

Cal wrinkled his face like he was mulling over what I said, but I noticed his attempt to disguise a laugh with a cough as he went through boring information about vehicles in general. My eyes wandered from his cool suit and glasses around his office until they zeroed in on a familiar emblem sitting on his desk. I knew what the triangle in the circle meant, I just couldn't quite imagine this Dallas hipster being a member of Alcoholics Anonymous.

"Hey, I know what that is," I said, interrupting him with an arm gesture toward his desk. Cal glanced over to where I was pointing.

"Oh, really . . . interesting," he said, eyeballing me with a raised eyebrow and a smirk.

"Yeah, my mom," I quickly clarified, as if to say, *no, not me, no way. I'm fine, really,* because I was scared he could see it in my eyes. Even as I sat there flirtatiously buying a pickup truck, I kept looking at him with curiosity from the corner of my eye. The guy broke the mold. Everyone else I knew in AA was old, and I'm supposed to believe my schmoozy sales guy didn't drink or do drugs? I wanted to know more but was too ashamed to ask.

Image is everything, especially when a person feels like they have nothing else. I needed to give the impression of a responsible adult capable of handling this current catastrophe for reasons beyond my pride. For most of us in a similar situation, we've already convinced ourselves we're failures. But if others glimpse or think we're doing okay by their standards, then we feel worthy of the space our bodies take up or the oxygen our lungs require for another 24 hours.

And if luck is on our side, a stranger pays attention when we dress nicely that day or our child doesn't have a meltdown at the grocery store. It makes us feel like we can keep going, so I did.

Shelby and I moved into a one-bedroom apartment near my mom's house and put two twin beds across from each other like we were roommates. Our little home had a subtle smell of secondhand furniture and old people. We'd come home in the evenings to sit on the floor at our coffee table for dinner, then play outside in the grassy courtyard. After her bath, we danced to music in our pajamas and read books in bed until her little eyes were ready for sleep.

"One more, Mommy," Shelby said, and I reluctantly reached down into the book basket, trying not to fall off the edge of the bed.

"How about *The Three Little Pigs*?" I asked, squeezing back in next to her while she nodded. Part of me always rooted for the happy-go-lucky pig who just wanted to build a house and get on with it, but not Shelby.

"He didn't listen, and you know what, Mom?"

"What?" I asked.

"He might get *kilt*." She whispered the death word like profanity from her little voice. I gasped in fake horror until she giggled and reminded me, "Mom, we read this a hundred times, he runs away."

Whatever the two of us were in that apartment, the unconditional love between us existed beyond the boundaries of mother and daughter. But there were things we never talked about that should have been said. Sometimes, true stories are the hardest to hear. And if I heard myself speak them, then it meant it was real.

Moments of bliss and normalcy genuinely occurred regularly. When Shelby fell asleep in my arms with her mouth open in relaxation and half my body draping over the edge of her single mattress, it was the best version of myself, and I wished it would stay. I had a worst version, too, like most people, but some of us have another separate place between those opposing versions of the same life. It stole happy moments between a mother and daughter and became a form of torture because I didn't know which side I belonged on. Wherever I was, whichever end or identity I chose came with unbearable angst. And it came for me that night when I slipped my arm out from under Shelby's head and tiptoed through the bathroom to the closet.

I was alone with the door closed but still kept all the lights off so nobody would see me get down on my knees and fumble around behind a pile of clothes for a plastic spicket poking out of a box of warm wine on a footstool. *I'm the worst person in the entire world,* I thought, picturing what I must look like kneeling in the dark like I was secretly worshipping at an altar. *Don't look at me,* I thought with every swallow I took from a big plastic cup I kept in the closet for times like this. The conversation taking place in my head was one end of myself screaming all the way over to the other end of me. That's what happens when we lose sight of who we are. Did I forget? Or was it that I never got the chance to know me in the first place?

This is the mind of a young woman falling apart while trying to keep it together. Despite growing up in the wake of alcohol's destruction, I kept drinking until my stomach was full. Then I crawl into my bed and let the alcohol sedate me to sleep. I did it because it worked. The sharp edges running through my head smoothed into the single blip of a heartbeat. My internal screams died down to a whisper, soft enough to hear Shelby's baby breaths across the room. I drifted to sleep, suspended in the impossible truth that the thing killing me was also saving me.

After I dropped off Shelby at daycare the next morning, the traffic snaking along the highway to my office gave me way too much time to crawl up in my head and think. Before I knew it, I was rifling around in my car for a sharp object to snap me back to reality. The pain and relief of a clean cut were exactly what I needed to flush out all the misery trapped inside of me. When I found an old razor from a bag I'd packed for my mother's house, I hesitated for a moment before breaking it open, my right foot shifting back and forth from the brake to the gas in gridlock. I didn't look when I did it. Blood appeared, but that was it. No euphoric relief, no pain, no sense of comfort. I was an emotional pressure cooker, a blocked geyser, a bomb with a hair trigger in a hot car.

About ten minutes from the office, I tried one last time before I had to sit at my desk for seven hours. One swipe of the razor, and I knew I screwed up. *I pushed too hard,* I thought. Glancing down, I could see open flesh down to the muscle as blood dripped onto my clothes and into my seat. *Shit.*

When I got to the office, I passed by a coworker and fainted right in the lobby. There, on the canvas of the sloppy brown paper towels twisted around my arm, were my coping skills on full display for all to see. I was literally caught red-handed. Thankfully, my coworker had enough grace to hide the freaked-out look on her face as she drove me to the emergency room.

In the hospital exam room, I told the nurse the truth. The divorce, the depression, the despair, that the unbearable weight of it all was crushing me, and I cut myself to externalize my internal chaos. She took notes with a confused look on her face as if this was the first time she'd ever heard of such a thing, then walked out of the room. When the doctor finally came in, he seemed annoyed and in a hurry. With a perfunctory glance, he blurted, "Why'd you try to kill yourself?"

"I didn't," I said, taken aback by his callous tone.

"Well, you have quite a gash. Are you suicidal?" He snatched my wrist up in his hands.

"No, I'm not suicidal at all. I'm depressed, and I've got problems, but I don't want to die." I searched his face for some form of acknowledgment. He dropped my arm like a dead fish.

"How did you cut yourself? What did you use?" We might as well be talking about toothpaste brands or golf. I told him what I used.

"Are you doing this for attention?" he asked. *What the hell, sir?* I wasn't going over all of it again.

"Didn't you read your nurse's notes? I told her everything," I sputtered.

"I did. Are you?" he asked me again.

"No," I sighed, deflated. Obviously, he had a problem with me. The condescending way he spoke after his cursory glance at my open wound, which was still bleeding, told me all I needed to know. Any bedside manner, compassion, or interest in me and my problems was dead set at zero. I slumped and waited to hear how many stitches my desperate mistake would require, but instead, he headed for the door.

"I'll send in the nurse to put some butterfly Band-Aids on you. Hopefully, that will do the trick," he murmured on his way out.

My mouth hung open in silence at the closed door. Before the nurse came back, I shrunk into the size of a little girl hiding in a woman's body that would forever wear the ugly scar. I was a hundred miles from the world, from my voice, from believing anyone cared to hear what I desperately needed to say. I said nothing, not to that nurse nor my coworker on the ride home. I went right back to stuffing emotions and drowning myself with liquid pain relievers, even when they didn't seem to work anymore.

I crawled into bed next to Shelby, listening to her sleep so I could remember someone loved me. I lay there listening to two dueling voices in my head, trying to decide which one I should trust. One was telling me to stay where I was and breathe like her, so peacefully, until my body grew weary, and I settled into sleep beside her. Another one told me what a loser I was, how I ruined everything every time, that I was born to be a failure. Then another voice chimed in, "I can make that all go away. I'll be your pain reliever, your comforter, your secret keeper, your friend." Each voice had different methods and different strategies, but their goal was the same: to manage the mess. I knew them all so well.

I got up and sat outside on my small porch in the dark, trying not to think about altars in closets or little sleeping angels. Right on the other side of my patio fence was a huge oak tree, and I watched its leaves wave back and forth in the silent breeze. The way those branches swayed made me wonder if God was trying to say hello. I hoped He wasn't and that He couldn't see me at all at that moment. I didn't want to talk; I had nothing to say. Another breeze came, and with it, a whoosh of wooded arms with hands out to say something, another feeling God was close. I was too uncomfortable for an awkward conversation, too absorbed in headcase arguments with myself and my miserable existence in Loserville, so I turned my back on all of it and went inside to wake up Shelby from her bed.

Carrying her as she slept on my shoulder, I grabbed my keys and my purse, then drove down the street to a gas station. I locked her in the car and dashed in to buy what I needed the most—a pain reliever, a comforter, a lifeline, a friend—then drove home and put her back to bed. As I slung back the wine alone in my closet, embracing the comfort I so desperately needed at that exact moment, I thought, "I can't believe I thought a tree was trying to talk to me . . . that's crazy." Then I opened my mouth to swallow my savior.

Because as much as I was in love with Shelby, she was no match for alcohol. Every morning, I woke up making oaths to get my act together starting that day, and every time, I failed. My truck pulled into places I didn't want to go, and my hands purchased wine I didn't want to buy. By midafternoon, I sipped my spiked cherry-lime from Sonic right from my desk, telling myself tomorrow was my quit day. Round and round I went, from one day to the next in a half-drunk fog of maintenance living. It felt like I was on a never-ending sprint, and I hated exercise. I could feel the end coming but not like a finish line, more like a landmine.

Cal, the car guy, came over weeks later while Shelby played at my mom's house, and we talked outside in lounge chairs by my apartment pool. He had nine months clean and sober, which seemed like an eternity. I stared up at the sky, looking over at the top of that oak tree I always watched from my porch. While I gazed up at the night, he talked about God like they hung out together all the time.

"I don't obsess about it anymore," Cal said when I asked about not drinking. *What a liar,* I thought, because it sounded so incomprehensible. Right then, a wind swept across my face then around my back. It was gone in the same instant I recognized the silhouette of my big tree and those familiar branches I'd been watching at night for months, this time from a different point of view. Its leaves glistened in the moonlight, waving at me, and it didn't scare me like it used to. Private and personal, even somewhat embarrassing, I knew whatever God was out there was trying to tell me something. I just didn't know what it was.

When I woke in the morning, I realized I hadn't snuck into my closet the night before to anesthetize myself with wine. At work, I didn't sneak off to my truck to guzzle hot wine in desperation during the day. The thought of it popped into my brain every hour, if not more, but for reasons I didn't understand, I stayed at my desk. No official decision was made, but later that evening, I dropped off Shelby at my mom's house and then drove to my own meeting, opening the discreetly marked door this time as myself, the one with a drinking problem, instead of the daughter of one.

"Hi, I'm Emily, an alcoholic," I said when it came to my turn, feeling the awkwardness of the word pass between my lips. I had wasted so much time drinking in misery to avoid hearing myself say those words—and now it was over.

I didn't die, and a sea of disappointed faces didn't huddle around me to scowl. Barely anyone looked in my direction, so I wonder if anyone saw my amazement at how good I felt to have a seat in that room. It was an utter relief to finally say out loud what I'd secretly known for so long. I was far from glowing, but it struck a spark of hope at the exact moment I needed to feel something other than darkness. This time, it came from somewhere inside of me instead of a false sense of worthiness from one of my fake attempts for approval.

Shelby and I celebrated our birthdays that year by going to see "The Lion King" musical in downtown Dallas. With one month of sobriety under my belt, we made our way to our second balcony seats, the ones I could afford, and waited for the lights to go out. She was so little; her seat would fold her up into a sandwich unless she sat on the edge. That was the game for fifteen minutes until the lights flickered, eventually going black, and froze Shelby in a state of apprehensive excitement.

I watched her face more than I watched the show. Her wide eyes barely blinked as she leaned toward the stage, every expression following along to match the characters on stage. I sat there staring at her glowing silhouette with a lump in my throat that wouldn't leave. All I could do was nod my head because at that moment, I knew. It was worth it; sobriety was the greatest gift I'd ever given us.

By the time we stepped into the late-night air, Shelby was asleep on my shoulder, her black Mary Jane shoes and little white socks clasped around my waist, her arms dangling down my back. I kept pace with the other patrons bustling to their cars to beat the traffic jam out of the parking lot when I realized I didn't want the night to end. My rush turned into a saunter, and with the smell of Shelby's shampoo under my nose and the starry night above me, I surrendered to the moment and took it all in; the crowds swinging back and forth and us in the middle of it all. It was magical, and for a little while, everything was as it should be.

CHAPTER EIGHT

2003–2004

R*iiinnng! Riiinnng!* The sound coming from a pay phone in the hallway sent bile creeping up to my throat. From the corner of a microfiber couch, a spot where I spent most of my spare time, I had a direct view across the common area. My only entertainment at the drug and alcohol rehab facility was watching unsuspecting strangers pick up the receiver. This time, a guy my age, late 20s, picked up and held the phone to his ear, then turned to his left and his right like he was looking for an answer.

"Emily?" he called out from where he stood. "Does anyone know an Emily?" I pretended not to hear him.

"Is it that crazy guy again?" a girl I couldn't see hollered back from down the hall. "He's a fucking stalker. Just hang up. He calls here every five minutes, and she's not supposed to talk to him."

I tucked my knees in tightly to my chest and sunk my neck into my shoulders, thinking if I could disappear into that couch, maybe my ex-boyfriend Chuck on the other end of the line wouldn't see me. *Is he watching me through the window? Did he bring his gun? Have I been here two days or three?* Sobriety turned up the volume on my intrusive thoughts. *In a week, I can call Shelby.* Thoughts flickered across the back of my brain with her image on it, but I just stared across the room, eyes glazed, pencil in hand, watching little blips of memories come and go.

My mind bounced between a numbing fog and unbearable awareness. When the booze wore off, I was left with the searing guilt at the notion that any half-decent mother would be mortified for winding up in a treatment center for alcohol addiction. What had I become? Shelby wasn't on my mind in a normal sense; she was inside of it—a pulse beating underneath the wrists I'd sliced to ribbons.

I sat there like a war-torn soldier sitting in his recliner, staring at imaginary battles in the distance. I'd call it shell shock but we don't use that word anymore. Now, it's PTSD. Both terms felt too extreme for me, though I don't know what you'd call my situation if not extreme.

Riiinnng! Riiinnng! The sharp trill shot pins and needles across my body. Another argument erupted.

"Just leave it off the hook," someone said, but several people were waiting for calls, and it was the only public phone available.

"Let me talk to the guy," an older gentleman marched over to take the receiver to try to reason with Chuck. "Mister, you can't call here anymore—" He was cut off by a rant on the other end of the line. *Don't listen to him, sir. Hang up! Hang up the fucking phone,* I thought to myself. *You will only make it worse for me.*

I considered what Chuck could be saying to the man who didn't know me, scared the stranger would believe his lies the way I had initially. I wasn't interested in defending the truth, so I closed my eyes for a moment to try and piece my nightmare together.

One year before, I sat in a noon AA meeting surrounded by a familiar crowd of retirees, stay-at-home moms, and professionals on their lunch break. It was summertime, hot enough to burn your hands on the steering wheel, but I wore jeans with my faded red tank top because the sight of my legs in shorts revealed too much about my ongoing battle. I crossed one scarred leg over the other and clicked the heel of a flimsy flip-flop, saying casual hellos, until a new face, someone in a crisp, blue button-down dress shirt, caught my eye.

He had a smile when he talked that made the ones listening lean in with mirrored excitement. When he caught me looking, my cheeks flushed into two bright red tomatoes, pulsing in rhythm with my pounding heart. I immediately glanced away but wondered if he was still looking at me.

When we introduced ourselves to each other after the meeting, I struggled to look directly at the guy without a dopey smile on my face.

"Hey, I'm Pete," he said, reaching his hand out to shake mine by the coffee pot. I noticed the way his shirt pulled a little tighter across the muscles underneath it.

"Yeah, I heard." I smiled, looking up at him. "That's my brother's name, Peter. He's funny, too, like you," I said, referring to things Pete said earlier to the group and forgetting to tell him my name.

"Well, in that case, I'm sure your brother's a great guy." We both started laughing.

"I'm Emily," I added, looking away again when the electricity between us zapped me.

"Oh, I know." His green eyes smiled when he spoke; I thought I might die.

My own mother, having met the guy before I did, used to talk about the infamous Pete, asking me when I got home occasionally, "Was Pete there?" Now I knew why. The chemistry between us was undeniable, embarrassing me to no end, the way I felt his presence the minute he walked into a room. I'd been through too much for daydreamy thoughts about a recovering cocaine addict/alcoholic with my brother's name, but there he was, always on my mind. To even entertain the idea that he thought the same about me filled my stomach with teenage butterflies.

And if Pete and I could have kept ourselves in a separate universe, it may have been the beginning of a beautiful happily ever after.

How many times do men and women fall into the trap of thinking that type of life is possible? Everyone looks their best when somebody new comes along and knows the least about us—and it didn't take long for me to find out my darling crush lived with a beauty who wore an engagement ring on her finger. Then he'd heard about my past relationships and met my little beauty when she came with me on birthday nights to sit on my lap and eat cake. Out of necessity, a friendship sprang strong enough to handle the truth as much as it lied about what we almost were.

We ran in the same circle of friends and went to lunch one afternoon when I brought up my job search. I needed to find a better-paying job and something that offered benefits.

"You should go into sales, seriously," Pete insisted. Our mutual friends agreed that I'd be good at selling cars. Without much of a thought, I walked into a Chevy dealership down the street from my house, got hired the same day, and went to training the following week. A couple of months later, I went with some coworkers to a private car show during work hours at Texas Motor Speedway. That's where I met a professional driver named Chuck, who explained automotive details in a language I didn't understand, but that didn't matter. I'd already learned I didn't need car smarts to sell one.

Before we left, he pulled me aside.

"Do you live around here? I'm only asking in case you know a good place to eat," he said from behind his mirrored sunglasses. There was something daredevilish about our interaction that piqued my interest.

"No, not really. And I don't go out to eat very often either, except for cheap places where I live. Sorry." I shrugged. Then he asked if I wanted to join him for dinner that night. I gave him my number, feeling flattered that the rebel wanted to take me out.

"So why is someone as beautiful as you selling cars?" Chuck asked me later at dinner.

"Why do I sell cars?" I repeated to the bleach-blonde Californian who'd moved to a little town outside of New York City. "I don't know. Some friends said I'd be good at it. I needed a job, and it pays well, but that's about it. Just a job—" It was hard to finish my sentence when he dug in his pocket and pulled out a prescription pill bottle. He unscrewed the cap and gestured for me to look inside. I leaned over and saw a stack of little folded papers inside that reminded me of a powdered aspirin packaging I had seen once. I didn't know Chuck was giving me a little test, and I damn sure didn't know heroin was inside the tiny, folded papers of his medicine bottle.

"Sorry, I need to take some medication," Chuck said. I shrugged and chewed on some fries across thc table, thinking, *so what?* He mumbled something about needing privacy and headed for the restroom.

I wondered what he was doing. Did it make him gag? Did he put it somewhere strange? I didn't ask questions when he came back to the table because I didn't want to make him feel uncomfortable, and I didn't care. Let him be mysterious. I didn't think about that medicine again until we were long-distance dating. One afternoon, he called and told me it was a problem and that he needed my help because he knew I'd been sober for 18 months, and I guess that made me an expert. As the magnitude of his issues began to surface, instead of running like my precious daughter's life and my own were about to burn to the ground, I chose not only to stick it out with Chuck but to try my best to save him.

I took a plane to New York for a few days thinking I'd help him choose a hospital, maybe a support group, only to find him in withdrawal, lying on the couch where he'd shit himself, curled up from cramps and covered in sweat. Thankfully, Shelby stayed in Texas with my mom. I went straight into caregiver mode, looking for clean towels after a quick greeting, where he explained he ran out of his meds.

"Yeah, I see that," I said. "What'd you say the VA put you on?" I knew he broke his back in the Coast Guard years ago and wanted to look up his medication. In 2003, I knew little about OxyContin when he said it, but when he told me heroin would get him through until his prescription showed up, I knew what he was asking.

"Holy shit, I can't do that," I said. Absolutely not.

"No! Just listen to me." He gritted through his teeth. "If you go with a friend of mine, she won't pull any of her shit and steal from me, okay? Just take my cash and keep an eye on her until you guys are back here."

It was midnight already, long past my bedtime, plus a cab dropped me off, and I had no idea where I was. Women like me are such people pleasers to men who never earned it, and it starts to make sense—how I wound up riding shotgun that night, going 90 mph down the Interstate with Gina, the junkie, to do a drug deal in downtown Newark, New Jersey, before I even took my shoes off.

I want to say I did it because I panicked at the moment, but in truth, I wanted to save face and keep it cool despite being scared shitless. *I'm a superhuman, sober woman.* When it was over, I felt more like a hero than a criminal and stayed the rest of the long weekend without either of us mentioning him snorting powder or shooting up in the bathroom. Things seemed normal afterward, and I assumed his plan to get clean would work out eventually.

It was insane of me to go back to New York, but I did, taking Shelby with me because the mother in me couldn't fathom being without her. Or her without me. For a few nights in a row, the three of us walked down the street to a nice restaurant for dinner, choosing to sit in the bar area because it didn't require reservations or fancy attire. The antique furniture and elaborate rugs gave it the feel of another time period, perfect for wintry nights and silly conversations. When we left the restaurant on the third night, the owner pulled Chuck aside to say a few words privately before we bundled up in our coats to walk back to his apartment above the market store. He seemed distracted, but I ignored it.

"I'm going out. Be right back," Chuck said shortly after we got back while I read a book to Shelby in a makeshift bed. I glanced up to see him dressed completely in black and got a strange feeling in my stomach.

The next morning came a knock on the door from a police officer questioning Chuck if he knew anything about all four tires being slashed on the restaurant owner's car in the restaurant parking lot the night before. It was that exact moment when I felt a new danger creeping into my reality. We were making spaghetti in the kitchen when I asked him that night if he did it.

"Yeah, and she deserved it. All the money I spend, and she's gonna tell me a kid can't eat where I want? The bar is set up for diners. Fuck her," he said.

Silence gets mistaken for approval when fear takes over. In the shock, it's the quiet that does the talking for us only because we're frozen, trying to figure out what to do. There's a lot to think about: *where is my daughter, where is the knife, is he watching me, who can I call, where is the phone, how far is the door, is it locked, where are our shoes, how much money is in my wallet, how do I leave without a car, what will he do if we go.* What's telling is that I thought of none of this before that moment, but in the silent panic, it all spilled into my head in a split second.

"You seem upset," Chuck said, pouring himself another drink as I grabbed a fork off the counter and stirred the pasta, trying to look casual. I shook my head and shrugged. The sound of cartoons on the television in the adjacent room drifted between us as I watched him take down another glass from the cabinet and fill it with wine.

"Look," he said. "I deal with that woman all the time. She's a bitch, and I'm not going to put up with her disrespecting you or Shelby." He slid the drink across the counter. "I'd kill someone for you." And again, I didn't argue with him.

I picked up the wine glass, and I took a sip. No one held a gun to my head. No thoughts of drinking like a "normal" person crossed my mind, nor did I consider the possibility that alcohol would make my nightmare go away. While making dinner, I drank the whole glass. This whole trip was one terrible decision after the other.

This too shall pass—the phrase can get turned upside down, revealing a darker side. A message of hope can be manipulated into a reason for sticking around. Take the abuse. *This won't last forever,* I thought, clinging to Chuck's original charm because I thought it would come back. Why didn't I leave? Because I thought he would change. There used to be a time when women had no choice but to stay, and now I'm a wrinkle in the clothes they used to fold. But did I really have a choice? Because all I've ever known, ever seen, is to stay, to "stand by your man." Even in my worst relationships, it was the men who left, not me.

After the first week in treatment, Chuck's calls to the pay phone dwindled to once or twice a day, and I no longer hid myself in couch corners. Instead, I migrated outside on a Saturday afternoon, waiting for a black Camry to drive into the parking lot. My mom was bringing Shelby for a visit, and the second I saw her, I flew to my feet.

"Shelby!" I shouted. She ran toward me, and I swooped her up with kisses and hugs. I didn't want to let go. What a sweet relief to have her with me again, to smell her hair and her clothes and feel her body next to mine.

"Oh my goodness, I missed you so much I could hardly stand it," I crooned.

"I missed you too, Mommy. And guess what?"

"What?" I asked as the three of us walked inside.

"I went to kindergarten." Her head held high. "And Ms. Gordon is my teacher, and she lives in Nana's neighborhood!" The sound of Shelby's sweet little voice was like instant medicine for my mother's heart. As her sweet voice made its way from my heart up to my head, a wave crashed over me. *God, what have I done? It was never supposed to be like this. I'm such a fucked-up mother. I missed her first day of kindergarten.* How quickly guilt can crumble us. It's why mothers are the hardest to convince to go to inpatient rehab and why we swallow the pain of our shame in the first place. To feel it all would strike us dead.

Pushing all my insecurities aside, I sat on the carpet with Shelby and my mom in the main room for a game of Bingo between the three of us. I watched as she gave us all the gift of her magic, her laughter, a happy distraction, and a sense of innocence that all of us longed for but lost somewhere along the way. *Where did I lose mine?* I wondered while Shelby told everyone about our favorite songs and how she already knew how to read and tie her shoes. It brought me comfort, for the most part, to see her doing so well in my absence because I knew my mom provided things I could not. Shelby was safe. All her needs were met.

I never realized that the discomfort bubbling up inside me that afternoon could be more than the simple awkwardness of what it was: a mom spending time with her daughter at a rehab during visiting hours. Because none of it felt normal, and I was emotionally raw.

As the knotted-up mess of my mental and emotional insides unraveled, it was hard to predict what would happen next. Was it right or wrong for me to want Shelby all to myself? Or was it more accurate to say I wanted my mother to myself? Is that why I was jealous of the way the two got along so well without me? These are questions I couldn't comprehend any more than I could have acknowledged three generations together on a Saturday afternoon at a rehab, all traumatized by alcohol. It wasn't until much later that it occurred. When I looked at five-year-old Shelby playing board games, surrounded by the consequences of addiction, I was also looking at a five-year-old version of Emily because I lived it, too. At that moment, I was the alcoholic parent, not my mother or my father. But with the clarity that only comes after stopping the steady supply of alcohol, pumping poison through my veins, I was connecting the dots. Thank God. What a horror to see how history repeats itself and that I'd become what I most despised.

"Is this your little house?" Shelby asked when I snuck her down the hall to show her my room.

"Not really." I laughed. "It's just where I sleep and do homework," I told her, then showed her pictures of us tacked to a bulletin board. "You know, I think about you all the time, and before you know it, I'll be home." Then I asked her if she knew why I was there.

"Yeah, you drink too much alcohol. You know, Mom, you're not supposed to do that," she said straight to my face with her eyebrows raised.

"You're right, it's a sickness, and I did a dumb thing. But I won't do it again, okay? Mommy's here to get nice and healthy again."

That was it for our sentimental heart-to-heart. Shelby skipped down the hallway to look for the cookie tray, and I followed behind her with a full heart. I'd worry about the dragon (Chuck) another time.

I wished he had never existed. It didn't feel like my bones could hold the weight of the memories. If I looked back to see how stupid I was to try and help him in the beginning, and how fast it spiraled into losing my sobriety. The shame I tried to leave behind me with a fresh start in Florida never left. It only grew. I want to look back and see how fast it all destroyed us. I wanted Chuck to get his life together because I cared about him and thought I could help him. But after losing my sobriety, a pretty house to rent in St. Augustine and a fresh start seemed like a good idea. My life in Plano existed around my sobriety, and the minute I was back on Texas soil, the drink came with me. I hid from and lied to the people and places where I once belonged until the shame of my secret was as big as the alcoholism raging again inside of me. My best thinking told me to go. It was easier to hide my problems if I kept a distance, and I couldn't stand the thought of those close witnessing another disaster. A new place came with the hope that we'd get clean and sober together—until Chuck's monthly deliveries of three big bottles of OxyContin showed up at our new address. I thought I'd made the best decision, but on a walk with Shelby, I saw a look of defeat on her face.

"Where the hell have you been?" Chuck said the minute we walked in the door. "And did you take your goddamn phone?"

"We went outside, relax," I said.

"You called your mom, didn't you? I know she hates me; she's trying to get you to leave me." But what he said was nothing new.

"I didn't call my mom, not that it's a big deal. We just wanted to get some sunshine, that's it." I shrugged. But the grilling went on for another ten minutes, building until he shoved me in my chest, making me fall backward. I tried to get up and he kicked me for being inconsiderate. All I cared about was that Shelby wasn't in the room.

But things changed later that night when I stood outside with Shelby's little hand squeezing mine. I noticed I was squeezing hers with equal force. We were out on the sidewalk, hearing his screams through the window, watching as the flashing lights came closer. I imagine if I were a passerby, it would have looked like the police cars were pulling up to not one but two scared little girls standing in front of that house because that's exactly how it felt. The officers went in and brought Chuck out barefoot, wearing only handcuffs and a pair of boxers that hung off his hip bones. How incomprehensible it was to feel responsible for the scene, to be worrying about his feelings like I would my own daughter's. I was so disgusted with myself. I couldn't wait for them to leave so I could go inside, hold Shelby until she fell asleep, then slip off and drink it all away. Something had to change.

When my mom offered to buy Shelby and me plane tickets for an upcoming family reunion in Minnesota, we went without knowing the ramifications. The flight departed out of Dallas, so Shelby and I needed to drive to Texas first. Chuck made me take his car instead of mine.

"That way, I know you'll come back," he told me, but I assured him he had nothing to worry about.

"Of course, I'm coming back. I love you," I reassured him with a smile.

Shelby and I hit the road for sixteen hours with a tank of gas, two suitcases and $20.00 in my bank account. My whole life was running on empty when I pulled into the driveway of my old house and saw the look of relief on my mother's face before I saw her smile.

"Nana!" Shelby shouted. She ran from the car and into the arms of her grandma while I watched, taking my own private moment to feel relief before I smiled at the sight.

"My girls! Oh, I'm so glad to see you, God, I missed you so much," my mom said to Shelby.

"How you doing?" she asked me when I walked up for a hug, but she already knew.

"I'm okay. Just glad we made it," I said. *I have to keep it together,* I kept thinking because the truth was the sight of my mom made me want to fall to the ground and weep uncontrollably until every pent-up sob escaped. I wanted her to hold me to her chest and wrap me in her arms, run her fingers through my hair like *I* was the little girl instead of Shelby.

But falling apart wasn't an option because the following day, we boarded a plane to Minnesota, back to my mom's hometown, to stay at the house where she grew up, where her mother, Fern, would greet us on the front porch like she'd done since I was a baby. It felt unreal to suddenly be in Brownsville, population 460, where little had changed in decades other than the price of gas.

Later, the four of us piled into Fern's Chrysler sedan and drove along dirt roads up to my Uncle David's house with my grandma in the passenger seat and my mom behind the wheel. Shelby and I sat in the back seat, taking in the scenery and listening to the two women talk about local town events and gossip, although Fern would never call it "gossip." Relatives like my aunts, uncles, and cousins who came from across the country were the kind of family that made it effortless to pick up right where we left off, whether the last conversation was a month or ten years ago.

Do we ever outgrow our childhood? Because I used to think I was a star when I ran around barefoot, climbing trees or shucking corn in Fern's backyard. They called me the good girl, pretty little Emmie, but as I greeted everyone with smiles and hugs, I clashed against the image of who I should have been. I hated what I'd become. A divorce, another marriage, another divorce, then a daughter out of wedlock—we played it all off in casual chitchat as one person after the other reached into a cooler and popped open a beer. I failed drinking, and I failed sobriety, too, and everyone knew it. All day, I hid my restless state from the people I adored, flitting around enough to fit in until I could disappear into the bathroom to secretly chug down whatever alcoholic beverage I stole from a cooler or cabinet. I wasn't drinking for a good time or drinking to be like everyone else who made it look so easy to manage. I drank because my body was screaming for it. I wanted to be drunk enough not to care.

It's painful to disappoint the people we love the most, but it's worse to see the look on their faces when they realize how bad it really is, which happened when Chuck relentlessly called my phone throughout the entire day.

But there was a moment when loneliness left me. I sat alone that evening on the back porch, thinking, *If only I could stay right here,* perched above the world on a hilltop where everything below me looked calm and gentle. A breeze blew against my sun-kissed skin, and I breathed it in while I watched the sky change from orange to deep pink. *Don't leave yet; stay a little longer,* I thought, as if I could stretch the quiet stillness inside me across an entire life. But silence can be mistaken for peace. And right behind me, through a sliding glass door, I heard my aunt's house phone ring three, four, five times until she picked up the receiver. When I turned to look, I could already tell by her distressed face. It was him.

"She doesn't want to talk to you," I heard her say. "None of us do." I hurried toward the phone, waving like a white flag of surrender. I had to talk to him myself or he'd keep calling.

"Hello," I uttered, my voice devoid of emotion.

"Did you forget my connections to the FBI? I told you I'd find you," Chuck bellowed. He was wasted. "You said you'd be a couple of *days*. And now you're already ignoring me."

"No, I'm not. I'm on vacation with all of my family. It's busy," I explained.

"Shut up! I need you here, darling, so you need to leave on the next goddamn flight or I'm coming to get you. It's that simple," he demanded.

No, it's not.

I wanted to stay forever and also leave immediately. But I knew both were terrible options. I felt relieved that Shelby and I had an earlier flight back to Dallas, separate from my mother, so I could collapse in private. Except nothing was private anymore. All my secrets kept spilling out, right up to a couple of nights later when we sat in Chuck's jeep at the airport waiting to pick up my mother.

"Do you want to come sit up front with me?" I asked Shelby because we had thirty minutes to kill before the flight landed. At least, I thought we did. I couldn't remember what flight she was on, nor could I remember driving to the airport. *Did I bring any water? I need to think.* I knew my mom would call when she landed, so I looked around for my phone. My eyes were so heavy from the alcohol I snuck throughout the day, despite having every intention to sober up by now. The only way to stop my head from screaming for a drink was to give it what it wanted, but the joke's on me because the screaming never stopped. *I didn't mean to get this drunk,* I thought, looking in the rearview mirror at Shelby before closing my eyes for a second.

Not a minute later, someone pounded their fists on my window like a gorilla, and when I lifted my hundred-pound head, I saw it was my mother in a furious, frantic state, trying to get into my locked car.

What in the hell is going on? I thought to myself in complete confusion before I realized what had happened. I passed out. For how long, I didn't know.

"What is *wrong* with you?!" my mom yelled when I unlocked the door, and she flung it wide open. "Get out of the car! Emily, I'm so furious, Jesus . . . you *drove* like this? With *Shelby*? I can't believe you!" She seethed at me before turning toward the back seat and talking quietly to Shelby.

I stumbled out of the car and made my way to the passenger door. I'd never seen my mom that angry. Her face was bright red as she told me how she couldn't get ahold of me, how long it took to find me in the garage, thinking I was dead when she saw me, how it's a miracle I'm even alive. I know she was scared. I should have been devastated and just as scared, too, but I was too used to the feeling, the feeling of nosediving into chaos.

Addiction is like a mountain that keeps growing until its peak pokes out above the rest of the range. The tallest part finally gets our attention more than what it takes to get there, and that night, my mom saw her daughter going over the edge. Instead of watching me plummet to my death, she made some phone calls to some sober friends, and on a Saturday, they drove me drunk and hopeless to an inpatient rehab while she stayed at a neighbor's house with Shelby.

We never said goodbye.

I'd been there almost three weeks by the time I walked into a conference room and saw my counselor, Rachel, sitting at a table with my mom and two brothers. I couldn't believe what I was seeing. *How dare you all do this to me?*

"Come on and have a seat, Emily," Rachel said in a lighthearted way that didn't fool me. One look at their faces and I knew I was in for an unpleasant earful.

"Wow. Peter," I said to my older brother, whom I hadn't seen in over a year. "You came all the way from California just for *this*?" I asked him from across the polished table.

"Yup," was his answer.

"So Emily," Rachel began, "everyone in this room cares about you, and that's why they came today."

"Yeah, that's fine," I said, noticing how my family wouldn't look at me.

"But they have some concerns." I looked hard at Rachel as she spoke. My palms broke into a sweat. "This is a chance for them to tell you how they feel without being afraid of how you'll react, and we've already gone over the tools we use for healthy communication, okay?" No one told me about this part of rehab. I crossed my arms like armor across my chest, bracing myself for what they had to say.

"I'll go first," Peter told Rachel, and she reminded him to talk directly to me.

"I'm going to get right to the point." He finally looked at me. "It pisses me off to see you here. Seriously, what the hell happened to you, Emily? Do you think about what you're doing to Mom? And what about Shelby? You have a daughter! You're her mother, and look at you." As he raised his voice, my lungs shrunk down to the size of a little girl's, holding her breath at the dinner table across from her father. But this time, I refused to cry. Like a reenactment of our familiar family pattern, my mom sat in silence with her eyes downcast, and Adam disappeared into the background. We'd just recreated my childhood kitchen.

"Chuck's calling everyone, you know. He wants to kill you," Peter continued. He stood up and walked over to me, all high and mighty in his khaki slacks and a short-sleeved, printed shirt tucked in like it was casual Friday at the office. He took my hand and pulled up my sleeve, exposing the trauma map of red streaks, bloody scabs, and scar tissue on my arm. "*Look* at yourself! Look at this, Emily. What is this? Grow up." The look of disgust on his face filled me with rage.

"Do you think I *like* this?" I shouted.

"You know what?" I heard him mutter when he sat back down,

"You're worse than Dad." And there it was, the razor-sharp phrase someone finally had the courage to plunge deep into my back.

"I'm done." I burst into angry sobs, unable to recognize whose voice was trying to convince me to stay. I didn't want to cry, not because I thought it made me look weak, but because I didn't want it to be mistaken for a plea for sympathy. So I grabbed my stupid bag filled with papers and workbooks meant to teach me how to live without needing to escape, and I thundered toward the door.

"Fuck you all!" I shouted and slammed the door behind me.

I'm pretty sure that's not how Rachel intended the family session to go. For an hour, I hid from the staff outside, crouching between an air-conditioner unit and boxwood shrub, with the hot Texas sun melting the sweat out of me until I knew my brothers and mom were gone. An open field of grass stretched out in front of me, looking like the closest thing to freedom. I wished I could lie sprawled out and let the heat burn off all my anger. Or maybe I could run away, find a place to empty everything inside of me and start all over again. Was there such a place? What are we supposed to do if someone hurts us and we can't defend ourselves or fight back? I'd hurt myself instead, but I wasn't allowed to do that either. There was nothing left to do but swallow my stubbornness and pride and go back inside. Besides, my brother said nothing I hadn't already said to myself. It's the confirmation of facts that stung the worst.

If my current circumstances resulted from my alcoholism, then sobriety is a logical answer. But is four weeks enough time to make a difference on a mountain like mine?

"Are you ready to go home?" Rachel asked at our last appointment.

"Absolutely. I'm not the same person I was when I walked in here, that's for sure." I meant what I said. I was a 29-year-old unemployed single mother thinking 31 days was enough preparation to tackle life as a sober, responsible adult.

The minute I walked out those doors and into the real world, I felt Chuck's silent, invisible presence lurking around me. It isn't always the screams or fists that scare a woman. But I didn't have time to think about that, not with a five-year-old angel running toward me, the blue sky reflecting in her eyes. Because this was it, the opportunity of a lifetime, my second chance, a restart for a new life where I'd be the perfect mother that Shelby deserved.

And again, I didn't get the option of keeping the two of us in a separate universe from the rest of the world. The bubble popped when reality hit it and I realized I'd have to go to Florida to retrieve my truck and our belongings, and the whole thing felt like a heist on my happiness. My stomach hit the floor thinking about it.

"Can't someone else go? Why does it have to be you?" my sober friend, Pete, asked me.

"Look." I sighed. "I hate it, too, and my mom and I went over this a dozen times. But nobody else will know what things to take from the house, what's mine and what isn't," I explained. We went back and forth over who'd take the trip with me because he wanted to be the one, but it had already been decided that my brother Adam would go.

"I don't want to lose you again," he said.

"Oh, my god, there's nothing to lose, really. And you won't. Believe me," I said with an eye roll.

Throughout the drive to Florida, while binge-snacking on barbeque corn nuts and beef jerky, I wondered what would happen between Pete and me in the future. I knew he was a good man, but I worried whether I was a good enough woman. That worry reached an apex when Adam and I reached St. Augustine, and I saw up close with clear eyes what dark, despicable living I'd done such a short time ago. It turned out Pete was right to worry.

It was a mistake to go to Florida. All those miles of distance pulled together too fast, and without warning, something snapped inside of me. The same feelings I couldn't handle corroded me, and the only escape I knew was the wine I snuck off to drink when Adam and

I stayed at a motel for a night. We were parked in front of the house, but I could not make myself go inside.

Instead, Adam took a list I wrote and carried out my belongings on multiple trips, my phone dialed and ready to call the police at any second.

Yes, I made it back home, and I didn't have to see Chuck at all. This time, I left, but it wasn't a victory, not by a long shot. He was still around, in phone messages or in my mind. It'd be years of random obituary searches whenever he crossed my mind until the day came when his name finally pinged, and I let out one final sigh of relief.

CHAPTER NINE

2004–2008

"Glad you're back, Emily," a woman, Kim, said with a concerned look on her face, and I nodded graciously *yes, yes*. AA encourages home groups, so we get to know one another and feel connected to the fellowship, but it also led to these types of moments. I braced myself as she swooped toward me.

"Yeah, been back a couple of weeks now, Kim," I said.

"So what happened?" she asked. "I noticed you weren't coming to as many meetings." *Ahh, here it comes, Queen Kimberly and her wisdom,* I thought to myself, trying not to stare at her badly sunburned cleavage, ready to reach out and smother me.

On the surface, it sounded like a thoughtful thing to say, and if I didn't know her, I would have gabbed her ear off like the first time we met, mistaking a busybody for a caring individual. But Kim wasn't a friend. Having known her for a couple of years, I kept it brief.

"A lot of stuff. It's hard to explain," I told her while I pulled my purse strap over my shoulder and gave her a quick smile to signal I was leaving the conversation.

"Well, you drank because you're an alcoholic, of course." She laughed, like I hadn't heard that line a hundred times.

"Yes, thank you," I said as I turned toward the exit. It's like any big family, really—love all and like a few. By another comparison, any organization or group of people, despite its size, was bound to have a few individuals who got on your nerves. No doubt, my name was on somebody's list.

Along the outside of our building was a row of dirty plastic chairs if you could find them through the cloud of cigarette and cigar smoke. I plopped down in the last one available, slouching into position to listen to the men and women around me share bullshit stories or, if I was lucky, someone's love life. The language was as unhinged as the laughter, and when my friend, Julie, handed me a lit cigarette, I was home again. These were my people, my side of the family.

There'd be plenty of time to dissect my relapse with a sponsor, but right now, I sat back and let a small group of drunks remind me of what a royal idiot I am sometimes. Because the proper time to whip out a war story is when someone like me feels their worst. It's a not-so-subtle reminder that my crap isn't special, and within minutes I was rolling with laughter at the ridiculous things my cohorts had done before they'd gotten sober for good.

"All's I had to do was reach down below my steering wheel, unhook that little tube, and take some good swigs. Cops never could find where I kept my booze," said Aaron, who'd been sober almost as long as I'd been alive.

"Yeah, 'cus nobody normal keeps alcohol in the windshield wiper fluid reservoir then rigs it to drink and drive, you fool," someone said through the laughter.

But I didn't stay for long, knowing my mom would wonder where I was if it took too much time to get home, and it's strange the little things I noticed now that I was back. Trust wasn't something I could order over the phone and have it delivered like a pizza thirty minutes later, so when I walked in the door that night, I talked her through my evening. It's hard not to feel nervous in those types of moments as I watched the extra care that went into my mother's normally casual movements or the way her eyes searched deep into mine while we talked about things like the traffic. I started shifting my weight from one foot to another, avoiding her eye contact and digging for leftovers in the fridge like I used to do in high school when I knew I'd been busted.

"Okay, I'm going to bed. What's your plan for tomorrow?" she asked.

"A noon meeting, some laundry, and I need to pay a few bills," I told her, but it left a lot of free time with nothing to do. Starting over wasn't easy, and while I loved to wake up and see Shelby eager for another day at school, there were moments throughout those seven hours when it felt like everyone was out in the world doing something productive but me.

I bounced between my AA family and the one I had at home so often that the two began to effortlessly weave into one. Not everyone likes it that way. Some choose to say Mommy was at camp instead of rehab or won't discuss what goes on at a meeting with their spouse. But since all of us at the group knew each other anyway, I found it comforting the way my sober family got excited to see Shelby on Saturday nights when she came for birthday night like a bunch of aunts and uncles. She'd cling to my leg in the crowd, saving her smiles for the people she knew best. One of them was Pete.

In my efforts to redeem myself as a sober human being, you can imagine how confusing our friendship suddenly became when I found out he was single. We have these unwritten rules like don't significantly change the first year and don't get into a serious relationship, so I caught myself stuck between trusting my gut or the gospel according to AA legend.

"Hi Pete," I said, but now do we hug? Because I hug everyone, it would be weird if I didn't. *Wow, he smells amazing, am I standing too close? Can anyone tell if I'm nervous?* My thoughts hindered any attempt at playing it cool, but Pete was so comfortable to be around that all my worrying was a waste.

"Hey, listen," he said one day. "I've got extra tickets to a show in Dallas this weekend. Do you guys want them?"

"What do you mean? You're giving them away or selling them? And what show?" I asked.

"Yes, well, no. No, I'm asking if you guys want to go *with* me. It's *Joseph and the Amazing Technicolor Dreamcoat.* I'll even drive. The three of you will love it." How could I say no to that?

I don't think any of us expected to hear Pete sing the entire hour-long drive, especially Bruce Springsteen's "Born to Run" at the top of his lungs, grunt sounds included. My cheeks hurt from smiling to the song I'd grown up listening to, and when I turned around from the passenger seat to look back at my mom and daughter, they were laughing. Good God, what a heavy price some of us pay for such moments of joy. Would the light be as bright if we hadn't suffered through the darkness?

My precious mother's expression showed signs of amusement mixed with relief. She finally looked happy for me. And it filled my heart with hope.

Because even though I was sober, I still felt like a drunk. If I had too much free time or not enough distractions, I'd think, *I wonder if I could get away with it.* Or someone would look at me in a way that convinced me *they think I'm lying* or *they're suspicious about my sobriety, she was trying to smell my breath for alcohol.* Whether I was right or wrong or normal in my assumptions, the secret misery was the same.

"I don't think that sounds crazy," Pete told me, and I don't know how he tolerated listening to me ramble.

"It's like any time I'm talking about something that people think is out-of-the-blue or I get really excited, or I sleep in or stay up late, someone suspects I drank," I shared.

"It's hard, Em, but you've got to believe you're not alone. You made it this far, right? God's not gonna drop you."

Oh, yeah. God. I could have taken the Group Of Drunks approach, but most were screwed up like me, and it didn't seem very reliable. Texas wasn't the greatest place for someone like me to go searching for God, and I say that because the Baptists and the Catholics are serious about who can and cannot pass the qualifications for being a Christian. As far as I could tell, I was already going to hell, but I was willing to try anything if it meant a better life.

"God, money, parenting, this stuff is hard. I mean, Shelby's happy, but I feel like I suck as a mother, too," I said one night to Pete. Normal life looked so easy until it all showed up at once.

"What? You're a great mom, are you kidding?" he reassured me.

"I just feel like I'm always so behind, like I can't catch up or keep up with what's going on at her school or if I'm supposed to organize a playgroup or something. I feel like a teenager out there." I felt as if all the other moms had proper training and were twice my age. Pete reached across the little outdoor Starbucks table and held my hand.

I wasn't looking for love when I found it. Heck, I still struggled to love myself, but I couldn't keep friend-zoning this beautiful man. I didn't want to. I was a mother and a newly sober one at that, but I was also a single 29-year-old woman. What part of me was ineligible for such a tender sign of affection? Because a minute felt like forever that September night with the two of us suspended inside a silence filled with anticipation and promise.

"You know I love you, right?" With those six words, Pete broke open the quiet space.

"Yeah." I knew it was true. I looked at his face, lit from nearby windows, where I watched people order coffee and sip from cups with friends. I couldn't stop myself.

"I love you, too," I confessed, wishing I'd never said it to any other man before the one who sat in front of me now. He smiled at me because he already knew it, too.

"Just so you know, if we start dating, we're probably going to get married," he said, half joking, half serious. To the outside world, it looked like another one of my spontaneous bad decisions. Relief washed over my body, not like a secret finally came out, but like an old familiar breeze blew across my face and told me, *you can breathe, you will be okay.*

"How does December sound for a wedding?" I asked on the way back to his car. He said it was perfect, then turned and pulled me in for a long embrace. I wanted to stay and make out like a couple of teenagers, but I had a kid who didn't understand the concept of sleeping in on the weekend.

Two months later, I woke up panting, covered in a light sweat. In the dream, I was falling off a cliff into a dark hole in the earth with no bottom. In a panic, I flailed my arms and kicked my legs, not to stop the fall, but to stop and catch a breath. Mixed inside all the joy and excitement hid an old voice telling me secret messages I'd kept to myself. *He can't possibly love the real you, Emily. You're not good enough for him. Something horrible will happen, and it's going to hurt like hell. He will find out who you really are and leave you.* The volume of those thoughts got louder when I tried to talk to God about them, so I stuffed down the old tapes playing in my head and tried to play out my perfect life.

Why would I want to look backward or give attention to dark things when the light finally felt so good?

It was never supposed to happen, not again. But my head was pounding with what the experts call anxiety, fear, perfectionism, shame pumping through my veins, and mixing in with a splash of PTSD, but I didn't care what it was called. I wanted all the racket to shut up for a minute so I could enjoy the good things happening. *Give me an hour or two,* my head said on my way to the pharmacy counter. I'd almost made it to the back of the store when the mouthwash caught my eye. Something made me think it was less threatening. So I bought it and drank a few swigs in my car driving home one morning.

I don't know why I spent so much time trying to insert logic and rational thinking into the insanity of addiction when it never made sense in the first place. That one decision to break the seal of sobriety I desperately tried to keep under wraps didn't end until a few weeks later when I came out of a blackout in a hospital emergency room with a police officer guarding my door. Pete was sitting next to me.

"Oh my God, I can't be here. I need to go; I have to go home," I cried.

"No, you can't, it's not safe. You need help," Pete said. How was I supposed to lay there knowing I ruined everything again? I wanted to ask him what happened, but I also didn't want to know. It turns out I went into a rage at the house that night, and my mom called Pete to come over and help her.

"You had a knife, Emily." His voice turning softer, and I buried my face in my hands. "And wanted to hurt yourself. You weren't very . . . cooperative when we got here."

Officers came and handcuffed me before putting me in the back of a squad car to escort me to a psychiatric hospital, Green Oaks, in Dallas for mandatory surveillance.

"Wait, this is a mistake. I don't belong here," I pleaded to the man about to lock me in an empty room. It had one wall made of plexiglass, exposing me to a massive room full of patients and a nurse's station on the other side.

"Sorry, but you have to wear one of these." He lifted a straitjacket, although he called it something softer, like a self-harm protector.

"Please, sir, don't make me do this," I pleaded, sliding my arms into the thick, white canvas sleeves with no ends for my hands to poke through. Instead, it sewed down into straps to wrap around me like a hug I didn't want. The buckle in the back made sure I couldn't wiggle my way out and wipe the snot dripping out of my nose until they eventually came and unstrapped me.

I was left for endless hours in the room with a disturbing

quiet—the kind of silence that sent a high-pitched vibration through one ear and out the other. When I pounded on the glass for help, it echoed like unbearable thunder, but no sound came from the other side. Nobody noticed or heard me. I was invisible, sitting for another 12 hours on the floor with no one looking in my direction. Locked in that room with nothing but my thoughts. *What if they forget about me?* The thoughts grew into an insidious shadow, suffocating me.

I wasn't just an alcoholic who hadn't learned her lesson yet. There were reasons I sabotaged every good thing that came my way, reasons as deep as that hole I fell down in my nightmares. The outside of someone's life rarely matches what happens within, at least in my experience. Emotions and reactions aren't labeled for easy reference, and it's hard to sort them out when they spill out in a jumbled mess. A mixture of primal needs and societal survival collided in the fear of never getting out, of being overlooked and forgotten because *if you forget me, I'm dead. What if they forget me* turned into *What if he leaves me?* And it scared me as much as *What if he STAYS?* I didn't know what to do with all that fear. This was Pete's fault, alcohol's fault, God's fault. *I'm such a fucking coward,* I whispered, because I knew I'd rather be numb than brave.

My hands were shaking when I reached up for my hair and pulled it as hard as I could, letting out the loudest, longest scream my voice would make until I gagged and spit on the floor. After the outburst, my lungs heaved like a worn-out wild animal. I stared at a clump of hair on the linoleum, certain I'd look up and see people staring at me. But nobody looked. Not a single glance in my direction. I paused, momentarily grateful and relieved, because for the first time in my life, I lost my shit, and no one blinked an eye.

Here comes your bride, I thought to myself when I finally shuffled out the doors in my hospital paper pants and awful breath into Pete's loving arms. He looked at me the way he did on our first date, and even though it made no sense I let him wrap me up in his arms and kiss me on the mouth.

"I'm sorry," I stammered, "I'm so stupid, I'm so sorry."

"Emily, look at me. I love you, and we're going to figure this out. I'm not going anywhere, okay? C'mon, let's get out of here," and together, we drove back to Plano.

Some wake-up calls can happen instantaneously, unfolding in a story that captures a lifetime in a flash and leave a magical glow after they're gone. Green Oaks was the more miserable wake-up call of slowly plummeting onto the pavement and lying there for a long time staring at the truth. I had to decide.

I chose to fight for a life that came with no guarantees and trust in something I didn't understand. Pete did the same, and with the odds stacked against us, we got married a month later, on December 11, 2004, in front of a small group of loved ones. We weren't outlaws or rebels, despite how some may have judged it. Not everything deserved an explanation.

Nine months later, nine-pound, four-ounce Rebecca was born.

In the mornings, I dropped Shelby off for first grade at her new elementary school down the street and in the afternoons. At the end of the school day, I pushed baby Becca in her stroller past the neighborhood playground, over the bridge, and back to the school doors, where Shelby came out to greet us. Becca's arms and legs kicked and waved at the sight of her sister when she crouched down in front of her, saying, "Well, hello, my cute baby sister!"—in a voice two octaves higher than her normal range.

"Hi honey, how was school?" I asked Shelby.

"Fine," she said, handing me her lunchbox and backpack before taking off down the sidewalk toward the park.

And this was motherhood. I'd finally settled into a rhythm where putting one foot in front of the other came easily. Later, I slid a 10-pound Mexican casserole into the oven after making a huge mess in the kitchen and took the girls out to the front yard to wait for Pete to get home from work. I paused at my reflection in the hallway mirror on my way to grab a blanket, noticing that I looked like I just rolled out of bed. My hair was a mess, and my shirt was stained with sauces and spit up, so I quickly changed clothes and freshened up my makeup and hair. I read in a book that when we spend time on our appearance, it makes our husbands feel special, and I wanted Pete to know he was the luckiest husband in the whole world. And I was the greatest wife of all time. *God, I want you to know I have no intention of fucking this one up.* Of course, I'd never considered myself one of those perfectly organized and careful goal-oriented women, but that's not to say I didn't try. An hour later, the three of us sat down at the dining room table to enjoy my dinner masterpiece.

"So what do you think? You like it?" I surveyed my new husband's face in search of satisfaction. "It's a new recipe."

"You know," he reached for his glass of water and commented, "I love you. I'm just not a big fan of this one."

"Oh," was all I could muster because I was devastated. How could he not love it?

Instead of taking his comment as nonchalantly as he said it, I interpreted it as him telling me he hated my cooking in general. I flunked my "greatest wife of all time" assignment and would surely be fired in no time. My bottom lip trembled. I was fragile over something so trivial. *Who would possibly want someone like me?* I thought.

Seeing him picking up toys or loading the dishwasher meant I didn't do my job. *I know he thinks I suck. Our mothers did this stuff better than me,* I thought to myself.

The start of a new family is really an extension of already existing trees, part his, part hers. While we focus on things like raising babies and saving money for a lawnmower, an underground web of traditions tries to survive underneath. The word "marriage" brought with it accidental expectations, like I needed to start baking bread and quit saying "fuck" around our friends now that I was a family woman. I thought I should collect table linens and that Pete needed power tools or maybe a men's bible study. But none of this was ever said out loud, and all of it felt ill-fitting to both of us. He came from a Catholic family and his father was a doctor, and sometimes, I called him Mr. Fancy to tease him. We knew from the start how lucky we were to live in our duplex, to have friends, and to place our kids at the center of it all. My pressures for mother and wife goals—those were light enough to pin in my hair, easy enough to stick in a drawer.

Within a couple of years, I was pregnant again with baby number three.

An old friend sat down next to me at a meeting one night, looking like she had bad news.

"I don't know if you heard, but Deborah isn't doing good at all," she whispered, a code that meant she'd gone back to drinking.

"Oh, shit," was all I could say.

"Yeah, it's pretty bad. She lives in her own apartment now, too." I envisioned what that meant for the husband she left behind and her daughter, who was the same age as Shelby. Not only was she the woman who generously watched Shelby during the day for free while I was at rehab and my mom was at work, but she was on the wait-list for a new liver the entire time she was sober.

When someone so deeply involved in recovery falls that far that fast, it shocks us all. Because they are our friends, they are our people, a family we love and who love us.

But after we moved from the duplex to a rental house a few miles north of Plano, I didn't think about Deborah much. Life was so good even as things got busier the more Pete traveled for work. Here and there, she'd come to mind when I was in the backyard playing with the girls. I'd converse with Pete or my mom, and her name would come up. Mostly, I thought about my freedom from that hell. And tried to leave it there.

My contractions started for our third daughter on an early April morning in 2008. Pete and I headed to the same hospital where Shelby and Rebecca were born.

"Oh, my God. She's so beautiful." I laughed through my tears when I saw our daughter for the first time and started to laugh through my tears at the sight of her across my chest. We named her Stella after my great-grandmother and our hearts filled with the joy of new life all over again.

As another quiet stillness descended on the hospital that night, the way it always did when the excitement died down and close family went home, we heard a soft knock on the door. Pete looked at me from the cushioned chair where he cradled his newest daughter in his arms, and I gave him a nod.

"Come in," he said, and I sat up in bed to see our dear friends Joan and Henry walk in with a vase of flowers. They were old enough to be our parents and had known me since I was a teenager. Their loving eyes soaked up the scene in front of them.

"Is this little Stella?" Joan asked in a whispery voice as she peeked over Pete's shoulder. "She's perfect."

"I can't believe you guys drove out here and brought flowers. That was so nice," I said. Henry patted my leg, his way of saying *you're welcome.* The four of us were talking about our kids and their grandchildren when they mentioned we might have other visitors coming by that night.

"We know some more people who'll be driving out here," Henry said, and for a second, Pete and I thought it was all in our honor.

"Deborah is at this hospital, a couple of floors up on the fifth floor. I don't know if you were aware, but she's been on life support. The family is taking her off in the morning." Joan's words sucked all the air from my open mouth. "She's gone." She sighed with tender sadness. "So there'll be some goodbyes tonight. But look here." Gesturing to the baby swaddled in Pete's arms, "then we've got this little miracle in your room to meet for the first time, don't we?"

On their way out, Henry said maybe Pete and I would get a chance later to go upstairs, but I barely heard him.

I lived in a world of recovery, where there are often tragic realities for people I love and who love me. It was the never-ending disease of alcohol where either you get to live or the monster eventually kills you. There is no middle ground. And I didn't know why I got to live when others didn't or why it worked out for Stella to be the angel of hope that our broken hearts needed on the night Deborah died.

The truth was I didn't want to know. And I couldn't bring myself to make the elevator trip up three floors. I never said goodbye to my friend. I was too comfortable in my miracle to pause for her tragedy, too lost in my state of bliss to take the time she deserved, to give my respects to the woman who helped me when I drank again but survived. She became another sad story we get used to hearing when we stick around a community that isn't built on guarantees, and that's where I left it.

I never considered it a warning, nor did I think too much about the daughter she left behind who was Shelby's age, or how close I came to making Shelby motherless like Deborah's little girl. I went home the next day with Pete and the beautiful family I'd dreamt of all my life, where I was certain I was safe.

CHAPTER TEN

2008–March 2010

In 1953, on a Thursday in April, behind the idyllic images of postwar happy homemakers, my grandma Fern sat motionless on the front steps of her pink two-story house on the corner of Main Street in a small Minnesota town. Within a time span of four months, the three significant men in her life had died. Her father died in December, and then her father-in-law passed away on a Sunday after a series of strokes. And then only two days before, just a couple of days after her father-in-law died, after health complications from being a prisoner of war during World War II, her husband, Rona, died. She stared blankly down the road that led to the Mississippi River, unable to comprehend the magnitude of change that had befallen her. Three dead men, three new widows. All the women lived in the same town in southern Minnesota. It was almost May, and Fern was four months pregnant with her eighth child. My mother was five years old at the time. Fern's quiet moment was cut short by hungry kids waiting inside. So she rose, turned, and went in to make supper. The grief would have to wait.

Years later, in 1981, my mom sat in her own quiet moment on the back step of a yellow one-story house where she lived with her husband and two kids, watching me climb a tree in the yard. She was in a state of despair, a chasm of stress in her chest. Her thoughts drifted around an unhappy marriage plagued with traces of his infidelity, the disheartening decision to move from Minnesota to Texas for her husband's job, and his escalating issues with alcohol. But it was the pregnancy she hid under her shirt that sealed her fate.

I was seven years old with a little brother on the way. She couldn't leave and could never financially afford a different way of life. It was unthinkable to disrupt the family. So she stopped considering a way out, got up from the step, and went inside. It was time to make dinner. The sorrow would have to wait.

Three generations of women intersected on a timeless map. My grandmother, my mother, and I were all 34 years old when a life event delivered traumatic results.

A connection exists with pinned points that pull us together with a delicate stitch. My grandmother didn't know, my mother didn't know, and neither did I. When the needle pierced me, our common thread hooked on a daughter's inherited heirloom, a shared understanding that women stifle their suffering behind closed doors, so the sight of a failing mother doesn't burden the children.

But the silence of three generations of women was growing impatient.

In late March of 2010, Pete and I lived in a white two-story house just outside of Raleigh after leaving Texas for North Carolina a year before because of his job. But I was not at home or sitting on porch steps.

"Can I help you?" a nurse asked.

"Yes, hi, I'm Emily Redondo," I said, leaning on the counter between us. "I got here this morning. I think I heard my name called." She flipped through a stack of paper to check the name on my hospital admission bracelet.

"Wait here for a minute," she said and walked away.

I looked for a place to sit down, my stomach turning over at the realization that I was in another psychiatric hospital, this time for medically assisted and supervised alcohol detox. My body still reeled after a long night with delirium tremens. DTs, as it's sometimes called, was the most severe form of alcohol withdrawal marked by the sudden, life-threatening imbalances that skyrocketed across mental and nervous systems inside a body more likely to function with the poison than without it. At the hospital, a nurse told me how rare the condition was and gave me information about my symptoms, but it solved nothing.

The morning wasn't any better. I still had to wake up and get three daughters ready for school like I always did, but something wasn't right. I was sicker than usual, and my heart felt like it lost its rhythm. A quick *pound, pound, pounding* in my chest, then I couldn't catch my breath. Pick up a foot, move it forward, put it down, do it with the other foot, and all of it with giddy little Stella tugging at my ankles. My arms were too weak to pick her up. *I don't want to die*, I thought, clinging to the stair rail and begging God to let me make it to the bottom. This time, there was no sitting on a stairstep in a moment of anguish and grief like my mother and grandmother. Instead, anguish and grief were sitting *me* down, forcing me to deal with it. This time, it would not wait.

Can I make it? Can I get up and pretend I'm okay? My body bucked in a resounding *NO*. I called out to Pete for help.

Suddenly, the nurse returned with the same expressionless face.

"It looks like they wanted to talk about your blood work," she said. I started going through each internal organ, wondering which one I ruined. She asked me, "Are you on birth control?" I responded with a blank stare.

"I mean, yes and no. Condoms, but we're not . . . intimate a lot lately," I told her. She checked the papers in her hand again.

"We do a lot of tests, so maybe you weren't informed of this one, but you're pregnant." Her perfunctory words were like ice cubes being thrown at my face. None of it made sense; Pete and I were barely speaking.

The possibility of inheriting more than physical attributes can seem like a pseudoscience until generational threads tie together in unmistakable patterns. Standing there in my hospital socks with a pounding headache, I didn't realize the connections between Fern, my mother, and myself. Radical life events had changed us all when we were the same age and pregnant, occurring 29 years apart. Was I marked from the beginning?

It doesn't excuse how I ended up in such a miserable place, but it contributes to a bigger picture of who we are. Most of us who are buried in mental mayhem or trapped again in alcohol's ferocious grip usually grab onto simpler answers and blame ourselves wholeheartedly. This is exactly what I did, sitting in a sober state of shame and remorse for being none other than Emily. And in most cases, we look no further than our own stupid choices that led to terrible consequences by our thoughtless actions. But what if it's deeper than that?

"So I guess I should call my husband," I said in a way that was both a statement and a question, exposing the fact I didn't want to do it. The nurse pointed me toward a phone on the wall with zero privacy. I ran my fingers through my uncombed hair and dragged my feet, trying to figure out what words to say . . . *I'm sorry, forgive me, I'm pregnant.*

"Hello?" Pete answered.

"Hi, it's me," I could tell he wasn't exactly thrilled to hear my voice when I called. "How is everybody?"

"Not great, Emily. Actually, pretty devastated." The word devastated crept into my ear, paralyzing my face in shame. "So what's happening there?" he asked.

"Well, I got some news from my blood work. I don't know if it's good or bad actually, and obviously, we have a lot to talk about—"

"What? What is it?" he interrupted, worried.

"I'm pregnant." As I said it, the corners of my mouth pulled into a subtle smile, like it forgot about everything else for a moment. It's hard to tell what he was thinking, but I got the sense we both yearned for a different time and place. The conversation was short, left dangling on a thin thread of hope I didn't deserve and couldn't explain. How can things go from being everything I ever wanted to everyone's worst nightmare?

It felt like only months ago, Pete mentioned moving when we had another vision of how this might have looked.

"Aaron wants to start a print department in North Carolina, and he wants me to run it," he mentioned one night while we sat outside playing gin rummy and listening to old country music on the radio.

Oh, my gosh was my reaction. His face lit up as he talked about a salary increase, more commission, and bigger opportunities. It was contagious.

"And no more traveling two weeks out of the month," he said, caressing my leg.

I wonder if my mother felt the same way when my father came home from work one day and told her about a job he found, with lots of potential and less traveling, that was in Texas instead of Minnesota. Did she argue? Because I didn't. The right thing to do was follow my husband and ignore the tug of my heartstrings telling me not to go. My grandma did the same thing, too, along with many other young brides during WWII. They followed their husbands from coast to coast, the image of the good American wife on proud display. Pete swung a fly swatter over my head and smashed fat June bugs against the window like my hero, and I thought, *this is marriage. Women do this all the time. It's not a big deal.* I had visions in my head of countless other mothers making cross-country moves and new friends with no problems. My mom moved to Germany and had my older brother in a country that didn't speak English. By comparison, this would be easy, right?

"Knock, knock." A woman entered my cold, sterile room and flipped on the light switch. "Sorry to wake you, but I need your blood pressure and more blood work."

"That's fine," I muttered, groggy from my night medication. "What time is it?"

"Midnight," she answered. I told her I always asked the time so I could picture what was happening at home.

"Oh yeah? Well, everybody better be asleep at my house, that's for sure," she laughed, and I agreed. This woman, whose name I never knew, talked about her rambunctious kids and the funny things they used to do that drove her crazy. "I mean, I love them, but I don't always *like* them, ya know?"

I nodded, so surprised that I suddenly felt like crying.

"Thanks for talking to me." I choked back tears. "Like I'm a real person. It feels good," and I wanted to say more, but my throat closed, and this stranger understood.

"Nah, I get it. C'mon, we all have something. It's going to get better for you." I believed it. It was simple but incredible all at once that a woman could see me at my worst and still talk to me as though I was worthy of her time, that I didn't need to be pretty or sober or happy to have value because I was none of those things, yet she offered me friendship. Someone saw me and sure, it was in a psych hospital, but I didn't care. It was Easter weekend, my mom was in town, and I couldn't see her. I missed my kids. I'd take whatever I could get.

For the first several months in North Carolina, I was home all the time. It was surprising how hard it was to make friends in the winter months. One afternoon, I slumped onto the couch, staring out the window at the rain coming down. We needed groceries, but I didn't feel like taking a three-year-old and a nine-month-old out in the dreary weather. Laundry baskets filled with clean clothes and scattered toys were sprinkled across the living room floor. The dishes I'd left in the sink from lunch and the cold mac-n-cheese, still in a pot on the stove, needed cleaning. Added all together, the scene showed signs I was struggling. There was too much to do, homesickness would have to wait.

"Are you sure you want to do this?" I remembered my mom ask me over the phone while I sat in the carpool line before we moved.

"I think it's going to be fine, Mom, really. I do," I told her.

"What does Shelby want to do, have you thought about that? I just know it's going to be hard on all of us. I mean, I know it's going to be hard on me." Her voice cracked as she held back tears. But I didn't want to hear it because I couldn't afford to listen. I was on a mission to make sure every member of my family was taken care of, reassuring them of all the positive sides to every concern, protecting them from pain and worry. It's what moms are supposed to do. I chose the best neighborhood we could afford, picked out a dance studio for Shelby within walking distance, and even found a house that came with a playset in the backyard. Becca was more than ready to start preschool when the new spring session started.

"Honey, I know it's not your old preschool, but you're going to love this one. They do art every day and have a big playground with *trees*," I chirped into the rearview mirror as I drove the unfamiliar route with her and Stella in car seats behind me. At 2 pm, when I picked her up, Stella wanted to play after an early nap, so we walked over to the playground where other moms and kids gathered before heading home.

My insecurities quadrupled when I stepped inside the fence and saw half a dozen circles of women socializing. How long had it been since I was the new kid? Because suddenly, I felt transported back to 1987 as an awkward middle-schooler with thick glasses and a home perm. I didn't want to be rude and barge into the middle of a conversation with my arm out for handshakes, but if I walked around by myself, I might look antisocial.

"The weather is so nice out today," I said after lurking around a particular circle of moms. *Jesus Christ, I sound like my grandmother.* Old people talk about the weather, not me. Some heads turned in my direction.

"Oh, hi. Are you new here?" a mom asked.

"Well, sort of. We moved here a few months ago from Dallas."

"Dallas? Texas is *so hot*," a blonde mom chimed in with a light chuckle. "You will *love* it here. Everyone does. It's just the perfect place to raise a family, you know?" *Actually, I hate it here, but thanks.*

"I'm Emily, and this here is Stella," I said, sticking my hip out a little to showcase the baby even though they weren't really looking at us. "And Rebecca is the one over there, playing under the monkey bars. I also have a fifth grader at North Forest Pines."

"Oh, okay, yeah," she said, looking out across the playground. "I think Rebecca's in Ms. Patricia's class. She's a pretty good teacher. My son has Ms. Rachel; she's actually *amazing*." For some reason, I felt slighted.

"That's great," I replied. "I'm still learning pretty much everything around here. I can barely get to the school without getting lost." I exaggerated.

"Where's North Forest Pines? Is that private?" someone asked. I shook my head and told her where we lived.

"Ohhh," she said, "so you don't live around here. Like, not in Raleigh." Apparently, I gave out information that would affect my status. I didn't know one neighborhood from the next, let alone one school, but I knew the feeling of women looking down on me. It was time to go.

Screw them, I thought as I drove home. *I will make this whole thing work out if it kills me. I'll find my own friends. The kids will be happy, and the house will be spotless, I'll join a gym and scrapbook every blissful family moment.*

Because it's not enough to be a mother anymore, if it ever was.

I'm a member of the first wave of daughters to come from a generation of women who not only embraced a new way of parenting but fought for women's rights. Betty Crocker cookbooks next to *Ms.* magazines, my mom also learned about the developmental needs of kids at different ages and stages while washing it all down with a glass of wine. A pile-on without loosening the grip of traditional definitions for a stay-at-home mother—the housework, bills, errands, activities, appointments, and being the emotional backbone of everyone living in the house. As for my generation and the women I silently sized up on playgrounds, our list was longer. Because tacked on to the never-ending list of what it takes to earn the Good Mother badge was the obsession with a thin, youthful beauty and excessive wealth. Too bad if you're an average American living paycheck to paycheck like we did. And if the stress of it all didn't kill us, the guilt when we couldn't do it all would.

My animosity toward other mothers was anger at myself for finding simple things so difficult to do. I was lonely and jealous of the friendships around me where I knew I didn't belong. It made me want to go home, as in all the way back to our home on Gardenia Lane in Texas. I wanted to escape so I wouldn't have to see women manage all the things I couldn't, right down to the shockingly clean interior of their family minivans. *What the hell is wrong with me? Why can't I do it?* It never dawned on me someone else washed their cars and cleaned their houses. It wasn't normal for me to think that way. We never paid a babysitter or hired someone to clean our house. I'd been a babysitter my whole life and worked as a nanny. After Shelby was born, I worked for a family that let me bring her with me. My mom or close friends watched the kids if we needed it, and I'd always been the maid.

I associated myself with cleaners and caregivers; I didn't hire them.

Of course, I didn't talk about feeling inadequate, not honestly. What a disgrace, no one did. Pete had enough on his mind already with his new job. I didn't talk about my problems at all. Some of us learn that from our mothers, too. After a handful of months pent up with homesickness and loneliness because Pete worked such long hours, I was ready to pop.

"You're later than usual," I said one evening from the kitchen when he walked in the front door after a 13-hour workday.

"Daddy!" shouted Becca, then the sound of bare feet pattering across the wood floor for a hug and hello. Coming home was his favorite part of the day.

Later, I cleaned up the thankless dinner while Pete got the girls into their pajamas. The sound of laughter coming from upstairs irritated me because he barely talked to me at the table, and now, he was riling up the kids again. We created a system for bedtime routines, hoping to cut the process down to less than an hour, and when the kids were finally down for the night, he headed toward the screened-in porch to relax and watch television, cigar in hand. That was Pete's routine every night.

"We're out of milk," I said, sticking my head through the sliding glass door. In marital terms, I meant one of us had to drive to the store because we needed it before morning. Neither of us moved. "I'll go." I sighed after losing the brief staring contest.

Alone in the minivan I despised, I couldn't decide if I noticed the silence because it was exceptionally quiet or if it was simply the absence of commotion between the seats that caught my attention. I let it ring in my ears as I turned onto the main boulevard toward the nearest Walmart and pulled behind a long line of cars at a stoplight, staring at the red taillights. All my distractions were gone. Most mothers would have basked in the moment of peaceful reprieve and let out a sigh of relief, and even though I looked calm and contained, the stillness made me want to come out of my skin. I felt a cluster of angst at the base of my spine rolling up to the top of my head, growing stronger every second I sat waiting for the light to change. Every feeling I'd stuffed down for the past four months webbed out across my body. My heart was racing, my fingers gripping the steering wheel like I was waiting for an impact to crush me. *I'm not going to make it,* I said to myself, seeing flashing lights from a traffic accident up ahead. *I wish we were home. Don't think about it. Don't think, not now,* I told myself. Because the pain would kill me if I let it out. The truth was I wasn't going home. This was it, and I hated it all. My wheels crept forward, and I looked over at the car next to me at a stranger I knew nothing about when a thought hit me. *Wine would fix this.*

It came like a life preserver thrown from the sky to save me. Just a quick thought was all it took. I could rid myself of the emotional storm and breathe again. A little wine to soften the overwhelming feelings suffocating me, and then I could move forward. I'd be the decent mom and wife I used to be. Not once was I afraid of the thoughts running through my mind. Quite the opposite. They offered me hope.

I pretended there was still some choice involved when I turned into the corner gas station and bought a four-pack of mini-Chardonnays for the first time in almost five years. I walked in thinking everyone in town was watching me on video surveillance, so I tossed in a diet Coke and a pack of gum at the register to throw off the cashier, who didn't give two shits what I was buying.

In the safety of my car, I drank a little bottle on the way to the store, carefully checking windows and mirrors to make sure no one saw me taking sips. It tasted so strong that the smell of it on my breath after one sip burned the hairs in my nostrils. But within a matter of moments, a familiar warmth hit the inside of my body and trickled through each vein like a bath of sunshine. Wine makes lots of promises and I felt them come true walking through the Walmart parking lot with my enormous discomfort shrinking down into sips I could swallow and forget. I let out a sigh and smiled through the aisles, wanting to skip and twirl like a pretty ballerina and not some mascara-smeared mom of three worried about the time. *I will be okay*, that's what ran through my mind after the wine. I could barely remember the last time I felt that optimistic.

Wine didn't look dangerous when I went to bed that night after getting away with the secret. It was nothing more than my "in case of emergency, break glass" moment of desperation, and I didn't drink the next few days or even the next couple of weeks. I passed the wine displays set up in grocery stores, gas stations, and drug stores, pretending to feel the way I did before I broke the seal of sobriety. But who was I kidding? In my bitter, homesick moments when I was tired of talking to toddlers and the loneliness set in, I thought about wine as an emergency option. I tried to believe that somehow, I beat the game, even with everything I already knew.

But all that changed when I pushed my cart past one more wine display on an insignificant day and put a cardboard bottle in my cart.

For the ones who can't relate, the obvious answers are everywhere—don't buy it, don't drink it, think about your family, get some willpower for Christ's sake. And if decisions like that were possible, I'd tell the woman rushing to the bathroom with the stomach flu to stop and walk away. *Ignore the urge to puke, no matter what. Hold it in with some determination or it will be a big mess.* It sounds ridiculous, considering at some point, we aren't in control of our bodies no matter what we think. Still, how could a mother plummet from multiple years of sobriety all the way down within weeks?

When the word "alcoholic" hits the ear, there's still the image of a man in tattered clothes with a bottle in a paper sack flopped under a bridge. Imagine adding the word *mother,* and the image flips to a house covered in filth, with kids who run around unbathed and unsupervised, while a worthless woman lies on a couch and clutches her cup. I see it, too. When stereotypes become weapons of disgrace and shame, they turn into stigmas that make us hide and prevent us from seeking help.

I hid because my world depended on it. I couldn't lose my children, and they couldn't lose me.

It didn't matter that I tried to quit every day or that I'd make it for a few days here, a week there; it was a lie to think I was anywhere near staying sober. No one, not even my husband, knew what I was doing despite me having multiple wines stashed throughout the house. Cheap chardonnay came in twist-top containers like fat juice boxes that quietly slid into winter coat pockets and overflowing laundry baskets to be later trashed in another plastic garbage bag I kept under the stairs in the garage. My weekly trips to the grocery store multiplied into almost daily excuses to run out for missing ingredients, and one thing about drinking is the effect starts to change when tolerance kicks in. The other problem is the mental toll because the drinking part is only half of it. I thought about how to buy wine and when I could get it, where I hid it and where else to hide it, how much I had left and how much I needed to get me through until morning because the fear of running out was comparable to death. Where's the line? It was only a matter of time before I got caught, and I knew it.

"Are you okay?" Pete finally asked me after work. That afternoon, I drank what was left of the wine I was saving for the next day. There was no reason other than I knew it was there and I split myself in two. As my hands grabbed the bottle, it looked and felt like someone else was doing it. Even when my head said *stop!* I still kept drinking.

"Mmm hmm, fine," I said, keeping my face turned away from him.

"Are you sure?" he asked and started walking closer. "Why won't you look at me when you talk?"

"Honey, I'm fine. I'm just trying to get dinner ready." And I bumped into him, heading toward the sink.

"Emily. We just ATE dinner. What the hell is wrong with you?" his voice shook with a mixture of worry and frustration. I was about to tell him that's what I meant to say because I lied about everything lately when I saw his shock turn to pain and spread across his face. He knew. My sobriety hadn't been questioned in years, so to see it crush him was unbearable.

That was it. The moment some of us live in fear of and some of us think will never happen. Addiction doesn't care if we tear up a family or break a few hearts. After he got the kids to bed and made me stay in our bedroom, Pete called some women I'd met from the sober meetings I had gone to. A few came over to the house and talked to me in our room while I was in a blackout. I woke up the next morning knowing something terrible had happened. Pete was not only devastated, I was too. I couldn't piece everything together, but flashes from my memory were enough. I felt the old familiar horrors of the disease on every level.

Well, maybe not every level. Because anyone who's been in a similar hell understands it can always get worse. And in the same way, relapse leaves a mark on our sobriety, and so does a curious case of amnesia.

The last place I wanted to be that night was a church basement for a sober meeting, but Pete made me go. Subtly, my eyes scanned the room from my folding chair in the corner to see if anyone might approach me and mention being at my house the previous night. No one did. I tried not to overthink the familiar woman who wouldn't look in my direction or the strange sensation that everyone knew my business. I left the second the meeting was over without saying a word, so it surprised me when Kate, a member of the group, called me later that evening.

"Hi, Emily. I heard you were at the meeting; that's good," she said.

"Yeah, I'm really having a hard time," I said. "Were you here at the house last night? Pete said he might have called you, but I don't remember. I'm sorry, I'm so embarrassed."

"No, I wasn't, but we need to talk," she stated. "I'm calling because I heard how rude you were. And that you said insulting things about me and a couple of other women." My face flushed as she kept going. "See, we don't do that kind of behavior here with the yelling and profanity, it's very offensive. I'm a little shocked since we've been so nice to you." Then she paused.

My mouth hung open in shock while I stood at the end of my bed with the door closed.

"I don't know what to say," I stammered, envisioning these women gossiping about me at my worst. I'd been in their position myself several times back in Texas with an intoxicated woman, primarily to keep her out of harm's way, so I understood how ugly it could get and didn't dispute my drunken behavior. I was more shocked by the judgment. They came to my house on their own accord without a shred of humanity for the suffering alcoholic mother in front of them, and the punch hit me hard when women like Kate did not remember the horrid things they'd done while drunk. I felt like I was about to get kicked out of a club that came with a new set of rules.

"And another thing," Kate continued, "I had your family *over to my house*." As if my recent bad behavior was a personal vendetta. "I don't recall a formal thank you for inviting you to the dinner party. It's proper etiquette to send a card to the host." I paused before the girls came scrambling into the room and gestured for them to *shoo, shoo!*

"Not now, girls, one more minute," I whispered to them, then to the scorned woman on the phone, "Why are you telling me this *now*? We thanked you profusely that evening, several times. Look, I apologize for everything, Kate. I'm sorry, I don't know what else you want, but I have to go." I got off the phone to go cry in the bathroom.

If I didn't hate myself yet, I did the next morning when my new local sponsor, Kelly, called and fired me a week later. That one hurt the worst because she was the only genuine friend I'd found. Our kids were friends, our families would get together for Green Bay Packers games.

"Obviously, I can't help you, Emily. I don't have what you need, but we can still be friends."

Our phone call lasted less than five minutes, and I hung up feeling rejected and utterly alone. Within a week, I would be admitted to the Raleigh psychiatric hospital, sitting across from another social worker, wondering, yet again, *How did I end up here? What else could go wrong?*

It's risky to tell the truth when the facts look like a tragedy. The social worker's name was Ann. She had gray hair and a laid-back attitude as she listened to me rattle on about the circumstances leading up to my detox. I admit, it didn't look optimistic.

I told her about the night before I arrived, how scared I was because my body needed alcohol and I didn't have one single drop in the house to give it. *God, please help me. God don't let me die,* I pleaded in prayers when my body started shaking. *I'll stop I swear. I'll tell him. I'll tell him, I will,* I kept whispering about the husband sleeping next to me who was unaware I thought I was dying. My mind jumped to frantic images of my daughters in their beds and their faces. *I can't believe this is me,* thinking about Pete waking up next to my dead body compared to the way we used to fall asleep entwined with one another. *I promise you, God. I'll go somewhere. Just get me to morning and I will do the rest. That's all I'm asking,* but I was begging.

I read about the effects of alcohol in high school during drug awareness week like it was a scare tactic for the party crowd of popular kids, but it felt exceptionally real when I heard a talk show playing on a radio somewhere in the house that night. I stumbled around in the predawn hours, going from room to room, up and down stairs in the dark for what felt like hours trying to track down the sound and turn it off. As soon as I heard it in one room, the voices started coming from somewhere else. *Who's doing this to me? What the hell is happening?* I finally gave up and got in bed. The stagnant air pulled sweat out of my pores as I tried to close my eyes for sleep. It took ten minutes before I sat up with a turn toward the headboard to realize I found the voices from the talk show. They were coming from inside the walls. It scared me into a sob I muffled with my pillow.

If there was ever a question about what kind of wine mom I was, it's safe to say I wasn't the type having one too many glasses of rosé on Girls' night out.

"The good news is your husband loves you so much, Emily," Ann said. "This can be a whole new beginning for your family," and I smiled at the thought. "I printed off all the things you asked for—names of different AA groups in the area other than the one you were attending, ob/gyn offices and some therapist referrals. I also made a follow-up appointment with a psychiatrist regarding your medication," she said.

"Thank you so much, really," I said. "I don't know how I would have figured this stuff out without you."

On my own, it looked overwhelming. Maybe that's why I chose to believe the pregnancy was God's little miracle, like a rescue mission just for me. Because the minute our conversation was over, I was done screwing up my life, done with booze forever. The contrast between the woman who stumbled into that place and the one who was walking out was all the proof I needed. It was hope, and the brightness of it blinded me to a flood of problems never mentioned to me by anyone in the course of my week-long stay.

When I walked in the house after being gone eight days, I saw Shelby's face first. She wasn't disappointed; she was far beyond that. I was unprepared to catch the guilt that spilled out of me onto floor. My heart sank at the sight of her, and I wanted to rush over and reassure her that I could handle all of it—everything she needed from me plus sobriety, her little sisters, her dad, and another baby—but the younger kids ran between us, and she took off up the stairs before I got to say it. *Just a setback,* I thought, *she'll come around over time. We all will, I'm sure of it.*

CHAPTER ELEVEN

2010–January 2011

I finally had the chance to lie down after fighting off first-trimester fatigue, first in Stella's bed then in Becca's across the room they shared with pale pink walls. At 8 pm, my back ached worse than my double-sized breasts and my belly looked like Jell-O. Occasional thoughts about my grandmother in her pink house raising eight kids compared to me with only three ran through my mind while lullabies played on a music box. *Who am I to complain? Emily, grow up,* I'd think to myself as my daughters drifted off to sleep in their cozy beds. Maybe some women, like Fern, were just better at being moms. I seemed to be losing my mind over it.

"You're being too hard on yourself," Pete told me when I went downstairs. "Cut yourself some slack, Em, a lot's going on. Sobriety, pregnancy . . . remember all those times you locked your keys in the car when you were pregnant with Becca? Or the migraines with Stella? It's okay," he said. I wanted to agree, but something felt different this time.

"I'll get over it, I'm sure," I said, trying to will myself into a better attitude about a new baby.

My maternal bliss still hadn't showed up when I reported in for another prenatal checkup. The OB/GYN reception area reeked of overpriced maternity wear and scented candles with background nature music meant for relaxation that made me want to pee. I looked like shit that day, praying I wouldn't get a pelvic since I forgot to shave "down there." I missed my old doctor like a grieving widow, mainly because he would have snapped some sense into me and taken some action. I would have listened to anything that man told me to do.

The fact I was so utterly desperate for help in combination with the how impersonal everything was in that place had me on the verge of tears within two minutes of being with the doctor.

"I'm sorry to be emotional like this," I said. "I'm just having a really hard time," I confessed while she looked at my chart.

"Date of birth?" she asked, and I told her.

"I'm not . . . well. As in, mentally. At all," I confessed. I needed someone, like a doctor, someone I could trust for support. Another baby seemed like more work—*who thinks like that?*

"Can you scoot down a little farther?" was her reply, apparently a required question for pelvic exams because my bare cheeks already hung off the table. I scooched and kept talking.

"You see, I don't have any family here, and I was used to that, and my husband works a lot," I continued. "We've got three daughters and to be completely honest, this pregnancy wasn't exactly planned," I stared up at the ceiling, pausing for her to say something in return. She rubbed a heartbeat detector around my stomach covered in gel. The thump carried along rhythmically to my one-sided conversation. "I've had a hard time meeting new friends." I sniffled up the snot coming out of my nose and dug tears out of my ear that quietly ran down the side of my face.

The woman wiped off my belly with a paper towel and said, "Okay, you can sit up now," so that's what I did. "The measurements are on track and the heart sounds healthy."

"That's great, really. Thank God," I said, staring toward the doctor and the mound that used to be my lap. "I was wondering if maybe, under the circumstances, I can schedule my appointments to see the same doctor each time?" I asked, sitting up on my elbows and scooting back on the table enough to sit up. "I know there's five of you and no disrespect, it'd just be helpful to have someone who knows what's going on with me."

I didn't want to sound especially entitled or high maintenance. I asked her because I was depressed. I'd never felt darkness so deep as a mother. She shook her head without looking at me while she typed into the computer. Finally she turned and looked me in the eye.

"We don't operate our practice like that, but trust me, any doctor you see is highly qualified and sees the exact same medical charts regarding you and your baby. We don't even know who will be on call when you deliver, so this way you'll get to know us all. It'll be fine," she said, standing up and opening the exam room door. I saw the way she looked at me. It shut down all the emotions inside me.

I left the office four months pregnant, got back into the driver's seat of my minivan and sat in silence for a minute. The option to move back home near family was financially impossible. The house we lived in was the first one we owned. We bought it in 2008, right before the housing market crashed. Even if we wanted to sell, we'd owe more than it was worth. Pete and I were lucky at the time to even qualify for a loan after separately ruining our own credit scores and working to rebuild them. I still had debt from student loans for a degree I never used, not to mention he'd have to find another job if we moved. It all seemed too much to consider. Money doesn't buy happiness, but it does provide options, which was what I desperately wanted. Besides, the girls were settled in now.

How selfish of me to feel so miserable.

"How'd your appointment go?" Pete asked when he called from work that afternoon. Between the little girl voices playing behind me with a battery-operated toy we regretted buying, I didn't have the energy to tell him the whole truth through the phone.

"It was okay," was all I said.

"So the baby's fine?" he asked. *Oh yeah . . . the baby*, I remembered.

"I got to hear the heartbeat," I told him, remembering the swooshing sound and feeling guilty that I didn't pay more attention at the time. "Everything's nice and healthy."

"That's so great! Awesome news, honey. Did you ask about the doctor thing?" he asked.

"Yeah. They won't do it," I said, then started to give a quick summary before he needed to take another call.

Pete wanted to keep looking for a better setup, but I already did an exhaustive search and decided, *I'm just going to deal with it*, feeling already halfway through the pregnancy. *I'll be fine* was what I told myself, without a medical professional to trust and confide in for the first time. It's worth asking, how good is anyone at self-evaluation? We can't exactly observe or analyze ourselves without some degree of bias or skewed perspective. Maybe if I woke up with something drastically wrong, it'd be easier than the slower slope into dangerous territory. It's why I can't see my children growing until their clothes don't fit, or why I don't notice my hair getting longer until suddenly, *wow, my hair's gotten long.*

In the same sense, it's hard to pinpoint when I started waking up every morning with a long list of things I needed to accomplish perfectly, only that I slid into it thinking the end result would be happiness. I committed myself to the challenge like I was under the gun, but the gun was mine.

"Mom!" Shelby hollered from the kitchen one particular morning. "There's no food in this house, can I buy lunch at school?"

"C'mon, there's plenty of food!" I hollered back from upstairs with a soaking wet pull-up diaper in my hand. "Dig around. I'm sure you can find something." I grabbed the closest pair of elastic-waist pants I could find and slid them up my legs.

"I'm not eating that lunch meat And all the chips are stale, Mom. Why can't you just let me buy lunch?" she asked as I rounded the bottom of the stairs.

"You know what, fine Shelby," I said, irritated because Rebecca and Stella started arguing over the Disney cereal bowl. The youngest sister reached out and yanked on a clump of Becca's hair as a cup of apple juice spilled across the table.

"No!" I yelled. "Stop it! Give me the bowl, nobody gets it. And now I've got to clean up your mess, I'm not happy *at all*," my bad attitude hung in the air as I grabbed a handful of paper towels. They ate in silence with occasional sounds of sniffling from crying.

"Bye, I'm leaving!" Shelby said from the front door as she headed out for the bus stop. I didn't get a chance to reply.

By late morning, Stella was her cheerful, chatty self with her bubbly curls bouncing off her head in her car seat when we dropped off Becca with her big smile at preschool. I, on the other hand, was torn up with guilt for reasons beyond the chaotic morning and my mounting short temper. A quick review of my actions while we drove home, and I'd already failed the day.

I don't know where the idealistic images of perfect mothers came from and in truth, it didn't matter what scenes of fictionalized women were smeared across my windshield. My state of mind was completely convinced that a reality existed where particular moms woke up and did everything correctly from the start. I wanted to be in that group, those girls, the winners. And the thought of someone effortlessly accomplishing things I continuously struggled to do left me in a demoralized state of failure right down to the deli-sliced turkey and goddamn Chip Clips. Simply put, it drove me crazy. *If I could somehow not always feel so overwhelmed, like I'm always running behind with everything, I could be like them.* What a lie.

I festered in that state of mind when Stella and I bought groceries that day. With her riding happily in the cart, I grabbed our usual items until my eyes landed on a wine display at the end of an aisle.

Those little chardonnays caught my attention like a bundle of former friendships telling me they'd play nice this time around. I knew it was a lie. But aren't there times we're just happy to get the invitation? I imagined we missed each other's company, that the big lie won't burn quite as badly, and in the middle of a single second, I pretended to forget.

The baby in my belly, the horrors I created only a few months prior, *God, when is it my turn to lose the memory of it all? How can I plunge off the edge of this cliff and stay alive?* I bought into it, then I bought it.

Digging through the grocery bags in the back seat, I found the wine before my car was out of its parking space. I was twisting the top off with a couple of clicks for the anticipation of life's resuscitation as I turned onto the street that took us home. With Stella's car seat directly behind me, she didn't see me take the first few swigs, nor did she notice my guilt was gone as soon as the liquid hit my stomach. Cheap chardonnay warmed me with a toxic irony by giving me a way to check out and help me focus. Avoid the truth and pretend to be like "them" at least for a little while. By dinnertime, the buzz was a thing of the past and household duties I normally dreaded actually got done. Any mom, and most doctors, don't fuss over a drink or two during pregnancy. Everything was fine.

But it didn't last. I went through the next day not needing a drink, but the day after that, the thought of one festered in the back of my mind. On the third and fourth day, those festering ideas turned into a mental brawl between me and something much bigger than myself. I didn't know what irritated me the most—my family, my body, my house or the nagging monster dying for me to drink.

But after about a week of obsessing over wine, alcohol wasn't the only thing on my mind when I quietly carried two twist-top bottles up the stairs late one morning. I bought them without a second thought, and as I reached my bedroom, I remembered how much I loved being pregnant in the past, right down to buying tiny socks and a fresh box of Dreft detergent. No matter how hard I tried, I could not conjure up the same emotions for the baby boy I was currently carrying inside of me. I tried to fake it, tried to think about things for his nursery, but nothing came, and the guilt was crushing me. The feelings of basic maternal attachment betrayed me. What could be worse? It's fair to say I quit thinking anything when I closed the bedroom door after shouting, "I'll be right there!" to the little girls turning on the television downstairs. I hypnotically walked into the closet, downed warm chardonnay to the count of five big swallows, and hid the remainder under a low hanging rack of clothes I never wore. *A shoe box will work. He won't look there. Or will he? What am I doing? I can't, this is so awful. It's fine, just this once.*

I used to love a good buzz from alcohol and the silliness that came with it, whether I was out on the town or day drinking by a pool with friends, but I admit those days existed briefly several lifetimes ago. Now, from the moment I took my first sips and felt a looseness rise up through my body, my never-ending job was to look, act, and sound completely sober.

It's reasonable to wonder if mothers like me got so good at our disguises that we accidentally played a part in our own secret suffering because the ones we hoped would notice were the same ones we worked the hardest to fool. I wanted Pete to rescue me. And yet I hid everything, thinking I was doing him a favor. I did the same thing with my mom and friends back home, believing that I was sparing them from worry. I didn't want to be a burden or take up too much unnecessary time or space because there were other things more important in the world than me and my problems. Now, of course, it sounds like poor, pitiful Emily the martyr. But I actually believed it was the right thing to do. *It's not that bad. I'll figure it out.*

The day before, I walked around the corner and dug my fingernails as hard as I could into my wrists in an effort to snap some sense into me. I thought about saying something to Pete, but I didn't want to upset him. *He's got enough stress with work.* The same words echoed over the television weeks later before I made the girls lunch.

"Should we do grilled cheese today?" I asked. They nodded their heads in agreement.

"Okie dokie, I'll make 'em in a minute," I said, then walked upstairs. *One swallow,* I said inside the closet. *I'm only taking one swallow, just to shut you up* but I was back the next hour, justifying the sips with stories I heard about all the pregnant moms who drank a generation ago. *Then I'm done. And I mean it!*

"Mommy!" Stella shouted from inside the house later that afternoon. Becca and I were by the back porch checking on the carrots we planted, so I didn't immediately answer.

"Bec, why don't you check this one? It's got the highest top, think it might be a real winner," I said. We'd been waiting anxiously for our first garden to produce, well, anything, so she bent down to closely examine her specimen before giving it a proper yank.

"Mommy," yelled Stella again, "I need you!"

"Come outside!" I said, trying to hide my disappointment at the dinky, corkscrewed carrot because Becca was glowing with pride. "Honey, you did it, amazing! Look at that," I said to Becca. From the inside of the house I heard Stella say, "But I pooped," and off I rushed to find Stella on her plastic potty in the middle of the living room.

"Well, hello there," I said as we exchanged smiles. "Good job, way to go," I told her before letting out a sigh and cleaning up. It comforted me to do all the daily deeds of a good mom because the reward was watching my children have a regular day. I even managed to find Shelby's missing jazz shoe after school with only seconds to spare before we left for the dance studio.

"Mom, you're the best," she said as she hopped out of the car when we got there. That's the part of me worth noting, the side I want remembered. That it wasn't always tragic. Most days, those uneventful ordinary kind, were folded under, accidentally, over time.

But out of sight from the kids, I was making trips into my closet for a swig or two, or four. *Okay, that's it, no more, seriously.* I'd start off thinking, *I feel good, this is great, I'm a fantastic mother today.* I was in the game, and the trick was to stay within the lines of reasonableness, so I'd pull out the breathalyzer Pete bought, thinking the digital number of a screen would hold me together. When we got home from dropping Shelby at the dance studio that day, I blew into it and saw 0.02 BAC. My blood alcohol level needed to be a solid 0.00 in an hour when Pete got home, so I poured myself a big glass of water and started drinking it. Exhaustion began to set in as the little girls dragged out poufy princess dresses and the war inside me started to rage.

"Hey Mommy, can we dance?" asked Becca.

"Sure thing, hang on," I said, knowing they wanted music. I put on Lady Gaga while their feet bounced around with happy dancing. *I'm a good mom.*

With my back turned to the party in the living room, I started making tacos at the kitchen counter, knife in hand, chopping tomatoes and getting angry. I guess when someone doesn't know what to feel, anger is the first choice. Chop, chop, chop, then I asked myself, *what the hell is wrong with you? How could you? Why would you do this to yourself? Your baby? Your fucking family?* Chop, chop. *People are worse off just for knowing you. You ruin everything and always will.*

I put the knife down to drink some water and rub my forehead, gearing up for the hidden nightly reckoning that always came. Clarity started killing me at the same pace the alcohol left. I wasn't sure which one was worse anymore.

My brother, Peter, and I used to arm wrestle, and for a moment I'd think I could beat him. Stronger or not, it only takes an inch in the wrong direction before you're screwed and there's nothing left to do but watch the back of your hand slam to the table. I lost every time. Peter was clearly stronger and toying with me. But still, it felt like, *maybe there's a tiny chance I can beat him,* the elusive *what if this time I won?* I was scared to death I was going down, where defeat meant getting caught or ruining something or another tragic consequence.

I always lost, just not that night. When Pete got home, we had a lovely meal. I was relieved because my final breathalyzer was 0.00 and the girls did most of the talking by filling in Daddy on events from their great day. With all that going on, nobody noticed the blood raging through my veins right under the surface of my skin. How could they? I looked like an ordinary mother with a baby belly and swollen ankles, a tired smile plastered on my face.

What a strange thought to consider all the people in my life who had no idea what was happening to me, including the one who slept next to me. Pete caught me multiple times under the influence since moving to North Carolina, and each time I lied about it even when the breathalyzer told the real story. Pete had to know, how could he not? It wasn't as if the man was an idiot. I wanted to scream, *Hey! Do you miss me,* even stared at him for what felt like an hour waiting for him to look over in my direction or come in and see where I was, but nothing. Was he worried about the baby? Or was he too busy with work to confront me? Too busy picking up my pieces? Maybe, like me, he just didn't want to look.

None of that meant I quit trying. I hear people say the definition of insanity is doing the same thing over and over expecting different results, and it's cute. It reminds me of another saying, "Ignorance is bliss."

At the heart of it, someone in the hell of addiction isn't expecting a whole lot. We can only see the second before us, and then the second after that—how will we cope, how will we survive, how will we feed our addiction in the next second and the next and the next? Make no mistake, the monster will get its meal. It's a chase scene with lives whizzing past us, on the run from another *tick* on a watch coming closer. I was running out of breath.

I sat across a desk from a psychiatrist and told her, "I'm an alcoholic, I'm depressed and desperately need help or I'm not going to make it."

I needed to hear a tiny speck of hope to get me out of my gnawing depression after making it a week without alcohol. She lectured me on the dangers of taking medications while pregnant, and I argued, "You've got more danger sitting in this chair right now."

She wrote a prescription for antidepressants on a fractional dose that equated to taking nothing at all, and I continued to see her despite the lack of improvement. I no longer woke up each morning on a mission to quit drinking for good. How absurd. It was every hour, at least, when I tried to stop what was happening, begging myself not to do it and sipping rations of wine like I was lost out at sea.

What's worse—insanity or the brink of it when a fragment of self still exists?

I still went with the rest of the family to the local YMCA outdoor pool on the weekends, wobbling through the gate with my shoulder falling off as I carried a huge beach bag stuffed with towels, goggles, snacks, and sunscreen. Pete carried the life jackets and found a table, then went into the water with Rebecca and Shelby. Every part of me was tired, so the cool water felt good when I sat down in the shallow end and watched Stella bounce around me.

"Mommy! Mommy, watch me go under," she said, and I nodded with a smile. She sprang up into the air in her bright pink bathing suit then face-planted with a splash, coming up with a triumphant look on her face. What a sight. Everyone looking in our direction would have seen a mother caught up in one of those moments old people love to remind us to enjoy. And I was, watching her look around for whom she'd pick to make friends with that afternoon as I glided my hand across the top of the water. With my legs stretched out in front of me, I scooped some into my palm and poured it on the plum-colored swimsuit stretched tight across my melon belly. To keep him cool. *Don't want you getting too hot in there,* I thought, eyes still looking outward at Stella, catching glimpses of similar smiling moms who had no idea I'd been reading about fetal alcohol syndrome late last night.

"Stella! That's a little too deep, honey!" I called to her. "Come closer to me please," and she sashayed over with two friends in tow. *If anything's wrong, I promise, we're going to take the best care of you,* I thought to the boy inside of me, and that was a tortuous place to be. It's beyond a regular person's comprehension to believe I can't just quit doing something that looks like a voluntary action. Goddammit, *stop drinking!* Like the time I had Restless Leg Syndrome and the inescapable urge to move my legs—*Hold still!* I scooped up more water to pour across my stomach, leaving my hand to rest on its top when Pete came over and sat beside me. He reached over and held my other hand, our raisin-ed fingers intertwining in the water.

"You having a good day?" he asked, and I knew it was loaded with subtleties that questioned things like self-hatred and cravings.

"Yeah," I said to him, "I am." The smile he beamed in my direction was worth the price of my half-truth.

My family looked happy, which was what I wanted and loved to see. Splashes of joy and laughter still glistened on the surface of my days. I kept thinking maybe God would save me.

We were down the street at a church service one Sunday in the fall when my bloated, eight-months pregnant body ran out of breath from singing hymns. Suddenly I was burning hot with sweat trickling off my forehead and into my hair.

"I don't feel good," I whispered to Pete, wanting to go home and lie down in front of a fan with a cold washcloth on my face. But it felt like I might be sick, so I made a quiet exit for the lobby restroom. I stood at a sink staring at the reflection of a red-faced woman soaked from the sweat of alcohol withdrawal and didn't recognize myself. I closed my eyes. *You're not going to save me, are you?* I whispered with my face buried in a wad of brown paper towel from a wall dispenser. It didn't matter if I cried, so I did. *I don't blame you.* Cold sink water soaked the paper pressed against my neck, but the heat felt unstoppable. *I wouldn't save me, either.* I couldn't cool off, so I took one last glance at my ungodly appearance and walked back to the sanctuary.

Pete squeezed my hand when I sat down and tried to figure out what was happening near the altar. The head pastor stood next to a man whose sad-looking posture gave the impression his day was going as well as mine was, but I couldn't see very well through the rows of people angling for a better view. Instead, I attempted to hear what the pastor was saying.

"A member came and informed our staff about Mr. Reynold's problem with enjoying his liquor a little too much," his hand rested on the man's shoulder. "He's lost his way, turned his back on his wife for a wandering eye and a lust for the drink. Would you like to speak to the congregation, Mr. Reynold?"

What on earth? In front of everyone, the humiliated church member mumbled an apology that oozed with a weird "thanks" to the crowd that raised a hand and voted in favor of his excommunication as soon as he walked out the door. I didn't dare move a muscle or look at Pete. My eyes stared a hole into the back of dozens of heads sitting in front of me and all I could think of was how many of them lucked out this time. I damn sure did. I wanted someone, anyone, to turn around and accidentally lock eyes with me so I could crush the hypocrisy with one look. I shut my eyes and pretended to pray before whispering to Pete that I'd meet him by the car. I bolted outside for fresh air.

Have I gone completely mad? I detached from myself, unable to grip the world around me. *How can I disappear without causing anyone more pain?* I knew it was impossible. *I can't live and I can't die. I wish Shelby had somehow been born to my mother, so I could have known and loved her without wrecking her. All of them actually. These poor girls, this poor baby. I wish God would deliver him right now and just erase me. Rewrite everything so I was never here.* I prayed that someday I'd be forgotten by everyone who ever loved me. But if I couldn't have it my way, I prayed for one more chance.

"*God,*" I whispered alone on a wooden bench near the parking lot, "*let me go back. I want to go back to the very beginning, but this time get it right. Please, God, just give me that. Give me a do-over,*" but I was too late. Sunday rolled into Monday's paperclipped set of schedules for the week.

"Honey, my water just broke," I gasped to Pete a couple of weeks later at the doctor's office. I hovered over the chair I'd been rising from wearing maternity jeans with a wet crotch. His eyes got huge.

"Are you sure?" he asked.

"What do you mean? Look! Yes, I'm sure. It popped. Get the doctor back in here." We stared at each other and started grinning. It was three weeks until my official due date.

We both thought there'd be plenty of time.

"Okay, you go home and pack my bag, and I'll drive myself to the hospital and meet you there," coaxing Pete to agree with the plan. I thought I was perfectly capable of the fifteen-minute drive until I found myself doubled over from a contraction going 75 mph on the highway. *This is serious shit,* wincing my way through a parking garage, thinking maybe we made a mistake. I hunched over and shuffled along the sidewalk toward the hospital's front entrance, thrown off by how many people ignored a woman in labor and how fast things moved compared to the hours of boring labor Pete and I predicted.

"Good morning, you doing okay?" hollered a security guard in my direction from the doorway.

"NO! Definitely not!" I huffed at his dumb question. "I'm having a baby."

"Ah, well, congratulations. Is this your first?" he asked when I waddled to the doors. I wasn't in the mood.

"It's my FOURTH." And as soon as the number left my mouth, he turned his head and shouted, "Wheelchair! Call up to third floor and someone get me a wheelchair, hurry!"

Nurses surrounded me the minute the elevator doors opened onto the labor and delivery floor. A million questions flew at me as I tried to breathe through contractions—age, birth stats, insurance, husband's name and number, allergies.

"Can I get an epidural?" I asked when a nurse checked my cervix.

"We don't have time," she told me. *Son of a bitch,* I thought, *I need to get it together.* With the sound of equipment wheeling around the room, I suddenly remembered a story I saw on television about men buried underground dying of thirst who confessed they would have killed the man next to them for a single drop of water. It popped into my head because when I writhed in the most excruciating pain a human can endure, I thought, *I could murder someone. If I had to do it to survive, I could.* Such a random thing to be thinking about on the brink of giving birth and so opposite of the violin concertos that softly played while my mom or husband stroked my hair when the girls were born, yet there I was contemplating homicide.

Then again, if women aren't warriors in childbirth, the human race goes extinct. Some pain is meant to make us stronger in the fight, and some pain means we're dying.

I knew them both.

I wanted to push, but two nurses rolled me on my side to wait for the doctor. I never realized the action was identical to one done for Fern over 60 years earlier while she waited for the doctor to arrive and Lynette was born with cerebral palsy. I only waited a couple of minutes, and then Pete showed up, flying through the doors with a look of relief on his face because he didn't miss it. And like the times before, a beautiful baby was placed on my chest, instinct took over, and I cradled him, touched him, kissed him, and cried. I looked at Pete, who was looking at me, and for a second I forgot that anything bad existed in the world.

Later, the two younger girls came to meet their new baby brother and handled him like a breakable doll. Each time he moved or squeaked out a sound, they fell further in love with him. Shelby stayed home, choosing to skip the visit like I did when my brother Adam was born. I missed her presence much more for my sake than for that of the newborn lying between two of his sisters. The picture in front of me was incomplete without her, but I knew I'd see her soon.

I was alone with Spenser that night after everyone went home. My new bundle slept across my thighs, and I stared at him lovingly, inspecting every inch like I'd done with each of his sisters. But that night, I searched for signs I had damaged him. I had read everything my heart could handle while I was pregnant. My fingers traced the outline of his ears and brushed across his forehead. I studied his hands, holding each one up to my mouth for a kiss before I moved on to his little feet and toes, finally lifting him to lie against my chest with his face tucked under my chin. He was so perfect.

The times I'd spent detached from whatever was growing inside me, when I thought about another child as just more work for me, were gone. I felt my heart turn a vibrant red again at the sight of Spenser as only a mother's heart could understand. I deserved all the devastating emotions wrecking the innocence of the scene in front of me, and I was acutely aware most people considered me unworthy to be in that room holding him that night. Still, I watched his delicate fingers grab hold of my own as if we belonged together. I could never make this right; I would never get over what I'd done. I knew it right then and started quietly crying in a way I wasn't sure would ever end. I wept for things I had done, and I sobbed because I couldn't undo them. I cried for the lost dream of who I wanted to be and for my overwhelming gratitude to God for saving my son. But I think He forgot to save me.

Does shame serve any purpose? What about failure? Motherhood can be devastating on its own, partly because it can't be mastered no matter how hard we try to get it right. Outside of the endless supply of advice suggesting ways to turn lemons into lemonade lurks a fog of grief. It surrounds the housewife born from a lineage with surefire ways to medicate the pain of expectations that ended in defeat. It didn't turn out the way we pictured. We know it was our fault.

But what happened to the woman before the babies came? *Am I still here?* It's a dangerous topic to mention out loud. *Please, quiet down, there's a baby sleeping.* We're not supposed to clamor about ourselves when there's a husband and children to care for.

"Hang on, *hang on.* Girls, back up and give us some room," Pete said, making his way through the front door with the baby carrier hooked in the crook of his elbow like he was bringing in a bucket of ice cream. My mom, who'd arrived earlier that morning, waited patiently by the couch, coaxing the girls to come sit down beside her.

When Shelby was born, I kept a daily record of every minute she nursed and every drop she peed. Now I stood wearing maternity pants pulled over the giant hospital diaper and watched my two-year-old drool over her new human doll. I was afraid she'd take off with Spenser and feed him plastic green beans from her play kitchen if I let her out of my sight, but Rebecca stepped in to mediate the situation with a "don't touch the baby" approach.

"Emily, come sit down," my mom said. "Where's your water? Are you thirsty? What do you need?"

"I don't know," I said and sat down on the other couch. Drifting above me were sounds of conversation—Pete talking to my mom, Becca talking to Pete, Mom talking to Stella—but my eyes fixated on the newborn being carefully lifted into his father's arms and carried over to me.

"Hey, honey? You should probably try to nurse him. It's been a couple of hours," he said.

"Okay, yeah. I'll take him."

For a week, I tried to get into the swing of life again, silently rehashing old affirmations to myself about leaving the past in the past and starting over with no knowledge that some of my struggles both pre- and postpartum involved the neurobiology of my brain. I'm not a scientist. My head simply told me I didn't deserve to even be there, which led me to always question why my family loved me back. But it was that perfect little swaddled baby who tortured me the most. I watched him sleep at night in the bassinet pressed next to the bed, and I swear I woke up every ten minutes the first night home to check and see if he was breathing. I pressed my cheek against his, being careful not to wake him, and took a deep breath to smell the sweetness of his milky mouth. Little miracles like the sound of Spenser breathing and Shelby warming up to him with Nana's encouraging words should have been a comfort, but all I felt was unworthiness and despair.

"I'm beyond miserable. I can't get over this feeling," I told our family doctor. He's the guy I saw for things like a sinus infection, but I was desperate to try even if I hated making that kind of confession out loud. I glanced down at Spenser sleeping in his carrier by my feet.

"It could be a hormonal shift," the doctor said. "Emotional mood swings are common in new moms." I wanted to punch him in the face.

"Maybe," I replied, knowing that was a crumb of my issues. "Does it matter? Look at me, I hate everything inside and out about myself. I can't close my eyes for two seconds without feeling like an alcoholic piece of shit who ruined everything, and no, I haven't drunk. Excuse my language, but I'm fucking depressed, and this isn't new."

"I understand," he said.

"Look at this," I said, motioning down to Spenser, and tears started rolling down my face. "He is *killing* me. I can't stand to be around him, but I can't stand to be away from him, either."

The doctor looked at me, completely baffled and replied that he couldn't, in his good conscience, prescribe any medications because I was nursing, not that I asked. I left with orders to eat better if I wanted to lose the baby weight, nap when Spenser naps throughout the day to get more sleep and try some physical exercise. How do I nap with three kids under five years old?

When I got home, the house was quiet, and dinner was baked in the oven. I looked out the back window and saw my mom outside in the cold, pushing the girls on the swing set while Shelby sat nearby holding Spenser bundled up in blankets. Why couldn't I be more like her? Each day of my mother's visit, she managed to complete tasks and schedules that spun me in circles. The thought of the nap came and went.

"I don't want you to leave," I said later that night while she packed her suitcase to leave the next morning.

"It's going to be fine. Isn't Pete's mom coming for Christmas? That's only a few weeks away," she said. "Trust me, this is hard for me, too. I miss the kids so much." I knew she did.

When the house readjusted in the following days, my mind went back to war. I walked around from room to room with Spenser sleeping on my shoulder, trying to dodge the chatter coming for me, but I became the critic, the judge, the protester who spoke in my ear every flaw to my character and past. Yelling at Pete, getting fat, losing friends, lying all the time, rejecting hugs from the girls when I was afraid I smelled like wine, Spenser, all of it, *STOP!* But it never stopped. The shame. *Is there anyone in the world as awful as me?*

Never had I heard a story of an alcoholic woman unable to stop drinking when she was pregnant. Even in the thousands of meetings I'd sat in, mothers mentioned how they didn't drink or use for nine months in their addictions. Lies or truth, I couldn't tell the difference. It kept me silent, knowing I was the worst.

Doubts or wishful hopes were no longer my problem. I knew I was an alcoholic when I drank again that day in December, home alone with my newborn baby sleeping like an angel. Any level-headed person could see what a terrible choice I made, but me? I wasn't level-headed at all.

It's unfair to apply rational afterthought to a relapse. Besides, what I wanted at that precise moment wasn't sobriety or a spiritual awakening for a new way of living. I wanted instant relief, meaning *I am in unbearable pain, make it stop.* I wanted something to rescue me, not to cure me for the rest of my life. I ached for a sober life but right now? *I am dying. Save me. There is no time for anything else.*

Simultaneously, somewhere else, the threads intertwining my grandmother and me began to unravel and disperse in new directions, but with my existence already on survival mode, I didn't pause to pay respects. Hundreds of miles away, Fern was dying, and a hundred times I thought about calling or writing a letter to tell her how much I loved her and say a final goodbye.

"I think it'll be soon, maybe any day," my mom said over the phone, and her words went in my ear and smashed against the long line of other tragedies waiting for me to think about. "She doesn't like hospice, and I know she wanted to die at home, but . . ." She paused to sigh. "We're all working, and God, I wish I lived closer so I could've driven up on weekends. But I'm glad I'm here now," she said, and for a second, I tried to remember the last time I saw Fern.

"I wish I could see her one more time, you know, to feel her and give her hugs. Can you tell her I love her?" I asked, and my mom assured me she would.

Fern took her last breath 26 days after Spenser was born with my mom and others by her side, and with it, ended the era of the old pink house on Main Street in Brownsville, Minnesota.

When family, friends and most of the town gathered in remembrance of a good woman who did so much for others and left this earth with many hardships unspoken, I wasn't there for multiple reasons—a newborn, the cost of a plane ticket, no childcare.

The idea of angels watching over me was now terrifying and when I thought of Fern, no comfort came. Instead, I wondered if she could see me while I hid and drank myself into another downward spiral and if she heard my determination every morning to stop. Did the way I disguised my heartaches remind her of someone else?

I tried to hide everything, but in January, I wound up back at the same psychiatric hospital for alcohol detox, the same place where the blood test revealed the start of my pregnancy with Spenser. The hope I created for a miracle less than a year before turned out to be nothing more than a hoax, just more broken promises to me and everyone else. It's a low blow when the devil himself has to come down further to meet your level of hell. At the nurse's station, I tried to hide my humiliated face.

"I think I remember you," said one of the attendants when I walked in with my duffel bag.

Funny, because I didn't remember me at all.

CHAPTER TWELVE

February 2011–March 2011

The nanny's name was Katie, and I hated her. I hated walking into my house after being in rehab for a month and seeing the way she sat in my husband's recliner, holding my son. She smiled at me, saying hello like a sweet, Southern missionary with dimples in her cheeks. Katie was a perky young bride whose husband attended seminary, and I wondered if my name was on their prayer list. She didn't stand up to say hello, causing me to feel like a guest who walked in on the substitute wife.

I held my composure as I got closer, smiling at the family, setting down my bags to prepare for hugs, and shifted my gaze down from her face to the baby, *my* baby, as she started to stand. She was so natural with him. A wave of jealousy washed over me, and just like a mother bear, I swept in to reclaim what was rightfully mine. *What if he rejects me? I'll die,* I thought, as I grabbed him, worrying if I even remembered how to hold my son. All eyes were on me, including Katie's, when Spenser squirmed like he was questioning who the new stranger was.

"It's me," I whispered into his ear. "It's Mommy. I'm home. Mommy's back."

I pulled him close to my face frozen in a moment thinking, *Will you ever forgive me? Will I?* and the moment was gone.

"Mommy, Mommy, Mommy, guess what?" Stella said, turning my attention to her high-pitched voice telling me about her latest adventure with her new tricycle. She grabbed my elbow. "Come look at it! I can go superfast!"

"That's so great; I can't wait to watch you," I said, seeing pure joy on her face.

"Okay, let's go," Stella said and shoved my leg. She wanted all of me right then. Meanwhile, Pete was talking to me, too.

"Katie needs to go over the kids' schedules," he tried to say, but Becca interrupted.

"Hey, Mom, I made you a picture and wrote you a story. Want to see it?" asked Rebecca, our four-year-old.

"Absolutely," I said, taking the paper. She watched me carefully as I read the story, studying my face for a reaction, but Pete kept talking, and Stella was pulling at my baby-free arm to go outside with her.

"Emily, I need you. Katie has to go home," Pete said. He wanted me to focus somewhere else or to engage in friendly chitchat, the kind I used to do.

"No, I'm fine, really," Katie chimed in.

Yes, okay, I can do all of this, I thought, and carefully got up to listen to the stranger tell me everything about *my* kids that I, as their mother, should know. It was similar to the way a mother walks a high-school babysitter through a checklist before leaving for the evening, except I was the awkward teen.

Shelby, who had been distant until now, tried to help calm things down.

"Stella, Mom's busy, leave her alone," she said.

"Girls! It's too loud in here," Pete shouted to get everyone's attention. He got mine because now Spenser was crying. I watched the chaos in front of me thinking, *Wow, rehab did not, in the slightest, prepare me for this.*

What can I expect from a type of institution that people often called "the bubble"? In some ways, those of us inside of it felt shielded from outside forces but for a few of us mothers, I'd call it another planet. It's the breathtaking view of Earth from space that makes it look harmonious and boldly alive in the floating silence and when I was away, home held the same amount of promise.

To think I woke up that morning in a foreign place with temporary friends I'd never see again. Was it even real? I wanted to pretend it wasn't until I remembered my first phone conversation from rehab with Pete on the other end telling me all about Katie.

"Hey, I've got some good news," Pete said. "I called that church and Becca's preschool director and told them what was going on with you being gone and everything, and now we're getting dinners practically every night. Isn't that great? Oh! And I found a babysitter, nanny, whatever you call her, so that's a huge relief. She started today," Pete said. "The girls love her."

My head tried to process all the news.

"Wait, you called the preschool and told them *what exactly*?" I asked with my stomach on the floor.

"Honey, I told them where you were, not the specific place, but at rehab. C'mon, cut me some slack. I had to. I'm desperate. But don't worry, the woman I talked to was so nice. All the moms have been really awesome, I swear. And Katie, the nanny, is too," he said.

Calls were limited to five minutes, so I asked no follow-up questions and instead stayed silent on the line while he passed the phone for a quick round of hi's and bye's to kids who didn't understand why their mother couldn't talk for longer. A line of people waited to use the phone and were ready to pounce on anyone who chatted over their limit, so I hung up and made my way down the hall to my room, where I hooked myself up to my breast pump for a quickie before dinner.

I don't know why I felt so uncomfortable about those women helping my family or why it felt like a form of aggression against me. *Get over yourself,* I thought, sitting on the floor listening to the rhythmic sound of my pump. It was the same day I'd taken a dozen assessments for who-knows-what and was questioned at my weigh-in for losing three pounds in a week. All that should matter was the well-being of my husband and children, and in case I forgot, *you did this to yourself.*

When they all came to see me on visitation day the next weekend, I imagined a storybook scene much like a picture-perfect vision of our planet, and when reality wasn't a match, it was my failure. I wanted to give all of me to each of them, and immediately I felt overwhelmed. The only way I could have done it was to chop myself up into five smaller pieces to pair up and take a walk. Or hover over them all like a breeze to blow around their heads and whisper in their ears all the secret sweet messages I had just for them because no human can master a three-hour window that passes in ten minutes. If I turned to look at Stella and listened to her stories, then someone felt ignored. If I turned away from Stella, then she thought I didn't care and talked louder, pulling on my leg. On it went for each of them as Shelby talked, and I looked at her, batting away the last time she sat on the couch pleading for me to come sit next to her, and I said no because I knew I smelled like wine.

I looked directly at her, engaged in every word she said to assure her I was listening until Pete interrupted. Her face sank, and I thought, *I don't know what I'm supposed to do. Who comes first? How do I do this? Whose hand do I hold when I only have two?*

What does overwhelmed mean for someone like myself? Because at 36 years old, not only did I say the word often, I could no longer describe or define it in those moments. I simultaneously felt everything and nothing. No one told me that people with a history of trauma normally have elevated levels of stress hormones and that by not addressing and resolving the traumatic experience, some symptoms can continue for years. Overwhelmed can become a chronic state of hyper-arousal, a term that comes with its list of symptoms I read one day. A high-alert nervous system means more impulsivity, irritability, and even some paranoia and insomnia, self-destruction, irrational thoughts and emotions, and heightened anxieties and fears. I mean, seriously, what happens to mothers without the tools or resources or time to fix it all? We shut down, space out, go blank in the head, and while there are multiple clinical words to define such things, it can sterilize how truly unsettling and sloppy the experience actually is.

When the five-minute warning came over the intercom announcing the end of family visitation, it was a slap across my face. But considering the infant maternal hormones desperately crying out for more time with a baby I hardly met, it was a fire inside me. They were taking my son away from me, and I couldn't let it happen.

"I'm changing Spenser's diaper before you leave," I said in a rush at the front door, then whisked him away for a moment of privacy, pretending not to hear staff members telling me no. In my room, time ticked like a bomb until a silence began to hum in my ears as I gently laid Spenser down on the bed. Slowly, I pulled out a fresh diaper and changed him, looking into the blue-green eyes of the son I barely knew as he stared back at me, studying my face as if I were a stranger. I remembered how Pete told me Spenser started smiling, but I couldn't get him to smile for me. And I started to cry.

Before I buttoned him back up, I took my hand and ran it softly across the skin of his growing tummy, his little fat thighs that were new to me and his tiny feet. I bent down close to smell him and whispered in his ear all the secrets I saved for him.

"I love you so much. I'm Mommy; this is your mommy's voice," I said. "I love you. I'm never gonna leave you, I'm never gonna hurt you." But I had to stop. "I'm sorry," I said.

I was out of time that day, but it was only a day. Three more weeks and now, back on planet Earth, I watched Katie leave and closed the front door behind her. She'd be back tomorrow morning. Until then, it was just the six of us again.

To finally be back in the house swung me in a circle, returning to the scene of the crime, and if I were prepped for the moment, it didn't stick.

"Did you call a therapist yet, like they suggested?" Pete asked me, knowing I hadn't.

"No, not yet," I said, leaving out the part about how expensive it was to go. Our insurance benefits wouldn't cover a therapist, and rates averaged $100/hr.

"Don't you think you should? And what about meetings?" I'd been home for five days and wanted to scream.

My sober aftercare plan was in place and thoroughly discussed, with a massive amount of obligations—ninety meetings in ninety days was the goal, plus therapy once a week, step work with a sponsor, prayer and meditation, journaling, exercise, and self-care. I even made a detailed schedule of what my days would look like now that drinking was out of the equation. Life looked, dare I say, positive.

My first couple of days home, the kids kept me within arm's reach and when they lost track of me, I heard the pattering of feet on their way to find me. It felt good to be needed and soothed the burning guilt inside me about being gone for so long. We were making up for lost time.

"The kids don't want me out of their sight, and you don't want me driving alone yet. Spenser takes a late morning nap, and then I nurse him. After that, it's carpool chaos and dance classes. And you know what nights are like," I said, meaning Pete wanted me home, too. "I'm trying to figure it all out," I told him. "Next week will look better." I meant it. After talking more, we agreed I could take Becca myself to her preschool the following Monday at a church in Raleigh, but only if I promised not to make stops along the way. Fair enough.

To be clear, Katie was nice. It was my fault I didn't know what to do when she was over because the whole situation confused me. Why would I ask her to fold the laundry when I'm sitting right there? Or make lunch for the kids when I could just as easily get up and do it? I can't begin to explain how empowering it felt to get behind the wheel that Monday morning and drive my child to school by myself. It may not have been much, but it was all I had. No one told me how to do it. Nobody advised, suggested, warned or even shoved affirmations in my face, and it felt refreshingly like freedom.

Before Becca and I got out of the car, I scanned the church parking lot, conscious of moms knowing precisely where I'd been for the last 31 days. *All right, here goes nothing,* I thought to myself, holding her hand as we walked toward the building. Becca smiled up at me, happy to have her mom with her again. I smiled back at her, and I kept smiling to hide my insecurities. *I'm a good mom, I'm doing it,* but as we got closer, the air felt different than I remembered. A stiffness or tension cut like an interruption when I said my usual "Hi!" to familiar passing faces and noticed some women refusing to even look at me. Formerly friendly mothers acted like they didn't see me, or if they did, quickly looked away with what seemed to be subtle unkindness. *Am I imagining this?* I wondered. Once inside, the same thing happened. Women rifled through their purses to ignore me or stared as if looking at a stranger in the crowded hallway. At Rebecca's classroom, her teacher met us at the doorway.

"Good morning!" I smiled at the teacher. "So good to see you."

"Good morning, Rebecca, come on in," she said, looking down at my daughter with a smile like I didn't exist.

"Oh, okay," I said to the teacher as she turned her back on me. Becca looked up and hugged my waist. We said I love you's and goodbyes, and then I watched at the door as she went in and began to play. I didn't want to turn around. The place was crawling with parents dropping off kids in every direction. I wished I was invisible or that I could take off running. Instead, I stared down at my feet as they turned the corner, slowing in the crowded stairwell to one footstep at a time. Finally, they made it to the welcoming refuge of my minivan, parked underneath sunny skies in the lot, looking like everyone else's. Only one woman, Karen, genuinely smiled and passed close enough for me to hear her whisper, "Good to see you."

Somehow, I mustered a smile for her with my eyes stuck firmly on the ground.

Sometimes, shame felt so real I thought I could reach out and hold it or peel it right off me. But that wasn't all that I experienced. Mothers shunning one of their own is a passive form of cruel aggression, so it's understandable why I drove home in tears that represented shock, humiliation, anger, and pain. We're supposed to believe women are caring and kindhearted when the truth is our aggression is equally ruthless. It's the kind that's subtle, like the way a woman smiled at me. If it were taken out of context, I'd be the one who sounded mean. Other times, like the drive home, it wrapped around me so tightly that I couldn't distinguish the difference between the shame and myself.

The women I encountered decided to make me feel as humiliated and ostracized as they could and inflict pain upon me, not with punches but with rumors whispered in my proximity, as a form of torture. What it lacks in a masculine punch across my jawline or straight to the nose, it makes up for in aggressions so politely spoken and discreet they can easily be denied for lack of proof. Gossip wasn't entertainment over tea anymore; it was out for blood. And in a snap, I never talked to any of them again.

"I don't get it, it doesn't make any sense," Pete said that night when I told him what happened.

"What don't you get? Everything they did, like the gift cards—the meals, the offers for playdates with the kids—all of it was for *you,* the poor guy stuck married to the drunk mother of his kids," I said while he stared at me. "Look, I'm glad they helped out. It was very nice, but those ladies won't give me the time of day." And he still couldn't believe it.

It's reasonable to believe I exaggerated the morning. Coincidentally, the same thing happened when I went back for afternoon pickup. Knowing the school had prior notification that I'd been in a drug and alcohol rehab left me more than a little self-conscious, and possibly nobody knew how to talk to someone returning from a facility for alcohol abuse. Pete had a good point, but there was something more to it. We don't always want to believe something's true. He didn't think I was lying. But Pete needed to believe things would work out between me and the moms over time. He thought I'd become less sensitive, and they'd become less hostile. He needed to keep the dream alive, the one where decisions like jobs and locations don't fail, where love always wins.

Unfortunately, as the weeks went on, Pete saw it for himself. This wasn't the land of promise, the best place to raise a family, and it wasn't a place for people like us.

And so life goes on. I faced those women day after day, not because I wanted to but because I was committed to showing up for my kids, who simply needed their mother. Pete stayed at the job he started to resent after commission cuts and broken promises about a salary increase came again for the third year.

My sole purpose was to be a sober mom to a baby, toddler, preschooler, and sixth grader, a wife and central caretaker of everyone's needs. I did my best as a dance mom, cook, maid and chauffeur, keeping track of groceries with a list of things like bread, milk, cereal, lunch meat, cheese, diapers, formula and whatever else was running low. I sought support for my recovery and cautiously looked for women to befriend. Then the phone rang.

"Hi, Em. Do you have a minute?" my mom asked when I answered. I could tell she'd been crying.

"Of course, what's up?" I said, holding the phone in the crook of my neck while I washed bottles and sippy cups at the sink.

"It's just a really hard day. I thought I'd call and see how you were doing and hear your voice." Her voice was soft. "I miss talking to you."

"Aw, Mom, I miss you too. Sorry to hear you're having a hard time," I said. "I wish there was something I could do for you." I meant it as I looked out the window in front of me, wondering what

I could possibly give her, detached from my grief about losing Grandma Fern. I figured that's why she was sad, but maybe not.

It was March, and the trees outside were turning green. We talked for a few more minutes until I told her I needed to go.

"But call me anytime, really," I told her before we said goodbye. Then I stood there feeling like shit.

Guilt tells me I did a bad thing, and shame tells me I *am* a bad thing; at least, that's what I learned at three treatment centers and two psychiatric hospitals. I think there's an ugly place somewhere separate that isn't so cut and dry, where our bodies and brains carry too much and yet, *I think I can handle it all. I think there's a little more room. I think I can rearrange it all to fit it and call her back and give a little more if I just squeeze a bit harder.* That'll take some of the guilt off. But if one more thing piled on top of me, I'd fall so far into the pit of shame I'd never feel human again.

A week passed.

"We can't afford Katie, and I don't like the idea of you asking your mom for money," I told Pete on Day Nine.

"Honey, my mom is fine, okay? And you need the help," he said. *But I shouldn't*, I wanted to scream. Call it ego or arrogance but I thought I could do it all, and why not? Women have been running homes since the dawn of time. I wasn't running anything, not even myself, when she was there. Each time I gave my duties over to Katie, it diminished my entire identity. I'd been a nanny for families as long as Katie had been an adult, but I fell into an awkward space, unable to think of her as an employee. It felt wrong. I was uncomfortable being in the room watching her fold laundry and then paying her with my mother-in-law's money.

A fresh start. It's hard to pull off in a house where the worst memories come to mind at every angle, across each wall in every room. I thought if I freshened things up with some new décor for the walls or placemats for the table, things might feel different, and the reminders of the trauma I created would dissipate. I left the house on an ordinary day a couple of hours before Becca's school dismissed to look for a discount retail store over on that side of town. I was excited over the idea, even putting on my nicest maternity blouse because my boobs were still too big for normal tops; then, I slipped my feet into a pair of black leather flats before heading out the door.

It was a nice day outside as I drove past shopping centers looking for a store with the potential for a colorful pillow to add to the couch or maybe a trendy wooden plaque for the wall. Really, what I wanted most had nothing to do with a purchase, and I wanted the freedom to walk around with nothing on me. Nothing to tie up my hands like diaper bags and little hands and family-size shopping carts. No laundry, cooking, conversations, guilt, or explanations. I wanted to simply enjoy time by myself. But I didn't realize how much I carried until I tried to set it all down.

Then I saw it. The familiar grocery store sign was five times bigger than everything else around it, and a signal went off in my brain saying wine could fix me for an hour, and no one would have to know. No mental dilemma regarding a choice, no consideration about calling anyone, nothing. It's a moment I'd be asked to dissect and analyze down to the second at least a dozen times. I pulled my car into a parking spot. I walked in, bought two big juice-box wines, which were more or less soft-sided bottles of wine with a twist-off cap, got in my car and drove away. How insane would I sound if I said it felt like half of me stayed in the car and turned my back on what was happening? Because it's true, and that's how I remembered it. I know I drank the first one fast. I know I went into a store and spent more money than we budgeted.

But the rest is a blur.

A hundred times over I was asked, "What were you thinking? Self-sabotage? Attention? Denial?" I never liked how strangers wanted to be experts on the topic of me. Sometimes "I don't know" is an honest answer because that day was supposed to be a good one.

When I woke up later that afternoon and heard echoing voices, it took me a minute to snap into the horrific reality of where I was and I began peeling myself up from the concrete floor of a crowded jail cell to sit and get my bearings. The two metal benches along the wall were already full of women in all shapes and sizes, none of them dressed the way I was. Some ladies sat in casual silence like it was a waste of their time to sit and wait, while others used the time to sleep or have short conversations. My mind raced, trying to piece together what the hell got me in jail. *Where was Rebecca? Oh my God, did I pick her up? What happened to her? Did Pete have her? Did he know where I was?*

Flashbacks started coming in bits and pieces as I waffled between wanting to remember and begging to forget. Repeatedly, I sat sweating with each new split-second realization as hours passed, and more women came in through the gate like cattle. I wanted to throw up.

Memories popped into my head as the slides of an old View-Master pointed straight at the sun. I remembered pulling the car over and telling Becca, "I need to rest my eyes for a second, okay? Not sleep, just a one-minute rest, I promise." Then, a rap on my window and police cars. Becca was crying loudly behind me, and at the same time, the officers were talking to me and peering in the windows. They opened my door and told me to get out.

"No, I can't," I said with a slur. "My daughter." There's little compassion for a mother in my condition. I tried to talk, tried to hold my eyes open and force myself sober, all while standing handcuffed on the side of a road with drivers slowing down to watch. I begged them not to leave with me, not like that.

"Hey! Anybody there? We got too many of us in here!" a woman next to me shouted out to get someone's attention. "Y'all need to move us upstairs or somethin'. Start another room, shit. We got an empty one right there, this is crazy!" she yelled to the guards, who ignored her from down the hall.

I looked around and counted. Twenty-two of us were crammed into one cell, and she was right; an empty one was directly across from us. The men were in cells with three, maybe four people. It was wrong, although I tried to look invisible when other women familiar with the process chimed in and started yelling.

"It's bullshit is what it is," someone said. I nodded. *What the fuck have I done?* There was a pay phone on the wall, but what was the protocol? Did it cost money? I already stood out like an oddball in my black blouse, black pleather flats and white skin; I wasn't comfortable enough to ask humiliating questions like, what was bail, and did I need it? *How do we know what we did to get in here? What are the odds I'll eventually need a shank?*

What an upside-down existence I found myself in that night. I called myself an outcast and felt like the scum of the earth, but I spent hours convinced I didn't belong *there,* among *them.* Despair is a terrible feeling, but it's unimaginable when I'm the cause of it. And when that amount of hurt combined with unused breastmilk from missed feedings for Spenser, my mind lost sight of emotional luxuries and went directly toward survival. *God, what was I thinking? This pain is unbearable, I wish I were numb,* I thought.

In the back of my head, I heard the cries of Rebecca from the back seat, unable to stop it from playing repeatedly for what was now ten hours of sitting on a concrete floor, and *I'm so fucked up. I'd drink right now if I could, just to turn off everything in this very moment. It's too much,* I said in my thoughts.

Part of me wanted to sprawl across the floor and thank God those things hadn't turned out worse, but I didn't want His attention. I hoped I was invisible for God, too.

I had no choice but walk over to the front iron bars and peer down the hallway for signs of a guard I could flag down. *How am I supposed to do this exactly? What should I say?* No one's going to have sympathy for the mom with mastitis in her engorged boobs.

"Hello?" I half shouted. "Excuse me!" I tried again, this time calling out louder down the long row of metal bars but with equal lameness as my first try. My voice sounded pathetic.

"Watchu need?" asked a woman sitting on prime real estate behind me. *Shit, I can't do a confrontation right now. I mean, I could if I had to, but please no,* I thought as I turned around to see a large woman who was shorter than me yet still somehow looked down at me. *Double shit.* Everything about her held a confidence I lacked.

"Uh, yeah, I don't know . . ." and my dam broke under pressure. Tears quietly tumbled down my face when I told her.

"I've got a, umm, physical issue I wanted to try and talk to someone about. Really, it's not a huge deal; I'm just in pain," I paused. The woman waited for me to say more, so I pointed to my chest. "A baby breastfeeding, and I don't know how much longer I can go." I stared down at the ugly black flats I wore on my feet with the stupid flower glued on the toe, waiting to see what she'd say.

"How bad are they?" she asked. I opened the neckline of my blouse exposing cleavage up to my collarbone.

"Oh, Lord, have mercy, you poor thing. Why you still here?" she asked me. It was late, and most women had gone. Those still around tried to sleep, so I answered her quietly.

"My husband's not coming," I said, and suddenly, heads began to lift to look at me.

"Are you for real?" asked a spunky young woman, shocked at the truth. A couple of girls stared at me blankly. A couple of others shook their heads and looked away.

"Oh, you got a baaaby," said one of them.

"Umm, yeah. Four kids, actually," I said.

"Hey, my baby's twelve. Watch them close, they grow fast," chimed in another woman.

The conversation lasted longer than I expected. I mostly listened, watching the way the women talked about their kids with a familiar glow of love mixed with the yearnings of regret. I smiled over the way we loved the same. And I suspected despite all the differences, we hurt the same. It was 3 am on a Wednesday, and none of us were home.

"Do they ever let you use a private bathroom?" I asked, getting some laughter mixed in with a resounding, "No."

Fuck it. My chest hurt worse than the heart buried in it. I got up and stepped over a couple of bodies lying on the ground, then unbuttoned my blouse in front of a small metal sink next to the toilet that we all had used at least once. What the hell happened to me? Someone must have questions for a girl who grew up to one day hunch over this bowl in the glory days of womanhood. I pulled one deformed mass out of my bra, and it was hard as a rock, humiliated like me as I stood there pretending I knew what to do. Hook me up to a machine and I pump enough milk to feed a village, but I was clueless about hand-expressing. Anything I might have remembered from a handout in birth class didn't work in a panic of embarrassment, but I kept rubbing and squeezing and whatever else I thought up for what felt like an eternity until finally, it worked. Milk began to delicately stream out and all I could think was *Jesus fucking Christ, it's a miracle.*

White droplets fell against the metal and tears fell down my face. I studied the way my pointless tears swirled into the milk the way they did in the rehab I'd left less than two weeks ago. Everything goes down the drain. Every painful squeeze bringing relief to my breast became a reminder of the piece of shit I turned out to be. Aching to cradle my baby boy, I squeezed. Missing Shelby and Becca's first day of kindergarten, *squeeze.* Hiding wine in a diaper bag, *squeeze.* Lying straight to Pete's face, *squeeze.* My mom crying on the phone, *squeeze.* You have no friends, *squeeze.* You just don't try hard enough, Emily. *Squeeze.*

By the time Pete picked me up the next evening, I'd been transferred upstairs after a soul-sucking body search where I squatted naked in front of a corrections officer. The orange pants, orange top, and used underwear that replaced my own clothes weren't as bad as the subhuman status that came with the uniform. Hearing how loud it was with women screaming and shouting, the hours with nothing to do but think, I could not fathom what it would be like to be trapped for months in that place. I was there less than two days. When Pete and I finally walked out of the building to go home, I was not the same. He and I headed to the car like strangers, the air between us so tight I thought if I moved too much, the windshield might crack.

"I'm so sorry," I said when I turned to look at him. "All of it, it's so awful. I'm so sorry, I don't know what's wrong with me." I didn't cry. Everything felt like a dream.

"I know," he said.

"How is everybody?" I asked him.

"Becca is completely traumatized," he fired off. I knew he was trying not to yell at me. "You have no idea. The cops left her completely alone in your car until I got there, Emily. They fucking sat in a squad car and did *nothing* for her for almost an hour! We are *all* broken up. Shelby won't even talk to me. Obviously, Katie knows. I doubt I can hide this from people at the office, and I have to go to work tomorrow. Do you have any idea what you've done? What were you thinking? You just got out of rehab twelve days ago, Emily! I love you, but you've got to stop."

"I know," I told him, with a fresh set of tears rolling down my face. What else could I say? He was right, and any attempt to explain myself would sound like an excuse. I earned his anger and disappointment, so I sat and took it. I let it all soak in with the rest of the things I already told myself.

The closer we got to the house, the more I dreaded seeing the kids' faces, with the fear and confusion in their little eyes and Shelby's disgust. But equally, I craved those kids. I wanted to feel the weight of them pressed against me in a hug; to smell the clothes they wore and hear their voices. I needed them close, keeping wordless company the way mother and child so brilliantly do. They needed to know I loved them, but in truth I needed to know I was loved.

What would I say to Rebecca? I still didn't have a clear picture of that horrible afternoon, but I remembered enough. I know I tried desperately to pull myself out of that drunken state. She didn't think I heard her screaming my name, *Mommy*, but I did. When the officers took me out of the car, I called out to her a thousand times, *Rebecca*, but I couldn't get my voice to come out of my mouth. I tried to reach her. I wanted to save her. I wanted to fight.

Stop, I can't think about that. It's too much because it was.

"Why'd you do it?" Pete asked me, breaking the silence as we pulled into the driveway. "Why'd you drink? And not call me? And drive? What happened?"

I'm not answering that, I decided. *It's too complicated to try and discuss, and we don't have long talks anymore,* I wanted to tell him, but I didn't. I wasn't brave enough to tell him the reasons. *Because I don't want to burden you or anyone else. Because you always have to be right. Because I'm tired of being a problem. Because I'm in the mouth of addiction like you were once. Because it works.*

"Are you going to answer me?" Pete snapped me back to reality.

"I didn't think about calling anyone," I said. He wanted a better answer, but I told him the truth. He wanted details and I wanted him to reach over and hold my hand. Give me some tiny sign I wasn't alone, that there was still a place between us where it was the two of us together.

That first night home, I sat by myself in my king-sized bed and stared at the wall thinking about the previous 24 hours. I'd almost forgotten what it felt like to turn around after exposing myself at a filthy sink to see a handful of women standing in a half-circle with their backs turned to me in a makeshift shield for privacy from passersby. Somewhere in the world, we all start as decent human beings until paths wander horribly off track. Mothers commit a crime and it's shameful, heartless. But for a moment those women whose names I didn't know treated me with a dignity I forgot even existed, like I belonged, and it felt good. Afterward, I could only offer a little smile in their direction as I went to sit down on the cement floor again, mouthing the words, "Thank you."

I wished I'd said more.

CHAPTER THIRTEEN

March 2011–April 2012

"Would you like to go next?" a woman named Susan asked while I sat on a folding chair in a church portable with other alcoholics on the opposite side of town.

Just my luck.

"Yeah, okay," I said. "I'm Emily, I'm an alcoholic." Then I hesitated. I stared down at my lap and examined the way my hands looked so old on that Saturday morning with their dry skin and big knuckles. I flipped them over, palms up, resting one on top of the other. My stupid tears fell straight down as if I were collecting them to make a cup of despair to splash across my face.

"I really don't know where to start," I finally said, making eye contact with Susan. "But I know what to say in these meetings, so I'm three days sober. I relapsed after getting out of rehab, got arrested for a DUI, and went to jail. My daughter was in the car, I am ruining everything and still, I can't stop." My confessions hung in the air of the silent room.

"I'm not suicidal, it's nothing like that," I said, "but I'll be honest. I can't do this anymore. My life is over. I don't know how I will ever get out of this, and it feels pretty hopeless." I told them I couldn't drive for at least a year and would probably serve jail time. "I don't want any of it—sobriety, alcohol, myself. I'm sure it will get better and yes, there's a solution, but not today. I'm sorry. That's all." The room remained quiet. I heard stories like mine and worse in meetings before, too, rendered speechless at how unbelievably reckless and sad it could get when one of us picked up a drink.

A common outcome of spilling your guts in a meeting was that others would chime in with their rosy outlooks, more commonly known as experience, strength, and hope and from what I gathered, people enjoyed it. I did not, but I stayed and suffered through the commentary, pretending to listen with appreciation.

"Wow, I'm so grateful you're here today, Emily," Susan said with a smile. The next person to talk after me was John, mid-fifties with a fresh haircut and dressed for a round of golf. "Your story is exactly what I needed to hear today. Hearing what it's like out there keeps me sober today, and that's how it works for me, one day at a time for the last 22 years," he said. *That's great, John. I'm glad my catastrophic state of hopelessness adds a little bounce in your step.*

"I needed the consequences and the pain to get honest, but I sure didn't like it. Selfishness was my problem, like the book says. And my goddamn ego," said another person, Charlie. "God's gotta run the show and I've gotta let him. It's all about surrender, and now I've got a life I never could have imagined," he said with a huge grin, and I nodded. Because none of it was wrong and none of it was new.

There was something sick about listening to people share. Celebrating the delights of sober living serves a purpose, but too much of it effectively ostracized the newcomer who could barely make it an hour without drinking. I wasn't asking for pity or another war story to make me feel better about myself. But when the party across the table made a gratitude meeting out of my misery, it wasn't much fun to watch. I felt increasingly alone as the hour ticked on and couldn't wait to leave.

Pete and the kids were in the car waiting for me when it was over. I walked with my head down through the parking lot full of conversations trying to avoid eye contact when a couple of women handed me a list of phone numbers.

"Thank you so much for what you said. I'm so glad you came today," a woman said. I looked down at the paper with handwritten names in blue and black ink just for me. Maybe I wasn't as alone as I thought.

"Yeah, I'm glad I came, too," I half lied.

"Please come back. We have a women's meeting, too. Here are our numbers. Call anytime."

"Ok, I will." I smiled and gave some sincere side-hugs, then I walked to the car. On the ride home, Pete drilled me for a full report on the meeting.

"So, what happened? How was it? Did you meet some women? Are those phone numbers? Are you going to call some of them? Are you going to go back?" he asked in rapid fire. *Hang on a minute,* I thought to myself. I needed time to switch roles in my head. *Who am I now?* I wondered, shuffling between the alcoholic, the wife, and the mother in me.

Because I felt like a child and Pete was my parent.

The kids in the back seat kept me from talking even though I felt like I owed Pete answers and explanations to everything I did now. He wanted me to say I loved it, that I met amazing women who were going to start giving me rides and helping with childcare. He wanted to see an old, familiar light in my eyes and a beaming smile on my face again. He wanted my quirky conversations, dance parties in the living room and side-aching laughter. I wished I could give it all to him. I missed me, too.

"It was fine. I'll call some ladies. A couple seemed nice," was all that came out before I turned around to talk to the kids and go on pretending we lived a normal life.

By the time we pulled back into the driveway, my family had been in the car for over two hours.

"Mommy, do an underdog!" Becca hollered from the backyard swing set after lunch. I pushed her high enough to run all the way under her seat to the sound of us laughing together, then turned around and watched the wind blowing back her blonde hair.

"Hey Mom, watch this," said Shelby from across the yard, and instantly she leapt into the air to show me her newest ballet leap. My cheeks hurt from smiling at the way she moved so gracefully amid the sounds of her squealing siblings.

"Oh my gosh, Shel, you get better every time! That was incredible," I told her. This was it, all I wanted, a sweet slice of life hidden from the dark space inside me. It felt so simple when I forgot to remember.

After dinner, Pete and I unloaded the dishwasher while the girls danced in the living room, and he reached around my waist, taking my hand in his for us to sway to the music in the kitchen.

"I love you so much," I whispered in his ear despite those words never feeling enough. I saw in his eyes how happy he was at that moment and my heart lit up over it.

Are we good? I wondered. Were the worst parts finally over?

We gathered in front of the garage for a family walk around the neighborhood, and the fresh evening air felt crisp across my face. I watched the girls while I carried Spenser in a sling across my chest and saw my entire world in front of me, safe in my sight as I walked a slow pace behind them—Stella on her tricycle, Shelby spinning on the sidewalk, Becca singing a tune to herself, and Pete leading the pack. *Leave the past in the past, Emily. Life is in front of you, not behind you,* I thought to myself because I felt something coming for me. *Help me, God. Please. Turn it off.* A puff of air burst out of my lungs after I realized I'd been holding my breath.

"Slow down, Stella! Wait at the stop sign," Pete said to the little daredevil before turning back toward me and saying with a big smile, "Come on, Mom, hurry up. We don't want to lose you back there."

I walked with more intention, looking down at Spenser and his perfect face sleeping against my chest, when my brain flashed back to a night when he was two weeks old and Pete snatched him out of my arms, muttering, "You're pathetic." Because I'd been drinking. *Jesus Christ, get it out of my head. I can't do this. Make it stop,* I said silently and put one foot in front of the other. I reminded myself that I was okay, and Spenser was right there with me. Paying attention to where I was, to ground myself, but memories kept slamming across my mind, even as Shelby walked beside me and put her hand in mine to tell me all about her new teacher.

What have I done to these kids?

There's a certain silence, a mangled sort born of shame and regret, that sits on the tongue with its barbs and thorns. The pain of spitting it out is too great, so it digs in and makes a home, infecting the voice until there is almost nothing left. I chewed on the shards of unworthiness and insecurities, trying to protect everyone I loved from the pain and ugliness of it all. But it became too big for me to hold. Everyone else filled the vacuum left by my silence with their own assumptions and stereotypes. Then I swallowed it all. *You're too much. You're so sensitive. That's a crazy idea. Calm down. No one cares.* I tied up my disfigured voice in a sweet smile so my suffering would be hidden, and I could stay pleasing. There are things we don't talk about. If we did, it might kill us.

I learned silence swallowing by watching my mom. One night, when I was in my teens, my dad was loudly flirting with our waitress at Red Lobster after one too many drinks. We were all mortified, but afraid to say anything that might set off his temper. I looked at my mom, thinking she'd make a comment, wave her off, or at the very least, glare at my dad; anything to put a stop to this humiliating spectacle. But she never did. Instead, she glanced up and offered one of those tightly tied smiles to both. I was amazed by what I perceived as her strength. I had no idea that the silence was ripping her to shreds on the other side of that smile.

My mom has always been smart. She was at her prime during the second wave of the women's rights movement in the 1960s, and I remember the *Ms.* magazines lying around our house. It was a tug-of-war she tried to muscle. My mother was raised from beliefs that women were better seen than heard. We are meant to be peacemakers, not peace takers.

The load-bearing thread of "a woman's place" weaved its way through generations of women. I felt the needle stitch right through me when my mother or grandmothers spoke about it out loud. In a letter from when I was younger, my grandma told me that my father would probably change if I showed him more appreciation. She wrote, "As a Christian, you must have read it's your duty to forgive," and added how much she hated to think of me as an antagonist to my dad. I needed a dictionary for the word, but her message was clear. Even the dearest women in my life taught me it was best to be quiet.

The kids were asleep upstairs. My mind was still attacking me while I stood in the kitchen, wiping off the counters before I turned off the light. I had so much to say. Peering through the window at Pete with his ritual cigar on the porch that night, I didn't know how to speak, not in this world, not even in my home. I knew nothing about repairing the broken parts between a husband and a wife. I'd never witnessed it, nor had my mother. Truthfully, Pete hadn't either. So I turned from the window, too exhausted to imagine something none of us had ever seen.

Screw it, I thought, grabbing my purse off the counter. I walked upstairs to my bedroom and plopped down on the side of the bed, staring at the wall for what seemed like ages. I don't know if I was simply following orders or making a conscious decision, but I closed the door and dug out a crumpled paper of phone numbers from the bottom of my purse.

I picked one with friendly handwriting and reached for my phone.

"Hello?" a woman said.

"Um, hi, this is Emily, I think I met you this morning . . ." She remembered me. The woman was glad I called her, and I was glad she didn't blurt out the dreaded question, *How are you?* For fifteen minutes, she was a friend on the other end of the line. She didn't try to save me or fix me like so many of us are tempted to do.

"I felt the exact same way when I got arrested," she said, and it sounded strangely like hope. I hung up and whispered, "I did it."

But it was never enough.

I asked my new friend for a ride to the next AA meeting, and she was happy to do it. But with my driver's license suspended for at least a year, I didn't feel good about bumming rides to a meeting so inconveniently far away from my house. It was too much to ask for anyone. I'd try and find something closer to home.

Nothing was out of the ordinary the morning Katie and I went grocery shopping, except I swiped a wine bottle off the shelf and stuck it in the diaper bag flung over my shoulder. My feet never missed a beat, and when I got home, I shoved it in my dresser drawer. Katie went home after lunch.

My living room, once a scene straight from the pages of a Pottery Barn catalog, was now littered with a stack of junk mail, graded school papers on the fireplace, a wadded-up sock, sippy cups, unfolded blankets, a bouncy seat, a baby swing, too many shoes, a half-eaten apple, two dozen books, a laundry basket, and a box of crackers on the couch.

All I could do was stare at it.

Many who take the twelve-step way get asked at the starting point on the sobriety train, "Are you willing to go to any lengths to stay sober?" That question nagged at me when I wondered what it meant for someone who needed a certain "willingness" to fit within the expectations of everything else. My second court date was coming up in a few days. My lawyer had appealed the jail time I got from the first judge. I didn't want to go back there. I didn't know where to start. And I did not want to drink.

I can't screw this up. This is serious, Emily, a big fucking deal now, I told myself, remembering how I'm casually reminded to ask for help, like it's an easy lap instead of a dark swim against the current in my veins.

I searched around for my phone and cautiously called Pete at work.

"Hey, what's up?" he said at the first ring.

"Hi! I'm just checking in and saying hello," I said. "How's work? Is this a bad time?" I asked when I noticed the tension in his voice.

"I'm so swamped, honey. I'll probably have to work on some stuff at home tonight, I don't know yet," he said with a heavy sigh. "You doing okay today?" I was so tired of being a problem, tired of being another worry in his day. So I lied, not meaning it as a trick to deceive him, but a loving and selfless thing to say.

"Yeah, I'm good. Not much happening really," I replied casually, reporting boring highlights of a stay-at-home mother's day and leaving out the wine in the dresser. Sometimes the truth is too much. So I swallowed the sword of silence again.

I lasted one more day before I went upstairs and drank the wine hidden in our room. Within a week, I was back in a place too dark to find words like *help*. My head thumped between two cement blocks, one of self-loathing, the other, indignance at the world, both weighing down my shoulders. It all came tumbling down on top of me one morning when Spenser and I were home alone. I flung open the stroller and buckled him in, walked out the front door and headed toward a little corner store to distract me from the feeling of my insides wanting to burst through my skin. Little feet in little socks dangled off the edge of his cushioned seat. They kicked around in a dance of pure innocence as Spenser enjoyed the walk through the late spring air, unaware his mama thought she was about to die. As I pushed the stroller, electricity zapped through my every breath. Panic.

The sun beamed across the cloudless sky, so my eyes needed time to adjust to the dimmer lighting once we stepped inside the store. A small crowd gathered in front of the little bakery counter to the right, waiting for morning pastries, but I turned left. I slowed to a casual pace and steered the stroller down an aisle. My desperate wandering eye felt so obvious that I was sure the other shoppers noticed the flood of relief that washed over me when I saw the wine.

"Sorry to pay in quarters, but I'm trying to get rid of some change," I told the cashier to cover the fact that I'd scrounged up money left lying around the house to pay for alcohol. He didn't care.

On the walk home, we strolled to the back of a little white church, and I sat on shaded concrete steps leading to a back door. It was quiet there and for the first time, I noticed an old cemetery hidden from the road and partially covered with weeds. I opened a juice box for Spenser and unwrapped the plastic from his string cheese stick.

Many times before that day, people told me to think through the first drink. Women told me to consider what would probably happen because sooner or later, it's a matter of life and death. I wasn't thinking about them when I tipped my head back and took the first swig of cheap, warm wine. What in the hell *was* I thinking? It's too easy an answer to say nothing was on my mind, because I must have been thinking something. Maybe a person can reach a point so low that the world turns upside down and living feels closer to death.

The wine gave me life. It was my savior, my god, and for a short time I was at peace. I could breathe again. What was killing me and destroying my family was also rescuing me, and that's the insanity so many of us understand too well. I filled my lungs with air, ate fruit snacks with Spenser, and walked home a little slower, with the sun at my back. I knew the reckoning was waiting, no need to rush.

The family routine carried on as usual when Pete walked in the door before dinner at his usual time. After a few tosses of kids into the air and hugs all around, he pulled me aside. Part of post-rehab aftercare involved Pete's ability to test my sobriety. *Building trust.* I blew a 0.00 in the breathalyzer for him after pounding water for hours, but any feelings of relief shifted when I saw the look on his face.

"We need to talk," he said. "I found out some news today." My stomach sank immediately thinking I'd been caught when he said, "It's Melanie. She has breast cancer."

Melanie was the wife of Pete's boss, Aaron. I studied the sadness in Pete's eyes as he told me about the diagnosis. Pete and Aaron's friendship dated back to childhood, long before the current arrangement. They even went to the same college. Pete was known as "Uncle Pete" by their kids, so the news felt especially hard on him.

"Aaron's devastated. I can't imagine what they're going through." Pete hung his head. The kids burst in to invade our intimate conversation while I stood frozen. "The whole office is trying to figure out how to help," he went on. "I was thinking we could take them over a meal. Maybe offer to babysit the kids while they're at the hospital, stuff like that."

"Yeah, of course." I nodded. Pete's genuine concern and compassion were why I fell in love with him in the first place, so it shouldn't matter that my struggles had long since stopped getting the same response. Melanie used to be my friend, or at least I thought so until my reputation went south. I tried to separate my feelings from the conversations and updates about her health. I listened earnestly at dinnertime when Pete talked about a foundation started on her behalf, donations people made, and a black-tie gala fundraiser planned for the fall.

That's terrific, so thoughtful, but I had little else to say on the subject.

Addiction brings out the worst examples of human selfishness. When I dropped off Rebecca at the Preschool of Humiliation, I watched from the window as my former friend was embraced by the circles of moms I once tried to fit in with. I thought of the last circle of women that surrounded me as I expressed my milk in the sink of the jail cell.

I got in my invisible minivan and drove home, thinking about the currency of compassion. And I felt bankrupt on both sides. That night, I sat alone in my bedroom and asked God to give me cancer. Because I was in it again, back at the wine, and every single morning, I woke up spending all day trying to quit. The never-ending obsessions about *one more sip,* the nonstop cravings that forced me back because I couldn't control myself anymore, the entire disease required as much if not more attention than the precious family who only asked one thing of me: *please, don't drink today.*

"Just swap it out," I whispered. "Give me cancer instead," I begged, hearing my pitiful voice. Yes, Melanie's cancer was awful; all cancer is awful. Still, I was jealous of it.

"Put me in the disease where people will be nice and won't blame me." I wallowed, my hands in a fist instead of a prayerlike fold, and I knew how awful I sounded. I wanted to believe these were two interchangeable diseases because they're both chronic and cruel. Except cancer doesn't make you get in the car with your kid while you're drunk. And it's less likely to get you thrown in jail or make you kill another person. I knew all of these things, but my self-pity didn't care.

A month later, Becca and Stella wanted to participate in the annual preschool Easter egg hunt and picnic. With a couple of weeks of not drinking and trying it that way, a loud crowd of children and judgmental parents was the last place on earth I wanted to be.

"You can stay home if you want, and I'll take the kids," Pete offered that morning when he saw my anxiety building up.

"You can't be serious." I sighed with a smile. "I love you, but the kids would be hurt, and I don't want to miss it. Plus, it'll only make the gossip worse than it already is."

We piled in the van, and he held my hand. Like any egg hunt involving a hundred little kids, it was a chaotic frenzy of dressed up children on a sugar high running around with baskets. I loved it all until we spread out our blanket and started to eat.

"This is weird," Shelby said.

"It's fine," I told her, knowing Shelby noticed all the socializing happening around us but not with us.

"Can we go home?" she asked when the two of us saw Melanie look straight through my daughter, who she used to dote on. I was pissed but tied myself up in the same tight smile I watched my mother tie when I was Shelby's age. And now Shelby was watching me.

As women, mothers or not, we have the power to help each other heal or the power to cause more harm to each other. It can happen in a second when we deny someone's existence or it can take place across a lifetime, but either way, the impact ripples farther than we think. I don't fully grasp how, as women, we can be so cruel and so wonderfully compassionate.

I know that wine has a fine line where, on one side, it's *yes, let's have girl's night and drink a couple of bottles of wine with friends because momming is hard.* But cross the line, and it's banishment and isolation. In the land of drinking, nobody is worse than a drunk mother. Any sin is made worse if that sinner is also a mother. I was taught to appreciate and forgive my drunk father, to give him grace and obedience. Sadly, nobody was lining up to offer me appreciation, forgiveness, or grace.

Sitting there, I never considered the possibility that those women had no idea what to do. While on the surface, I looked like the women who were unable or unwilling to support me, I wasn't like them at all. I couldn't be.

I didn't actually want Melanie's diagnosis; what I wanted was support. I wanted her circle, and I didn't want to have to go to jail to get it. The women in that community didn't have the compassion to see beyond the shit I did when I couldn't control the urge to drink. It was women I'd barely met, one who knew what it was like to be in the shit too, whose understanding stretched beyond where others could go. All this newfound awareness held a shared conclusion—no one knows hell until they've been there. And those of us who've been there do not forget.

I backed myself into a corner instead of a huddle, holding everyone at arm's length so my stigma wouldn't wear off on the ones I love. The result was a self-inflicted isolation fueled by the insanity of alcoholism. It's not pretty when someone loses their shit. The proper way to do it may be to scream into a pillow or break a few dishes on the kitchen floor. My method was implosion. I turned all my pent-up emotions against myself because something had to pop eventually. I guess that's what happened that warm night in June.

A whole scene erupted in the front yard with devastated daughters and an angry husband. I remembered nothing when I woke up with my clothes on and thought right away *I fucked up again.* But what the hell happened? How did I get so much wine? Because getting wasted was never, ever, ever the agenda.

I walked downstairs that morning, hoping it had all been a dream, and found Pete sitting at the kitchen table.

"Emily," he spoke softly when I sat down, stretching his arms out to grab hold of my hands gently. Something awful happened, but I didn't want to hear it.

I shook my head; tears stung my bloodshot eyes.

"Look, this is serious," he said. "Jerry was here." *My counselor, Jerry, from my Alcohol Drug Education classes for my DUI? Showed up at the house?* I panicked. "And one of the girls told him that you left them alone in the house yesterday." I shook my head defiantly, unable to imagine myself doing something so careless and stupid.

"What? Who said it? Maybe they just couldn't find me. There's no way I'd leave the kids in the house," I stammered, my head racing as I thought about who I'd become again. How could I try this hard to be a good mother, a good wife, a good person, and get out of this hell, but all I did was dig myself in deeper?

"I just need to start over," I said. "It's really hard, honey. There's just a lot going on." My voice trembled, too scared to tell him everything. "But I can do it, I swear."

"I think you need to go back somewhere." His tone was gentle, but firm.

"What?!" I said in a panic. "No! I can't leave again, no, please, God, no, I can't. I'll do it better this time, I swear."

"Jerry's required to report you to CPS," Pete warned. "Child Protective Services, Emily, that's how bad it's gotten. He told me the only option you've got for those kids is to go to treatment again." And he said it in such a kind and loving way, I wished everything was different and he was saying something else. Either that, or I wanted him to get mad so I could be, too. Here he was, with the look of a supportive and tender-hearted husband I longed for, but he was telling me to leave.

I got up from the table and ran to the living room, flinging myself onto the couch to cry into a cushion. *Don't look at me* was the message I gave him. *I don't want you to see me falling apart again.* The thought of leaving my babies again shattered me into pieces of unspeakable pain. I couldn't breathe. Without them close to me, I saw no reason to live.

"I can't do it." I was begging Pete to think of another way. "I won't make it; I know I won't!" But he'd already made the decision.

We had no money, no savings left, and I didn't want the burden of more guilt, *dammit! Who's going to take my place this time? What's going to happen with my probation? It's too hard on the kids without me, too hard on him.* Pete sat down beside me on the couch and put his hand on my back. Everyone's judgments and assumptions that I'd been swallowing for months rose up in my throat. *Well, Emily, you should have thought about that.*

I left the next day for another rehab, only three months after I got home from my last one.

For a week, little footprints from my children made their way around the house, scampering from room to room with a trail of toys and dolls, but I wasn't there. Nights went by without a bedtime story or goodnight kiss from Mommy, then sunrises without a good morning greeting, meals cooked and eaten, lunches packed without me. Endless hours without the sound of my voice or the touch of my hand—no kisses or hugs, no direction or correction, no laughs or listening to stories about their day. I was a ghost again.

One week tumbled into the next and was followed by the next. At six weeks, I completed the program, but Pete said I couldn't come home. All rights were revoked, and my voice was muted due to my counselor expressing her doubts about my wellness to him over the phone. Living in a treatment center that disconnected me from my life source . . . you bet I was unwell. There's little room in those places for people with children, especially mothers. More weeks until it was another dozen without my presence, my embrace, my voice, or anything at all of me in my house.

Spenser made first-year milestones like learning to crawl and cutting his first little teeth. He said Dada, learned to wave and say bye-bye. He grew into new clothes I didn't pick out. Becca started kindergarten, and Stella cut her face and got stitches for the first time.

I missed it all.

There are traumas we experience and traumas we create. All wounds take time and proper care to heal thoroughly, and if the trauma were broken bones, we'd get protective casts to shield us from more damage. While adversities in life that leave a mark or two are normal, a series of unrelenting breakages is not. Some of us can't distinguish one crack from another and forget how it even started. It's hard to see it until little fragments of our injuries start poking through the surface of our skin.

When it happens to a mother, like it did in my case, I got fresh glimpses of our scars every time I looked in the eyes of my children and saw how I failed them. I wonder if my mother ever did that with me when I was young. We couldn't get it right. Sometimes, we make it much worse.

So what's it like for a mother coming home after rehab? Or for a child when Mommy finally shows up at the house? And what's it like for a husband when your wife transitions back home again? Because what we needed and what we got were different things. We all wanted me to walk through the door, cured of the invisible sickness that lived inside me, like bones having been healed or a curse being reversed.

I returned with a new passion for creativity beyond my usual homemade décor, staying up late at night experimenting with paints and pastels. I'm a terrible artist but it was the act of self-expression through bad art and even worse poetry that ignited me. I felt alive, but I wasn't cured of the menacing thoughts of alcohol during the day. My sobriety wasn't perfect. There were slips and next-day restarts, but my days without drinking stretched longer—44 days, 67 days, 62 days.

Pete sat down next to me on the front steps one evening, his arm reaching naturally across my shoulders and my head instinctively leaning in to rest near his neck, both of us looking out at the kids playing in the driveway. He let out a deep breath.

"Maybe it's time," he said, "you know, to think about moving back."

I picked at the pink polish on my toes, unsurprised. We'd hinted at the idea multiple times, so the decision to finally wave white flags at our three-plus years in North Carolina came the way most wars end. We simply realized we could not win.

"Is it possible? What do *you* want?" I asked him, even though I knew what he'd say.

"I want you to be happy, honey. I want all of us to be happy and healthy, and it just didn't work here," he admitted.

Pete was right. Things were better, no doubt, but after all we'd been through, they weren't exactly good. Neither of us thought a couple of months without a major crisis qualified as a celebration. I stayed sober, but it was hard.

"You and I both know we've got a better chance in Texas—with your sobriety, with more family support—I have a good feeling about it." His voice sounded hopeful as he kissed the top of my head.

It's only natural to wonder why Pete stuck around. I can't count the number of times I've played back the horrific moments of our life, like I'm watching bad reality TV, wanting to shout at a screen, "Leave her, you fool! Kick her out and change the locks." But we were living in our reality, a couple of complex human beings.

Why stay? Is it codependency? Compassion from a person in recovery himself? Is it love for his children and their bond with their mother? Or something else that involved the mysteries of love, when a heart refuses to forget who we are underneath the storm? It sounded like a lie to say he never considered leaving me, but that's what Pete told anyone who'd listen.

"I never thought about giving up on you, not once," he said sometime later, and the answer wasn't enough for me either.

In the Spring of 2012, we made quiet plans for our departure when I got an unexpected phone call from my dad. I let it go to voicemail.

"Emily, this is your dad. Give me a call," said a hoarse, scratchy voice I barely recognized. *I'll call him tomorrow. Maybe.*

A week later he called again during *Sesame Street. Shit.*

"Hello? Dad? Is that you? Hang on." I scrambled, hearing a raspy voice stifling a cough on the other end. I stuck Spenser in his highchair with a handful of graham crackers and stepped out to the porch so I could hear better.

"Can you hear me? Is this better?" he asked, and it wasn't, but I lied.

"Yes, much better. Wow, Dad, this is a surprise. How are you?" I asked because it wasn't a significant day, not a birthday or holiday. We never called each other. Ever.

"I need to see you," he said. "No, I want to. You think you can stop over?" I paused in confusion. I pictured him in Plano in his one-bedroom apartment, a few blocks from my childhood home, looking out his window and thinking I lived close enough to swing by that evening.

"Well, Dad, I live in North Carolina, remember?" And when he did, disappointment hung in the air.

"Oh, right. Okay." Silence.

"But hey, you're in luck. We're moving back, actually, in a couple of months. To McKinney. I'd love to hang out with you when we get there," I said. Then I asked about his throat because he sounded so awful, and no matter how hard I strained to listen, I couldn't understand the words he said, nor did I have the heart to make him repeat them.

"Okay, well, I'll call you the day we get in town, I promise. I love you, Dad," I said. I thought he said it back.

When I mentioned the phone call to Pete, his expression turned into a *here we go again* look.

"What do you think he wants?" he asked, and I answered truthfully.

"I have no idea."

I don't know why Pete never asked me for a separation or divorce, nor could I grasp why my father decided to call that day and nestle into the back of my mind.

Love can exist within the folds of alcoholism, in the lesser-known crevices where the human heart is exposed, in the places where I am just Emily. All six of us piled into our big bed each night for an episode of *Backyardigans* and snuggles, where we felt safe in the comfort of a loving home surrounded by our favorite people on earth, without reasons to lie or pretend to be something other than ourselves. Love was in every look, embrace, and sing-along. This was my family, and we knew to protect such sacred spaces and tread lightly. *Do not rustle the blankets, do not wake the beast.*

CHAPTER FOURTEEN

July 2012

What does it do to a child to have a parent who refuses to love them? How does it feel for a child of any age to wonder what they did wrong, then spend a terrible amount of time trying to crack the code and win their parent over? A smattering of memories, along with photographs from when I was very young, proved a loving bond once existed between my father and me. But in a blink, and I never understood why, I no longer lit up his eyes. It's not unusual for a little girl to want affection and attention from her dad. His approval confirms that we matter in this world. Because no man is more powerful than our dads when we're young; they are the head of the house, providers, and protectors. I loved having him in my corner, and my best days were the ones when I made him laugh until his shoulders shook. I could see that he liked me. More importantly, I could say that I made him happy.

That I kept growing ruined what we had. I could see with my seven-year-old eyes the way my dad lit up when Adam was born. My mom was right when she said a new baby brought us happiness when we needed hope, but I wonder how much of "we" included me. My little brother was immensely lovable. He crawled around the house with that blonde hair barely visible on his bald head, and both my parents would follow him with their giddy shit-eating grins. I'm surprised my dad never tripped over me to get to Adam as he videotaped his every move with an '80s camera, almost an entire VCR slung over his shoulder. As the years progressed, I realized that Adam, who I loved, was the favorite, which I hated. He was my dad's perfect chance to start over as a parent. My mother was similar in more subtle ways, but clearly, in our house, Adam received the better side of Dad than my older brother, Peter, and I did. He got a different childhood than us. That's what happens in families like mine when kids get caught in the insanity of addiction combined with emotional and verbal abuse by different versions of the alcoholic mom and dad. I couldn't recall a single time when my dad's fury shot off at Adam. Never had I witnessed my father humiliate or insult my little brother in public, nor did I see him brought to tears at the kitchen table, and the effect it all had on me complicated the way I thought about myself.

To be fair, the collapse of my relationship with my father stretched well beyond Adam. But at night, when we gathered in the family room to watch television, all five of us stuck in the tension of togetherness, I stared across the room at my dad in his recliner with Adam tucked beside him in the space that used to be mine. I wasn't mad at my brother. Not even my dad, because that's not the way a child thinks. I was mad at myself and the parts of me that caused the rejection. Did he get bored of me? Bored of brushing my hair at night? Was he disappointed I never played Little League sports like Adam? Did I get too fat in fifth grade? Too ugly in middle school? Did I yell at him too much as a know-it-all teenager? That first wedding invitation that didn't have his name on it? Or was he still mad I blew the cover off his drinking? Because it takes an awful lot of anger to fault a family member for the way life turned out, which is precisely where we ended up. I blamed my father for everything when I was younger, and he blamed me, too. But I was also his daughter, endlessly searching for the one love I could not seem to earn.

Over the years, I gained little insight into my father, Dan. Once, in seventh grade, I asked him why he never went to church with us, and he told me he didn't believe in God. "Because if there was a God then He wouldn't have let my buddies suffer and die in Vietnam." I was twelve. Conversations with Dad felt like trips across a minefield; I had to get close enough to wave a flare in front of him. *I'm not that bad, really, I promise,* I wanted to tell him. And I thought he wanted to say the same thing. It was just a matter of time.

I was 28 and sober the first time I tried to see things from his point of view. We'd been estranged for several years when I wrote him a letter apologizing for things I'd said and done that were heavy on my conscience. I expected nothing back from him. When a card showed up in the mailbox, I didn't want to open it, thinking I was in trouble for something again. Written in his familiar handwriting were just five words: "I always loved you. Dad."

All this time later, my guess is he didn't feel loved as a child. Maybe he, too, wondered what he did wrong to make it so hard for a parent to love him. But I didn't think like that when I when I was younger, and I didn't see it when I read his card. *Forgive and forget,* I thought, even when his future actions never quite lived up to the words he wrote.

It shouldn't matter; I wasn't a child anymore.

But it did matter. A fundamental part of me still wanted my dad to care about his daughter, to just love me as Emily. In the absence of it, I got well-meaning words of comfort from people who weren't him. *Of course, he loves you; he's your father, Emily. I've seen how much he cares. He has his problems, you know.* Yes, clearly, I knew. But I wasn't interested in understanding the way history punched a kid named Dan long before he was a husband or a father. I didn't want to acknowledge how his pain synced up with my own. Admitting that would be admitting to my own inherited bloody knuckles and a self-confession that I was a 38-year-old alcoholic woman doing the same thing to her kids. And the shame it required to withstand that kind of truth? The vitriol I had for myself? *Shut it down, stop everything, I can't look.* Don't ask me to relate to my children's experience, not at that level. Deep down in places we don't talk about, I knew what their pain felt like and what they saw in me. I was intimately familiar with the ways their love could tip to hate and the agony between because I'd been there. I *was* there. And I wanted a different story. My entire life depended on it. Not for me, but for them. I wanted a different story for my children, a future filled with my deepest hope—that they would turn out nothing like their mother.

And if I didn't have a hundred other things on my mind when we finally arrived at my mom's house after the two days of driving from North Carolina, would I have understood? Of course not. I'd brush away my silly thoughts the way I did with a wild dream I remembered first thing in the morning. It all sounds so irrational when it pops to the surface. *My god, you get so dramatic,* I tell myself. The only big picture I cared about was our moving van being several days behind us.

"Good thing we packed extra clothes in the suitcases," I told Pete early that evening.

"Hey, we made it. We're back; that's what matters," he said as we dug around for pajamas to lay out for Becca, Stella, and Spenser. I grabbed a fresh diaper and handed it to him.

"No, you're right. I'm just stressed." I sighed. "There's so much to do." The overwhelm crept in when I thought about how much work went into unpacking an entire house.

Adam, now 30, lived nearby and came over after work to stay for dinner before the two of us headed over to our dad's apartment a few miles away.

"When's the last time you saw him?" Adam asked me while he drove. I watched the traffic in front of us, trying to remember.

"God, I don't know. Christmas last year? He's sick, isn't he? He called me a couple of times, which is so odd, and he sounded horrible. Does he know we're coming?" I wondered. Adam nodded.

"Yeah, it's pretty bad," he said. His short answers didn't land well with me.

We arrived, and Adam knocked a couple of times on the door before we let ourselves into my dad's small apartment. Two couches lined a corner and shared an end table with a lonely lamp on top. The place was dimly lit, but my stomach still lurched at the sight of someone on the couch. My father looked unrecognizable except for his sunken blue eyes. The shock of what I saw immediately made me wonder if the soldiers who rescued prisoners from work camps felt a similar reaction seeing living bones wearing skin.

How is he alive? My mind was reeling. *Is this real?* Were it not for the sound of his fluid-filled breaths, I would have thought the scene was fake.

"Dad!" I said, unable to stop my chin from curling into a quiver. When I rushed in for a hug that proved too physically painful, I dropped to my knees in front of him and stifled a cry.

"I love you so much. Oh, my god. I didn't know! I love you, Dad. We're back in Texas, I'm here."

"No grandkids?" he said while Adam bent down and gently hugged him.

"Not this time, no. But I can bring them over later," I said, then we sat down on the other couch near my dad. I took the corner spot to be closest.

"I've got cancer," he finally said. I nodded, still trying to merge the man in front of me with a lifetime of images of my dad. What I was seeing clashed so violently against the powerful man of my childhood that I shook my head to try to find a balance.

I can't do this, I thought. *He can't die; I won't make it.*

"Hey, I'm going to take care of you, okay?" I reassured my dad. "We'll figure it out. You've got a lot to live for, right?" My hand reached for his hands, so desperate to be the one to manufacture hope in his eyes. I hung onto every movement, waiting for some small sign in his face to prove my dad was in there; just one tiny flicker of familiarity so I'd know what to do. I wanted to help, to mean something, to earn my place in the pack. At the very least, get him comfortable and out of pain.

So, I asked him what he needed. Could I get him water? Patiently, I waited. Was he hungry? No, he wasn't. Did he want a blanket? No one spoke.

My ears filled with the sounds of my dad's wet attempts to clear his throat enough to say something to me. It seemed like minutes ticked by with me leaning toward him as if it would help ease his burden to see me there. *Look, here I am. Take your time, I'll try and help. It's your daughter, Emily.* How helpless it felt, waiting for his lungs to clear enough and fill with fragments of air so words could come out of his mouth. When he finally spoke, everything changed.

"Stop staring at me," he said with a look I knew to my very core. He was mad at me.

"No, it's not like that, Dad. I'm not staring at all; I was just waiting for you to finish your sentence . . ." I stammered, moving to the edge of my seat so he could see the sincerity in my face. But he wouldn't look at me.

"Just go," he said, but I couldn't understand the words and asked him to say it again. After an effort, he told me, "Get out." Which would turn out to be his final words to me.

"What?!" I asked, panicking instantly. "No, wait, please, what did I do wrong? Let me explain. I love you, Dad, I can't *leave* . . . We just got here."

An exchange took place between father and son while I sat on the couch as an outside observer. The way Adam helped him off the couch, gently held him and slowly walked as they left the room toward the bathroom, I knew they'd done this before. He'd been here.

After a while, the two were seated again, and no one said a word.

"Please, Dad," I started again, but he hadn't changed his mind. I turned to Adam, who was staring at the carpet in front of him. We exchanged looks, mine begging, *we need to stay! How do we change his mind? You're his favorite, Adam, say something, goddammit! Defend me for once, just once, so I can stay,* but he didn't speak up.

Instead, the three of us sat in a frozen moment—two minutes or twenty, I do not know—while I thought maybe something would change, but of course it never did.

"I think we should go," Adam said softly. I shook my head and stood up from the couch, letting it sink in for all of us that I hated what was happening. And then we left.

Ten minutes later, Adam and I stood in the driveway of the house where we grew up. I felt myself trying to stretch from the inside and be in two places at once, unable to stop time from racing past our house to take away our dad. *Why did I leave him there alone?* What the hell were we thinking?

"Adam," I argued, "he couldn't even walk. Dad could barely fucking breathe! We should have called an ambulance; we *still* should call one. He needs a hospital or, at the very least, someone there with him."

"I don't know, Em," he said, "I mean, he wanted us to go."

"He is *dying*! Alone in that apartment. What the hell are we doing?" I wanted to grab my brother by the shoulders and shake him.

But this was the role Adam played his entire life. The good son. It's all he knew to do. He would not upset my dad. And he would never take my side. He couldn't relate to me because he had no wrongs to right, and it made that family blood boil under my skin. It was like we were a couple of kids in the driveway all over again. And as usual, my dad and Adam aligned in an unrelatable bond, maybe because I looked too crazy for a brother who preferred things agreeable. We still lived with our family roles.

I thought all night about going back to the apartment by myself but not even Pete or my mother thought it was a good idea. They probably believed it could wait until morning to figure out. I dug through my suitcase, brushed my teeth and crawled into the bed where I used to sleep as a girl and hear my dad snoring down the hall.

For a split second the next morning, I woke up with a haze like it was all a bad dream. Maybe last night never happened. Once again, I'm at the mercy of denying the previous day's devastation. Sunlight was already peeking through the thin plastic miniblinds when I got out of bed and got dressed. Down the hallway toward the kitchen, I heard my mother's voice talking quietly to the early risers, most likely Stella and Spenser, and a sense of familiarity covered me.

"Good morning, everybody," I said when I walked into the kitchen and headed toward my mom for a quick hug.

"How's my daughter this morning? Did you sleep okay?" she asked me in our embrace. I stood in front of her with four months of sobriety, feeling fragile but still in one piece. There'd be time again for long conversations, but I looked at my mother and saw she was scared. I knew immediately she was worried about me, but tenderness was too much at the moment. It was a weight I brushed past with light conversation as we slowly got ready for the day.

When we got to the apartment, I led the family to his door and knocked a couple of times. I motioned for everyone else to wait.

"He might be asleep," I whispered and walked inside. The quiet stillness, broken only by the television's soft volume and the distant sound of traffic on a nearby street, confirmed my suspicion. There he was, on the couch, sitting in the glow of a tabletop lamp with his head slightly tipped back for a snooze.

"Hi, Dad," I said gently, tiptoeing through the living room. "Dad, we're here," I said again, casually dropping my purse down on the coffee table as I scanned the place he now called home. The kitchen had a window looking out to a courtyard. *That's nice,* I thought, *he should open the blinds and let in some sunlight* when I noticed a red light flashing on his answering machine from the countertop separating the kitchen and dining room. My stomach turned over.

"Hey, Dad," I said a little louder, sitting down next to him. I reached over and rubbed his arm in the dimly lit apartment. Something wasn't right. I looked at my hand on his arm then at his face and the way his lips were parted, then upward at his eyes. They were open, his blue irises replaced with clouds of gray. I started screaming.

"Oh my God, no." And stumbled backward, shouting, "Don't come in here! Get out," as I raced toward the door, still open with anxious family outside waiting. "He's dead, oh my God, my dad is dead!" I cried. My kids stood frozen with looks of fear and confusion while Pete and I shoved them back toward the breezeway. When I saw them, a switch flipped.

All I could think was, *Get the kids away from here. Don't let them see him, don't scare them, don't be hysterical, goddammit.* Instantly, a plan was made in my mind. I looked over at Pete.

"You take the kids back to my mom's house. I'll stay here and call 911. Can you call my mom at work from the car? And my brothers?" Before Pete drove away, I thought I glimpsed worry in his eye—not about whether I could handle the situation, but whether I would drink. I brushed it off like a speck of lint on his shirt sleeve, annoyed by the distraction. A moment of crisis had narrowed my sights on the usual cause for this chaos: my drinking. It never crossed my mind that Pete might be looking with compassion at the woman he adored who just lost her father. I could have glanced at a look of heartfelt concern and misinterpreted it through the distorted lens of alcoholic shame and my fear somebody might see me at all.

Back inside the apartment, I dug my phone out of my purse. *What am I doing?* Was I allowed to turn off the television or would I be leaving my prints at a crime scene? Do I ignore my dad on the couch? The body spooked me, like I was standing in a haunted house and any second he might pop to life and scare me. *Please, don't,* I thought and dialed 911, suddenly nervous. I wasn't crying, *Should I be crying?*

"911 emergency. Do you need fire, ambulance or police?" the dispatcher asked me.

"Hi. I don't know what I need. My dad is dead. I'm in his apartment," I blurted, hearing the taps on the keyboard get faster.

"Are you sure he's not breathing?" the dispatcher asked.

"Yes."

"Did you try CPR?"

"No." I looked over at what used to be my dad, the man who tossed me in the air at the local public pool, the one who taught me how to throw a baseball right-handed even though I'm a lefty the one who read me *Charlie and the Chocolate Factory* when I was in kindergarten.

"I'm sorry, he's dead, I'm sure," I told her softly.

She told me to wait outside until the paramedics arrived, so I hung up and walked out to the fresh air, closing the door behind me. The world seemed so different than the one inside, with a summer sun so bright it hurt my eyes. I stood on the sidewalk looking left and right for an ambulance or fire truck to come tearing around the corner. *Is this really happening?* I wondered. *Or have I lost my mind?* I only had to stand there and wait. A simple request, but I couldn't stop thinking about my dad all alone in there and how I left him. *I can't do it,* I decided and turned around to go back.

Death has an unforgettably awful scent, but regret lingered on me with an equally unpleasant stench. A part of me hoped to ease the fact I wasn't there when I should have been, as if "better late than never" could work for the dead. So, we rested together, he and I, staring blankly at nothing in the calm before a storm of strangers knocked on the door.

"Come in," I said when they arrived. The apartment filled with paramedics carrying unnecessary lifesaving equipment, followed by a slow parade of uniformed police officers and detectives dressed in suits. I watched the steady rhythm of their movements and hushed tones of communication with one another as if to show respect for the sad scene. It could have been a minute or an hour. I felt myself floating above the room, watching it all play out. Everything I felt stayed locked in a place some people call shock until a man wearing a white dress shirt and tie approached me as if he were about to defuse a bomb.

I needed to leave the room. They needed to take the body. I forgot to say goodbye.

Maybe it would have been easier on everyone if I'd admitted I felt like I was falling again. If I told my family, *I can't do the funeral, can't go through pictures for the slideshow. I can't go back to the apartment and clear out his things. I can't help with any of it. It fucks me up, I'm sorry . . .* but I didn't. I clung to the last bits of my dad's existence, trying to earn points from a dead man. I thought it was my duty to help, spending hours in silence sifting through his apartment in search of something to connect me to the man I used to know. A Christmas ornament I gave him a few years back of Santa with a fish dangling off a fishing pole was the only thing I found, and I took it thinking maybe I never knew him at all.

Then, one afternoon, I found a 12-pack of hot beer in his garage and popped the top off a can, saying goodbye to another round of sobriety and feeling like my father watched me do it. *Could it get any worse than this?* But I could not stop myself. I drank faster, knowing soon I wouldn't have to care. *Right now,* I said to myself, *I don't want to feel anything at all* and choked down three or four hot ones. Obviously, a shitty decision, but I had a brain hard-wired to look for the smoothest, quickest path to an escape, and that's exactly what I did. Even if I thought about the consequences, I could not change direction, not in those circumstances.

I'll get it back, I thought. *I just need a day or two.* And what a joke it is to try and lie to myself after so many years of this crap.

Is it all that surprising that I relapsed when the odds were already stacked against me, even before the bomb blew up in my face the first day I set foot back in Texas? My body expected to drink under extreme stress and emotional overload because that's the message it got from my brain, like a well-traveled road in the Wild West. Only this time, drinking didn't work. It wasn't enough. I tried to tune out the tightness consuming my chest over the next week, whether I was sneaking wine or not, until it radiated into my guts, my back, and down my arms. The strange new nervousness was impossible to ignore when my hair started falling out, and my appetite disappeared. I was suddenly scared to drive. *Get it together! At the very least, Emily, grow up,* I told myself. *Stop being such a baby.* As if scolding myself was going to work this time. Things predictably got ugly within weeks, and by mid-August, I was back in rehab with a handful of diagnoses and a substance abuse disorder.

It was a Wednesday, two days after Shelby and Rebecca's first day of school, when I walked into my first trauma group. Nothing about us looked unusual, but I displayed a decent amount of irritation and chose a black plastic chair to fit my mood in the circle. *Only seven of us? Great,* I thought, *I'll have to talk.*

"Are you ready to share, Emily?" asked the counselor after we introduced ourselves and did a check-in using a feelings chart. *Absolutely not,* I thought to myself.

"No, not really," I muttered. "But I will."

"Okay, great," he said, and I looked at the faces eagerly waiting for a story that wasn't their own.

"My dad died last month, and I relapsed. It happens." I shrugged, unable to put my finger on what to say next. I stared toward the floor when it suddenly dawned on me that everyone had shoes with laces crisscrossed and tied in bows. *That's weird,* I thought in my short distraction and glanced down at my faded Converse sneakers with empty eyelets. *They took my laces but not theirs.* I reached for my wrist to cover the neon green bracelet meant to alert staff of self-harmers, but why bother? We all knew what it meant.

"Hang on, let me start over. I found my dad dead in his apartment a month ago," I clarified, and the three women inhaled sympathetically. "And I'm pissed. I'm really fucking angry." I hoped the man running this group would give me a pass, but he didn't.

"Go on," he encouraged, and in a liberating flash, I realized I could say anything I wanted. I even received a permission slip. For some reason, I couldn't do it.

"About a lot of things, actually, but with my dad, there's a part of it I can't talk about." I looked down at the carpet. "I don't know, it's like I'm so ashamed to say it, but I saw him the night before." With each word, I unfolded myself, letting it all stumble out of my mouth. We're allowed to be sloppy, hysterical if need be. Not a day goes by inside an institution where someone isn't momentarily losing their shit while the rest of us glance over and keep walking. It's a sweet relief to leave our efforts at disguises at the door, but it comes with a cost when our secrets start to spill. On a bad day, it can feel like unflattering public nudity.

I felt partly responsible for my dad's death, not the "how" or the "when" of it, but the way it unfolded. Several months before sitting in that circle, my older brother, Peter, called me in North Carolina, distraught after he visited my dad with Adam. He told me about the cancer and warned me about how awful he looked. I took the information and filed it away in my mind as something I'd deal with later. Peter wasn't specific, and we didn't talk for long. I'd just gotten out of another rehab, and for whatever reason, the word cancer didn't immediately freak me out.

Some things have to be experienced, I guess, to be fully understood because not until I saw my father in the flesh did I realize how wrong I'd been. And I hated myself for it, rehashing repeatedly all the ways I could have done the last few months differently.

Suddenly, a man named George, who wore round glasses over a furrowed set of eyebrows, cleared his throat from across the circle of chairs.

"So wait," he said, putting a hand on his temples. "You knew? About the cancer?"

"I mean, sort of," I admitted, feeling the guilt bubble up and coat my face. "I guess I didn't have room to think about it. Or call Adam to find out more. I should have, though. I should have done a lot." I looked down at my hands tightly folded in my lap. The counselor told me to continue.

It's the relentless idea of one day getting "it" right that drives someone crazy. It's a type of perfectionism based on the belief that I began with a deficit, and my mission is to be good enough to break even. I didn't have to be better than anyone, just good enough. I told the group how it felt to fail in my final hour with my dad.

"I mean, the irony is laughable." I didn't want to dig any deeper than that. "Look, it doesn't have to make sense to be true," I thought out loud. I kept losing my train of thought. Or maybe I was avoiding it because I didn't like the way I kept drifting back into my dad's apartment and sitting in his living room again. I closed my eyes and spoke.

"I wanted to somehow grab every particle of sickness, like I could somehow collect all of it and cure him right there, so he didn't have to suffer," I said. But the more I thought about it, the more I knew the truth was deeper. "And so I didn't have to suffer, either. God, it's so selfish, isn't it? But that's what it felt like to look at him. I can't really put it into words. Maybe it's like seeing your worst nightmare or seeing a reflection of . . . I don't know."

"Keep going with that, Emily," the counselor urged in a drawn-out way, but I didn't want to do it. I didn't want to say what my audience was waiting for, and I didn't want to lift the curtain for anyone to see me at my core. *Dammit! Why did it have to be me?* I wanted to be someone else.

"It was me," I sputtered, bent over with my hands covering my face to hide the shame. He asked me to repeat myself, and I raised my voice, saying again, "It was me, okay? There! I said it, I saw *myself* on that fucking couch, ending up dead all by myself. I wanted to save him, see him happy because then I could have those things, too, instead of dying and breaking everybody's heart."

I hated the way the room sat in stunned silence, watching me, but sometimes it's unnecessary to fill a space with words.

The tap on my shoulder was the woman next to me, Charlene, holding out a box of Kleenex. I preferred treatment centers that required us to get our own tissues.

"Do you want a hug?" she whispered. Hell, no, I didn't want a hug. I wanted to punch someone.

"No, thank you," I whispered back.

"Your dad got cancer. Poor you. Hurt people hurt people," came a comment from across the room.

"Fuck you," was my reply.

"So what happened?" asked George, gently. "Did you stay?"

The blood stopped moving in my body when I realized they didn't know. All eyes in the circle waited for me to speak.

"No," I said, aware of how cold my answer sounded. "He was dead the next day. Right where we left him."

"Holy shit." George's face drooped as he sat back in his chair, his body representing the mood of the room. It was over. All of it. We were out of time, and there was nothing else to say. I cleared my throat and reached down for my water bottle to take a long sip, refusing to look at the seven faces. Class dismissed.

It's agony to face some truths about ourselves. I blew it with my dad. No chance for do-overs, another visit, another apology, no *I love you and I'm sorry for all of it,* from either of us. A lifetime of loose ends wrapped around my neck, reminding me there'd never be that happy ending I'd hinged my life on.

What if that's my story, too?

Anyone with a past like mine understands when I say we eat, sleep, and breathe the hope that one day we'll get out of this mess and get the chance to make things right. *Please, please let it be tomorrow,* only to screw up again. And there's a point where death comes to stalk us and will not leave like a constant shadow reminding us our turn is approaching. My dad was 64 years old when he died. Too young, too soon, if you asked me at the time, but the truth was my dad outlived the statistics for someone with his lifestyle by at least ten years. I'd be lucky to make it to my 40th birthday. One thing was certain, I wouldn't make it as long as he did before the darkness came knocking at my door.

CHAPTER FIFTEEN

Spring 2014

In 2013, the American Psychiatric Association updated its Diagnostic and Statistical Manual of Mental Disorders with a fifth edition, the DSM-V, by changing terminology and criteria relating to alcohol. Alcohol Use Disorder became the unifying term to describe an illness that centered in the brain, with individual scores ranging from mild to severe based on eleven indicators. Answer "yes" to two or three questions, and it likely indicated a mild case of Alcohol Use Disorder. Over six "yes" answers and a person leaned toward a severe case. I answered "yes" to all eleven.

Within the last year, have you:

- *Had times when you drank more or longer than you intended?*
- *More than once wanted to cut down or stop drinking, or tried to, but couldn't?*
- *Spent a lot of time drinking? Or being sick or getting over other aftereffects?*
- *Wanted a drink so badly you couldn't think of anything else?*
- *Found that drinking—or being sick from drinking—often interfered with taking care of your home or family? Or caused job troubles? Or school problems?*

- *Continued to drink even though it was causing trouble with your family or friends?*
- *Given up or cut back on activities that were important or interesting to you or gave you pleasure to drink?*
- *More than once gotten into situations while or after drinking that increased your chances of getting hurt (such as driving, swimming, using machinery, walking in a dangerous area, or having unprotected sex)?*
- *Continued to drink even though it was making you feel depressed or anxious or adding to another health problem? Or after having had a memory blackout?*
- *Had to drink much more than you once did to get the effect you want or found that your usual number of drinks had much less effect than before?*
- *Found that when the effects of alcohol were wearing off, you had withdrawal symptoms, such as trouble sleeping, shakiness, restlessness, nausea, sweating, a racing heart or a seizure? Or sensed things that were not there?*

Sometimes changing an unhealthy drinking pattern is enough, or a person gets sober at an early stage of AUD and avoids a future of alcohol-related consequences. Sobriety in my little world started off as a word that made my eyes roll every time my mother said it. Eventually it grew into some massive entity that weaved itself through social circles and belief systems going all the way back to ninth grade. It's not like I didn't understand how it worked or see it every single day by way of my mother with twenty-five years sober and Pete with nearly a decade. We hung with a crowd who'd known Shelby since she was a baby and watched Becca take her first steps at a meeting. We all were accustomed to addiction and watched it turn otherwise decent, intelligent people into someone almost unrecognizable. Alcoholics say and do things when we're drunk that our sober selves would never consider doing in our right minds. Then the next day, we're so disgusted by our actions, thinking *How could I do that? What kind of person does something so mean?* And it's a terrible shame to carry. We become sneaky liars and connivers capable of turning situations completely upside down to get whatever it is we want. Then, of course, we fall for the lies coming out of our own mouths for the same reasons the people listening to them do.

Because the nature of the disease is to deny its existence.

Twenty years of my life was spent with a recovery community, and from the beginning, I heard relapse is an option. It's never required. Years later, I heard it's part of the process and many of us experience it, maybe once, maybe more. It's harder getting sober after a relapse than it is first time, and the ones who love to argue with me about it are the ones who never went out. Still, who really wants to listen to what someone with my track record says about sobriety? For me to get mad at a program or the person next to me was like criticizing free life jackets while I kept drowning. It looked so easy. But I could not get one to stay on.

What's that about? Truthfully, I wanted to never hear another word about sobriety. It was always there, always everywhere. I was stuck in a mind of constant craving with a body unable to properly function without the chemical components of alcohol in my system. My brain didn't know how to regulate my organs without it, and every sip I took to stay alive, I knew it was killing me, too. I wasn't drunk. All of it was too real. My heart pounded out of my chest each time I looked at my family thinking, *What have I done? How could I?* Regardless of what they were doing—laughing, playing, dancing, fighting—the flashbacks of damage I caused wrapped around my neck and held me in a clarity where being sober felt like torture. Because it forced me to see the reality of what I'd done. The inescapable truth was killing me, more than the wine.

None of it was noticeable on me from a safe distance—no rash, no bruise, no fracture.

It was an ordinary spring morning when I dropped the kids off at school and drove myself to a parking lot at 8:30 am to stare out my windshield, this time in front of a grocery store. I wanted the war to be over. I wanted the peace I couldn't find in drinking nor in unbearable sobriety. *At last, let me be that woman who looked into the eyes of her children and instantly stopped.* Thinking I still had a chance for a private redemption before I turned off the car. But I couldn't even do that. My god, it was unimaginable pain. The kind that drives a person to believe no one will ever understand, because even I didn't know what was wrong with me, either, other than *I've ruined it for all for them. I got it all wrong and I can't fix any of it.* I was two weeks sober and capsizing, desperately trying to squeeze in with recovery women or neighborhood moms who inevitably reminded me I don't know where I belong. Who inevitably reminded me I was tired and wired, jittery and worn down to nothing from carrying an impending implosion when I unbuckled my seatbelt. Prescription pill bottles rattled in the purse I slung over my shoulder when I walked inside the store. I only wanted a light anesthesia to target the places it hurt the most, but I knew I was lying to myself again. Like a gun going off at the start of a race, I felt momentum build inside me with the first slug of wine down my throat. Well, no shit, right? *Don't take the first drink, you idiot!* But logic was late that morning, and I was stuck inside a woman doing things I didn't condone, walking a fine line of intoxication the rest of the day, trying desperately not to plunge over the edge.

It seems impossible no one caught me drinking. In over twelve years, I'd never bought nor sipped wine from stemware, never uncorked a bottle in my house, never drank in restaurants or out with friends. Pete and the kids certainly saw me after the fact, and when I think about the work it took to always pretend to be sober, always have enough hidden somewhere, find excuses for going to the store, sneak money from the house, look for new hiding spots, remember hiding spots, stash the empties, dispose them discreetly and *not* get caught? It's exhaustion from a secret full-time job. And it was stolen devotion for a disease that wanted to kill me.

Then to gaze through the windows of local boutiques spotting wine clichés in playful fonts etched across glassware or embroidered on kitchen towels? Women called it *Mommy's Juice* or *liquid therapy,* and grocery stores decorated the wine department on Mother's Day saying, "Give her what she really wants this year," and I didn't know how to feel.

Hearing giggles about day drinking when school moms chatted on the playground after school boxed me up in my own little world. I didn't belong in theirs.

This time when I drank, it was too much. Then again, it had always been too much.

"Kids, get in the car. I need a couple of ingredients for dinner, hurry up," I said late that afternoon and loaded the kids in the car, driving to a grocery market down the street. "I'll be right back." I locked the car doors on their unhappy expressions before running inside. It was only supposed to take a minute for me to grab a wine or two and stuff them in my purse. I couldn't run out of alcohol. I'd be sick; I might die.

"Excuse me, ma'am, you're going to have to come with us," said a stranger behind me when he grabbed my elbow.

"No, I'm sorry. I can't, I have to . . ." I started to say as I pulled back my arm.

"We saw you. And you don't have a choice," said another man next to him. The three of us walked through the front of the store to a doorway with stairs that led to a second floor. *A second floor?* I thought, terrified of the consequences waiting for me at the top. A group of adults were already seated around a large table when they ushered me to a chair across from someone I assumed to be the general manager. He asked my name, then explained I'd been under surveillance for a couple of months for shoplifting wine.

There was concern for the safety of my children.

"You got yourself a designer purse there, so I'm sure you can afford the wine. And I can tell you've been drinking today, okay?" he said, and I didn't deny or defend myself.

"Don't cry. I sent some managers outside to talk to your kids. They're scared to death, won't unlock the doors or even roll down the windows without their momma, but they're safe." Whatever else the man planned to do, I wished he'd just do it so I could run outside as fast as I could and give my kids one last glance. A wave of assurance, blow a kiss through the sky, anything. If I were lucky, I'd give hugs that said, *hey, we will all be okay* before the police came.

The bulky man pushed his chair back from the table and folded his arms across his chest, giving me a long stare. Time was on his side, not mine.

"So I can arrest you right now," he said, "or do you want to tell me what's going on?"

"I-I . . . It's awful. I'm so sorry . . . I hate this." I barely got the words out before crumbling into a cry. *Goddammit, Emily, not now, stop it,* I thought. "I'm sorry for what I've done, I know it's over. I don't want to do it, but I do . . . I'm an alcoholic. In a really bad relapse," I admitted not as an excuse but to give up the truth. I knew I needed help and that I couldn't stop what I was doing, and I confessed to all of it while I looked him in the eye.

I was stealing because in some sick part of my mind, it made it less real, that none of it was happening and that everything bad was locked in some imaginary place I didn't have to acknowledge. To a sane person, it clearly sounds delusional. But to me, it all made perfect sense.

"Do you live close to here?" he asked me after giving some thought.

"About two blocks," I said.

"Can you promise me you'll drive home and stay there? Talk to your husband and get yourself sorted out?" he asked, and I told him I would.

"Yes, sir," I promised. He was letting me go.

"I can promise you this, you ever step foot in here again, I'll have you arrested, do you understand?"

"Yes, of course. I can never thank you enough. I'll repay you, I promise, I am so sorry," but he just shook his head and had me escorted out the front door.

The relief of the sight of my children consumed me when I got to the car. I don't know how the mysteries of motherhood work or what kicked in to keep my voice calm and my words soothing as I talked to the kids on the drive home. Because I really wanted to grab hold of them and run away. I wanted to scrub every worry and fear off them, then lock us all somewhere safe when I thought about how close I came to losing everything. We sat together in the living room for a few minutes while I worked overtime to tenderly maneuver their fears in a different direction, so they could believe things were normal enough to leave my side while I finished making dinner.

It took everything in me to hide the remorse and humiliation from kids who suffered the consequences of their mother's actions. And I knew I was the cause of their pain, even as my mind drifted into the unfathomable regret of leaving that store without the wine. Because I still needed it.

We can try to pretty it up, but alcoholism or AUD, as some prefer, will always be ugly. Change the terminology, get offended, it's all a part of it. I wasn't a terrible person, but I could do terrible things. And I continued to get away with it.

Addiction doesn't discriminate, but we sure do. If I looked different or lived in a different neighborhood, I know my chances would have run out years ago. Maybe the store manager saw something in me that reminded him of a sister or a cousin instead of a criminal, and that's a privilege both of where I lived and what I looked like. Assumptions fall in my favor, like thinking a purse my husband splurged on one year at Christmas made me a rich McKinney housewife. It worked in my favor until it didn't. Because all the little free passes—someone letting me off the hook, pretending they didn't notice, or never suspecting in the first place—ended up as curses that kept me going further down the tragic spiral. Eventually, the scale was always going to tip, but until it happened, I was going down to the bitter end.

Either way, I knew I was running out of chances. When I told Pete what happened later that night, he didn't take the kids and leave me, but my secret was out. A new round of interventions would soon begin. I heard it's lonely at the top, but it gets lonely at the bottom, too. Waking up covered in a dewy sweat of remorse, whether I drank or not, began to feel like death wanted my attention.

Every morning I wondered if it's better to know what I've done or be left in the dark. *What happened? What did I do this time?* As much as I wanted to know, I couldn't bear to watch them tell me if I asked.

On one of those days, I made my rounds through the house to assess the emotional damage I'd done the night before, a sort of temperature check, without having to come right out and ask, *How did I hurt you?* I stopped outside of Shelby's bedroom door. My head pounded to the beat of my racing heart and when I reached out my hand to knock on the door, my arm trembled to my sweaty palm. Gently, I tapped twice.

"Can I come in?" I asked, and she said yes. Shelby sat on the edge of her bed, leaning over to leaf through a stack of papers on the floor. She knew why I was there and didn't look up when I started to talk.

"Shelby." I sighed. "I'm so sorry. I know you've heard it a thousand times, but I really am," I said, and rubbed my hands over my face as I took a few steps closer. "I know how much this hurts you, I want to stop, I swear I do, and I will," I told her. "I know you're mad. I don't blame you. I hope one day you can forgive me and—" Shelby stopped what she was doing and cut me off.

"Mom, stop," she interrupted. "I can't do this anymore. Just stop." She sounded tired. "I know you're sorry. Okay? I do. But I just can't hear it anymore."

Shelby was turning fifteen years old, and I nodded when she said it, oblivious to the moment of the connection to myself at the same age; how fed up I was with my parents, the mixture of rage and sadness it created.

"Okay, honey. I love you," I said, staring down at her long brown hair.

"Love you, too," she said without looking at me, flipping through papers in her lap. I quietly walked out of the room and when I got to the bottom of the stairs, a thick layer of denial blew up in my face.

Until that moment, I thought my heartfelt apologies helped my family heal from the pain I caused them. I believed my insurmountable guilt was for them, and my remorse somehow compensated for the bad behavior, as if I could wipe the slate clean.

I stood barefoot leaning against a hallway wall and took a long look at my offensive reality, thinking it might kill me instantly. I almost wished it had. Because I wasn't facing a mirror of myself, this was my children's lives, innocent and trapped in the chaos of a terribly troubled mother. It hurt when friends rejected me but by no means did it prepare me for the rejection by a daughter who loved me deep down.

Courage. When I think of the word, I picture the cowardly lion from *The Wizard of Oz* bolting down a dark castle hallway and diving through a window. Not exactly an ideal example. It clashed against the stories of women who symbolized strength and determination from pioneers to wartime wives, I was the coward who wanted to turn and run. I knew this moment would come when I'd be forced to see me. I stood in a daze for a minute and felt my feet clinging to the edge of a cliff with the guns of all my consequences drawn at my back. How long can I withstand it? *I can't do this,* I thought. *I'm so tired.* I could stomach getting sober long enough for a temporary peek but if I had to stay and deal with this mess, I'd rather jump. I'm so sorry.

What are we supposed to do with a woman like that? Because I would have been fed up watching her, too. My husband and my own mother, who had the same addiction I did, sometimes looked at me in disbelief and asked, "Why can't you stop? Why can't you *not* take that first drink when the thought pops in your head?" Their questions deserve recognition. We get judgmental watching someone self-destruct and I do it, too, sometimes to simply create a safe distance. It made sense why our televisions at rehab tuned in every night for bedtime crime episodes of *Forensic Files*, because there's comfort in knowing someone is worse off than you. But what if that someone turns out to be you?

We need to talk about selfishness beyond the trap of self-pity or blame, but it's risky to associate with such a cold, uncaring word. From a mother's perspective, the word lands like a weapon at our core. I like the feeling of acceptance and approval, and it's scary to say that most of us are selfish. All addictions are selfish. But it blindsided me to discover a sick twist in my guilt, because I genuinely felt remorseful toward the people I hurt. When Shelby didn't need my apology, I came apart because I needed her to take it. I wanted the weight off my chest. I realized my morning-after apologies and empty promises smuggled in a selfish motive for making *me* feel better, not them.

We couldn't afford more treatment. Weaning myself off wine wasn't working. I walked into my bedroom wearing clothes from the night before and heard my mother's voice repeating a grandmother's proverbial wisdom, *If the shoe fits, wear it. Beggars can't be choosers. If you wanna dance, you gotta pay the fiddler.* Is it selfish for me to leave them to feel abandoned again for weeks or months and expect my husband to pick up the pieces? Is it selfish for me to stay with my kids? Yes to all of it. *What am I supposed to do now?* With that thought, I stepped into my closet, fumbled around for the leftover wine I stashed, then downed it all before I got dressed, to ward off withdrawals. Clarity was not a cure. It was another infection snaking its way through my veins. I saw the disaster and the dead end, where the price of arrival was all the selfish work it'd take to turn myself around. If it was just me, then the entire story would be different, but those kids made me a mother the second they were born, and I wasn't a mother who gave up.

Close to dinnertime, Pete hollered, "Leaving!" from the front door, off to pick Shelby up from dance practice. I stood at the stove and poured a can of Manwich into the skillet of sizzling ground beef for the easy midweek meal. Behind me, past the refrigerator covered in paper masterpieces, the kids started annoying each other for entertainment. They were restless and hungry at the end of a long day, but I thought to myself, *I'm doing great. Look at me, a normal mom making dinner,* like a pat on the back for being ordinary.

"Stella? Becca? Hey girls, dinner's almost ready. Go wash your hands," I told them over my shoulder and got no response. "Now," I added louder, and heard them shuffle away from the television.

It was the brink of summer 2014, the night I filled hamburger buns with sloppy joe meat while crinkle cut French fries baked in the oven when, for a second, my balance glitched. *Weird,* I thought, as if a bend of space warped across the house. I felt a little light-headed and dizzy but thought it was hunger or possibly lingering symptoms of my recent sobriety. I blinked a couple of times.

The next blink, I was buckled on a stretcher in front of my house. A strange fog slowly melted out of my head like I was being pulled up from underwater. Somewhere, I heard my kids franticly calling out but only saw my neighbors staring at me in disbelief. Why were they outside? I couldn't lift my head.

"Ma'am, do you know your name?" a man asked, hovering close to my face in the whirling lights of an ambulance. I stared at him because I didn't understand the question.

"What city are you in? Do you know where you are, ma'am?" he asked me, and I drew a map in my head until I found the word.

"Texas," I answered, noticing the taste of blood in my mouth.

"Do you know who's president?" Of course, I knew who the president was. I just couldn't remember his name. *What's going on?*

Pete pulled into the driveway with Shelby in the passenger seat. The panicked sound of his voice, on top of my scared kids and the strange spectators, made me want to cut loose from it all and pretend that nothing ever happened. I stuck my hand out into the air, the way mothers beckon their children to *come closer, come to Mama,* but it just hung there, empty as the wheels beneath me dropped. Slam! Slam! Two back doors closed me inside the ambulance. *I didn't ask for any of this,* I thought, wanting to turn back around and go home, not to another hospital.

"You had a seizure, ma'am, likely what's known as a grand mal," a paramedic told me on the drive. By the time we pulled up to the automatic doors, it had barely sunk in.

I learned pieces of what happened based on what Pete was told. I'd fallen to the kitchen floor in convulsions, banging my head on the tile and biting through my tongue. My three younger kids saw me and tried to "wake me up" before they ran out the front door screaming that their mommy was dead in the kitchen. Someone came inside and called 911 while neighbors ran over to console the children until Pete and Shelby drove up.

The terror they must have felt. What unimaginable horror for a young child to believe they are watching their own mother's death, and no one is there to save her. I pictured the look on their faces, and my insides still curdle from the vision of Spenser, Rebecca, and Stella because I want to go back and comfort them in the scene every time.

"It could have been much worse," an ER doctor warned after running brain scans and other tests on me that night. He called me lucky right before drilling me over my drinking history cataloged in a hospital computer on top of his rolling cart. As he talked about my medication and nutrition, an apathetic nurse checked my vitals, looking down at me like I was a waste of space, and I thought she looked familiar.

Maybe she was a mom from the elementary school. *Had our kids been in class together?*

I wonder if it's possible to accept ourselves at our worst, the point when suffering tips us over the endless cycle of sick and tired of being sick and tired, and we just lie there.

I knew what was happening when I let go in the coming weeks, and I used to wish I could describe it in a way that sounded less tragic, less dramatic. But I glimpsed freedom when I waved goodbye to hope. A sense of peace breezed across me when I fell from the cliff knowing the white-knuckle war was over. I stopped pushing against the weight of death and let it have me, thinking it was only a matter of time, but I loved it just the same. And for a moment, I was untethered, cut loose without my hands clenched in fists behind my back. It felt like I was flying until I opened my eyes on the way down. Unbelievable grief and rage came out of nowhere. Destruction so horrendous swept across the horizon that it forced me to wonder how all of it could be my fault.

Hitting bottom wasn't optional; it was inevitable. But this time, instead of thinking I would hit the ground and start over, my legs buckled out from under me at the precise moment of truth, and it dropped me to the ground like a broken baby. I didn't think I'd survive a single breath with that thick, black ache covering me in a century of insufferable shame. Motionless, I wallowed in the years already wasted, and I watched how the days continued to slip past me.

Time drifted like a dream, even when I heard my own voice calling, *Get up,* but I couldn't. *Get up, goddammit* and I did nothing. I didn't want to. I wanted everything cut off me that pulled me apart. Again, *Get the fuck back up and keep trying,* and the argument kept on. I didn't want to take responsibility for the truth but if I didn't, I would die. And then I saw them. Even in the most hopeless state a human can endure, I was still a mother. All the wishes for self-destruction became pointless because the connection could not be cut. The bond was unconditional. It wasn't my life, not completely anymore, and mothers have known this since the beginning of time. Children cannot save us. Mine could not save me. No one really saves us, it had to start with me.

I got up.

CHAPTER SIXTEEN

Spring 2014 Pt. II

"Rise and shine," I said gently when I walked into Spenser's bedroom. "You get to go to school today." At the sound of my voice, he sat up instantly.

"Mommy!"

"Good morning, my favorite son," I said, only to hear him repeat the same thing back.

"Good morning, my favorite son," and both of us smiled for separate reasons.

It was a Monday and Pete was already at work, taking Shelby to school on his way to the office. Spenser and I walked downstairs to find his other sisters zipping backpacks and rifling for matching shoes in the hall closet.

"Did you guys brush your teeth? We're leaving in five minutes, okay?" I said, grabbing a hairbrush off the counter and the nearest headband. "Stella, let me do your hair."

"No, I want the flower headband!" With that, she ran off to go find the one with a massive blue flower glued to it.

I still had lunches to make but, like always, we got to school on time and within the hour, I dropped Spenser off at his preschool across town. On the drive home, I fumbled with the radio. I didn't like dead silence. Somehow it made me feel like everyone was out doing something useful but me, and the ringing in my ears from the quiet back seat felt like a whistle calling me to *do something.*

Close to lunchtime, I pulled into the parking lot of a respectable brick building with thirty minutes to spare before my psychiatrist appointment. I'd left the house ridiculously early, not from fear of being late but my fear of what I called the *rush,* when life sped up a notch more than I could keep up with. Reaching into my bag, I grabbed my worn little notebook and a stubby pencil with a gum wrapper stuck to it and wrote a few sentences. *At Dr. Novak's. Really going to try and stay positive today. Hope I don't kill anyone. Thanks, God. More soon,* clinging to the thought these are the baby steps for the normal life I desperately wanted.

"Hi, Emily Redondo, here to see Dr. Novak," I said at the desk through a glass window opening. Without looking up, the receptionist loaded a clipboard with a stack of papers I'd filled out at least a dozen times already and set it on the counter in front of me.

"We'll call you back shortly."

"Do you know if he's running on time today?" I asked. The woman looked up.

"We'll call you back shortly." *Okie dokie.* I snatched the clipboard and searched the lobby for an empty leather chair. I scanned the faces around me to see how I measured up in comparison, but we looked pretty normal, as far as I could tell. I did this every time, with a twisted side of me hoping for a whack job to walk in the door to liven up the place. Dr. Novak was a decent psychiatrist for all ten minutes I saw him each time, but his office ran like a nightmare. I waited in that chair for almost an hour before I made it to the back to sit in separate room the size of a closet for another hour. *What the hell is taking so long?* I opened the wood-stained door three times to look around, then slammed it shut. Each minute that ticked by brought me that much closer to being late to preschool to pick up Spenser and got me thinking, *I'm not doing this again. Screw this place.*

I'd known Dr. Novak since my first run with sobriety and the days of single motherhood in 2002 when depression seemed my greatest challenge. He was a nice, patient man, and was my psychiatrist for several years until we moved out of state. Back then, my med check appointments were every ninety days, and they were usually rather uneventful, which was a good thing. Naturally, he was the psychiatrist we thought of when all hell broke loose after moving back to Texas. Besides, he knew my entire history, something a stranger off the insurance-approved list did not.

I can look for a new doctor when things settle down, I promised myself, and the man finally walked in the room carrying what looked like 200 pages of my "chart."

"Hello, Ms. Redondo, apologies for the delay. How's your day?" Dr. Novak said in a voice void of urgency, as if he had the rest of the afternoon to spend with me.

"This waiting is ridiculous. I don't think you understand how absolutely stressful it is," I said. He apologized again, and we moved on.

"You look better today, I'm encouraged. Maybe a little less restless?" he asked, and I thought, *let's not go overboard.* "How are the intrusive thoughts?"

"I don't know," I told him, trying not to look at his frizzy hair sticking out in different directions like he just woke up from a nap. "I don't go looking for them. They just come find me, always the very worst flashes and I can't get them to go away without walking around or doing something—blasting music, dishes, driving, sometimes I yell at them—the memories," I said. He nodded and scribbled on his notepad while I wondered if I made any sense.

"Anxiety? Irritability?" he asked. *Absolutely, what a stupid question.*

"Maybe a little," I lied. "I mean, yes, actually, both, but I think I'm doing better at keeping it inside."

We talked about medications as if I knew the names and purposes of each one.

"How's the fatigue? And what about your mood swings?" Dr.

Novak asked, and I slapped my hands against my thighs. Who thinks about these things throughout the day? Every mother on the planet has mood swings and gets tired. Aren't most people enduring daily ups and downs without ever being asked to figure out how much, when, and why?

"I don't fucking know," I blurted. "How am I supposed to measure a mood shift versus a swing when everything blends together? I'd love a nap, but it's more like exhaustion than fatigue." Dr. Novak gave me a long glance.

"If I get weepy or pissed-off, I can't say 'Oh, I'm mood-swinging.' I barely even know how I feel in general," I snapped, then apologized for being snappy. He told me it was fine. "You know those big fireworks that go off on the Fourth of July? The way they shoot up with a boom and then tiny flecks of fire start popping in every direction? It's almost like stars exploding. That's what it feels like. In my chest." I hoped I was making sense.

"Anything else?" he asked. I looked at the clock. I had issues, big ones, with unworthiness and crap like that, but I liked to think I was good at reading people's minds. I thought Dr. Novak wanted me to hurry up and thought I was wasting his time babbling on like an idiot.

"The drinking's going okay, I guess," I told him. "It's been three weeks? I don't know, maybe longer. It's hard to think straight . . . I had some wine one morning and immediately regretted it, as usual. It was one day this time."

"Are you going to your AA meetings?" he asked.

"Yes, two or three a week." I nodded.

Dr. Novak masterfully gave me a long explanation for normal symptoms and temporary side effects to meds that could help with panic attacks, mentioning words I'd never remember and drugs I couldn't pronounce along with science I didn't need. Still, it comforted me he cared. I knew he had my best interests in mind even though I'd stopped listening after five minutes of his spiel. My patience ran out and it was my turn to be late by the time he handed me a written paper from his prescription pad. I didn't read it or ask questions before shoving it in my purse.

My favorite son was waiting.

Soon enough, Spenser sat buckled in his car seat eating goldfish from a Ziploc baggie and over-squeezing his juice box down the front of his shirt while we drove from preschool and headed toward the elementary school to wait in carpool line. I quickly glanced over at the passenger seat, double checking the snack basket and dance bags I filled the night before with leotards, tights and proper shoes—ballet for Rebecca, jazz for Stella.

"Hi girls!" I greeted Stella and Becca as they hopped into the back of the car. Conversations about their exciting day began right away, and as I drove the car a short distance to park along a curb, I made a note to myself to stop by the pharmacy and drop off my prescriptions after classes, the way a mother stops for a loaf of bread or a gallon of milk.

"Mom! Miss Garza put me at the front of the line today because she said I was being the best behaved. And then she winked at me!" Becca was bursting about the teacher known affectionately as Garza the Great because in her eyes, the woman could do no wrong.

"How awesome! You're such a good student, I'm proud of you, Bec." I handed her a granola bar and Capri-Sun along with her black satin dance bag. Stella's bag was shiny and gold.

"I'm a good student, too, Mommy," Stella chimed in. *Yes, honey, of course you are.*

If someone drove by us and saw what I was doing, they'd probably wonder why I stopped with my kids in the car instead of driving a mile to our house. The truth was it made perfect sense to me. I needed mental stability, and the kids needed a sense of normalcy, but I knew from experience how agonizing it was to get everyone back in the car if I unleashed them at home. We adapted to our own system of balance, which also explained why some days I needed to arrive extra early to the dance studio, due to my paralyzing stress from the overcrowded, chaotic parking lot.

For hours each week, I sat in front of big glass windows watching my daughters dance, all while keeping Spenser entertained with a makeup bag filled with miniature trains in cramped hallway spaces until it was time to go home and make dinner. The noise of dance mom conversations, of Spenser hollering over crying babies, or ringing phones and doors slamming put me on edge. I needed air. I wanted to peel the skin off my body, and sometimes, I wanted to walk out the door and into traffic. But then right at the perfect time, I'd look through the glass window and gasp, frozen in a moment as Stella did a leap or Becca did a pirouette in class and immediately, they turned toward the window to look for their mom. And I'd be there, having seen it, exchanging a smile that said, *Yes, I'm here. I see you.* That was all I needed to comfort my mind, like the soul of a mother resetting itself. Meanwhile, Spenser made silly faces with a girl his age, bouncing from chair to chair, until he sat next to her and offered her a train car as a sign of friendship. Thankfully, she accepted and I laughed from across the room because again, *yes. I can feel it. I'm alive.*

All the emotions. I didn't think I could bear it, whether it was the mind-blowing belief that love kept getting bigger and brighter or that despair slithered around in a darkness with no escape. It's like flying a Cessna without training. My autopilot brain kept telling me *you are about to die either way,* and it was hard to ignore. I loved a life that I found to be unbearable at times, and so I tried to hover in the middle.

By nightfall, Pete picked up my new prescriptions and put them on a shelf next to similar looking bottles of unfinished antibiotics and medications for his colitis disease. The cluster of drugs looked ordinary next to Children's Tylenol, generic Advil, off brand Band-Aids and a bottle of expired multivitamins. We did the same routine as millions of families spread across the country: said a prayer at the dinner table, ate a Crock-Pot supper, tucked the kids into bed after baths.

"So how'd it go today with Novak?" Pete asked later that night.

"Same as usual. I waited forever, but he seems to have a plan for the anxiety and sleep stuff, so that's good." I hoped.

"Hey, great, honey. The guy really cares about you." He seemed optimistic. I shrugged, not expecting any miracles as Pete changed the subject to fill me in on other news. My medication wasn't a new or interesting topic. I'd been taking something for my mental health the entirety of our relationship, and the only times a red flag waved a warning to Pete was when I stopped taking something against medical advice. Dr. Novak specialized in addiction, so appointments and med changes were simply necessary nuisances like an oil change or a dental exam. Pete went outside to smoke his cigar, and I grabbed the new prescription bottles and added them to my weekly pill organizer.

Again, I found it strange how loud silence could be. Standing in my house that night with the kids asleep, my ears rang loudly on a single high-pitched note. It sounded like a coded call sent out for all my demons to come find me, so I shuffled around making a clatter to throw them off. Adam told me once that when he and his wife Kristen spent a day at our house, the volume of activity and voices was such a shock to their system that they needed to drive home in complete silence to decompress. I laughed when he said it, because what he considered loud and noisy sounded like nothing to me.

What was balance back then? It was everything or nothing, and despite my sobriety I still looked unstable. I felt it, too, coming like a bullet right between my eyes around dance recital time. It sounds ridiculous to admit, but as a parent with multiple kids in multiple dances for multiple shows, I obsessed about it for weeks. Trying to stay organized, I had a color-coded system for my schedules at one point, until I misplaced it somewhere and cried when I couldn't remember how to start over. What mother isn't constantly going over some list in the back of their mind? Recital fees, costume fees, certain colored tights for which kid with which costume. I hung on by a thread with a horrible habit of holding my breath when stressed.

"Mom, breathe!" Becca yelled, and I exhaled a huge puff of air across the windshield.

"Oh, yeah, sorry," I said to the rearview mirror. "I'm good!" But traffic was heavy, we were late, and parking was a bitch at the convention center. *What door do we use again? Shit, where's the packet? I'll kill myself if I forgot the packet.* And this was only dress rehearsal. Something inside of me felt unsettled, off-balance, like too much coffee after an all-nighter of studying or waking up disoriented after a three-hour nap. It happened off and on for weeks, so I talked to Dr. Novak about it the next time I was in his office.

"I'm like a baby. It's not depression, not like that," I said to Dr. Novak at one of our appointments, "But I swear I want to sleep for days. Is that normal? It's like there's nothing in me anymore. And I know you gave me something for sleep, but when I finally go to bed at night, I wake up every hour." I started crying. "See this? God! I just want to be a regular fucking person, but I can feel myself holding it all in, and it's not good—" He held up his hand for me to slow down. I sat with my arms folded across my chest and tipped my head back against the wall.

"Hmm, okay," Dr. Novak mumbled. "Holding what in? What does 'holding it all in' mean? And I'm also going to schedule you for a sleep study," he said.

"I don't know what 'it' is. I bet I wouldn't be in this situation if I did. It's the thing right before a person explodes," I stammered. He was the doctor, not me, and lately I'd been getting confused about my state of mind. My head was all over the place and my memory kept faltering. Was this Post-Acute Withdrawal Syndrome? My anxiety disorder? Part of a panic attack? Something else? And who has time for a stupid sleep study?

"AA Meetings?" he asked, and I told him the truth.

"Yeah. One or two a week. A couple of women gave me a hard

time for not going every day and I hate that. 'You drank every day, didn't you?' is so stupid. I mean, not sure our deadly drinking patterns are the best predictor of what our recovery should look like. Anyway, I'm shooting for three or four."

Novak adjusted some medications and a week later, I felt Pete looking at me from the driver's seat while we ran errands.

"What?" I asked him, feeling the stare.

"Your hands," he said. "Hold out your hand and look at it." When I did, it shook uncontrollably. My stomach sank.

"It's not what you think, I swear. It must be from some medication, I don't know." He had no definitive reason to believe me.

"Honey, it's not just the hands. I've seen other signs," he said, and I asked if we could do this later. As we drove around, I wondered when the last time it was that I drank. I didn't remember buying anything or drinking anything in the past couple of weeks, but maybe I did? Was it possible? It was all so hazy.

Naturally, suspicions pointed to the possibility that I was sneaking around in my old alcoholic habits. Rightfully so because it's what I often did. And we already know what happened—a relapse that led to the shoplifting bust, more heartbreak, another psychiatric hospital, and an infamous grand mal seizure. Afterward, I'd have days of wishing I could sit for hours and think. *Can I figure out how to be a well-adjusted adult when I can barely follow a recipe or remember what I was doing ten minutes ago? Why do I keep planning my funeral? How do moms keep things written on a calendar? Do I believe in God? Where will I go when they all leave me?* But a mother can't stay gone in her thoughts for too long.

On the way home from school one day, I stopped by the pharmacy drive-through to pick up two new prescriptions, and when it was my turn at the window, I gave the familiar clerk my name. I waited longer than usual for her to return. The kids were getting restless.

"Hi, Mrs. Redondo. Can you confirm your date of birth?" asked a different woman I didn't recognize, and after I told her she said, "I'm the pharmacist here and I wanted to discuss these medications."

"Oh. Sure, you mean like a consultation? That's fine," I said, despite the kid's complaints. Cars waited behind me for their turn and I thought, *just make it quick.*

"I have concerns about your meds," she said, "and I'm hesitant to fill them for you." Suddenly, she had my attention. This wasn't an ordinary consult, and a swarm of bees went off in a frenzy inside of my body.

"Umm, I'm sorry, what? Are you talking about a prescription for Redondo?" I asked, thinking maybe she grabbed the wrong name. "Which medication?" She mentioned two drugs with meaningless names, her look and tone told me she suspected I was a pill popper shopper dropping scripts at local pharmacies to sell on the streets. *Me?*

I knew some people from rehabs who did that sort of thing, even forging signatures and printing fake prescription pads, and it all sounded terrifying. I was offended.

"This is a lot of medication for one person to take," she said.

"It's directly from my doctor, so I don't know what to tell you. Maybe you can contact him?" I asked. But it was four o'clock on a Friday and I needed the pills plus my refills. "In the meantime, since you have the prescription, can you just fill it?"

I'd need to come back in an hour. The incident disturbed me and after telling Pete what happened, I called Novak's office and left a message explaining the situation that took place at the pharmacy. Thirty minutes later while I watched Stella and Spenser draw hopscotch squares on the sidewalk in front of our house, my phone buzzed inside my pocket.

"Mrs. Redondo? It's Dr. Novak."

"Oh! Thanks so much for calling, sorry but did you get my

message? About the pharmacy and my medications?" He did. He informed me he'd spoken directly to the concerned pharmacist and my prescriptions should be filled and ready within the next hour.

"It was just a bit of over caution and some miscommunication on her part. My apologies for the confusion," he said, sweeping in like a casual hero to brush all our worries away. Pete picked up the medication later that night and as he set it down on the counter, he mentioned the unfriendly pharmacy techs.

"It's like they think we're up to something, I don't know," he shrugged, and I nodded in agreement before the subject changed. It was 8 o'clock on the Friday before Mother's Day. Three kids just finished bath time. And with the squeals of freshly scrubbed, pajamaed young ones bouncing on the bed, Pete and I wrote a grocery list and planned a Sunday trip to the zoo, eventually realizing we were shouting to hear one another. Families are loud, and kids are unpredictably funny. Watching the silliness made me laugh. A peaceful warmth surrounded us despite the chaos, and I thought, *I will not drink this weekend. I will not ruin these lives.*

Still, I'd catch myself in the misery of hindsight, pointlessly pretending it was supposed to go a different way. I went over it a thousand times, and every single time it was me. I was the train wreck. We know this. It's why no one's surprised when I ended up at a fifth inpatient rehab facility a few weeks later after getting kicked out of an outpatient program for knowing as much as the instructors.

"She's too smart for this," they told Pete. I could have taught the classes, except *please, no.* I begged everyone, *please don't send me somewhere else.*

That's how fast it felt to suddenly be down in Texas hill country, sitting across the desk from a new doctor, Dr. Holder, in charge of my medical care for the next month. I glanced around his office, noting multiple framed degrees and certifications hanging on the walls. The office looked like an interior designer got their hands on it, instead of the usual institutional vibe. But the man sitting across from me dressed like he had the day off. After our short introductions, he got right to the point.

"I want to discuss your medications. Dr. Novak, I see," he said, looking up from my papers, and I gave a *mmm-hmm* response. "About how long have you been on Xanax?" Dr. Holder asked. My head did a double take.

"What?? I'm not on Xanax," I corrected, in a shocked but matter-of-fact way.

"Yes, you are," he said casually. "I have your chart right here," and the sound of rushing water filled my ears. "You're taking a couple of benzodiazepines actually," he said. "Plus two addictive sleep medications, and a dangerous stimulant for narcolepsy, also addictive. Did your psychiatrist, Dr. . . . Novak . . . did he know about your history?"

I stared at the man in front of me staring at me, and a dozen emotions crossed over my face.

I froze in a stillness while his words spun around my head until they found a place to sink in. *I've been taking Xanax? Me?* Because look, I didn't know a lot about pills, but everyone knew about that one. *Holy fuck,* I thought, *what have I done?* The same high-pitched ringing filled my ears and I cut it off with a startling cry.

Dr. Novak, it turned out, was a psychiatrist with a reputation for overprescribing or wrongly prescribing his patients. Whether or not those qualities were the reason for his chronic lateness and bustling practice, I'll never know, but it took two years for any one of us to ever hear the words "benzo" or "Xanax" or a warning regarding the addictive or dependent nature of my medications. Maybe that was part of his game.

However, the information was out in the open, unlike the secrets I tried to keep with my drinking, but no one noticed despite multiple encounters with a medical community given signed access to my entire list of current and former medications and health history. Doctors, nurses and others at hospitals, offices and institutions—all of which required full disclosure and review of official documentation regarding past and present medications—and no one ever said specific words to either Pete or myself about the pills prescribed, not even the concerned pharmacist who spoke to each of us separately.

"Reading over your papers, some of this makes more sense, but unfortunately it will complicate your detox and recovery treatment. This is serious, but we'll take good care of you," the doctor assured me.

"I just don't understand," I said, feeling too much all at once. "How did this happen? How did I NOT know?"

Because it was *always* about the drinking. *Always alcohol,* until that day.

I sat in shock and listened to the sound of my blood pounding in my ears as I clenched my jaw shut. I was accustomed to the noise the way locals barely blink when a freight train comes roaring down the tracks a stone's throw from backyard fences. Our whole life was so loud and there was so much happening, we could only focus on the immediate catastrophe in front us. We didn't understand what was underneath us the whole time. Seeing it that way, it's understandable how much we overlook, either by pure accident or for the sake of getting by.

Only now when I look back at those years, I see that the sun was not in my eyes and the memories are muted. I can see what's coming in the distance, and I know what happens. Take a pin and mark this spot because this is the brutality of truth that tortures a soul. It's an unrelenting engine blowing billows of smoke across the blue sky with a long line of boxcars racing along behind it, each stenciled with letters spelling words like Risperidone, Edluar, Armodafinil, Alprazolam, Seroquel, Clonazepam, Latuda, and Eszopiclone. I want to change it all, to go back in time and scream at myself for not checking the horizon or watching my step along the tracks, the same tracks where my great-grandfathers worked the rails and the same steel line where my cousin stood watching the thunderous sound blow past his waving hand with a foreboding siren. Because where there's smoke, there's usually fire. I wasn't looking over my shoulder up there in the midst of my distractions, none of us were.

But Novak was a hundred-mile merciless train that ran me over and, in the end, it was just another train wreck. And the train wreck was me, Emily.

That's how these stories always go.

CHAPTER SEVENTEEN

Summer 2014

"You want to believe you're terminally unique, Emily, and that's an ego problem," Jerry, my rehab counselor, told me one afternoon.

I looked at the stapled stack of papers on the desk between us covered with my scribbled handwriting and his red marks, bored by his statement. *All the work I put into my answers and that's all I get?* I thought to myself. Generic 12-step lingo was helpful but at this point it was Groundhog Day for me. I could have said it all myself, regurgitating all the right answers if I wanted a stellar grade from the heavyset man with wire framed glasses across from me.

Instead, I left his office and walked to the top of a hill where an outdoor chapel overlooked the Texas summer hill country. Before my next scheduled class, I felt the humid air as the sun came out to warm my skin. A wooden cross hung in front of me from the rooftop like a silent presence waiting for me to see it, and I did. I stared at it, thinking about my treatment team at the bottom of the hill, scattered in different buildings, encouraging me to fly to California for three more months of intensive treatment. Then I pictured the young faces who just wanted their mother to come back home. I thought about my overwhelmed husband, who didn't know what to do, and the handful of women who, once again, stepped in to fill the space of the caregiver, driver, and cook I used to be. And it's one massive ball of confusion, impossible to keep simple because it was complicated. I wanted to figure out the magic formula that let us all win, but I couldn't afford to fail myself again, aware I might not make it back. I finally gave up and talked to the God who'd become a stranger.

"Just take it. You decide. You figure out what I'm supposed to do because I can't. If you make it work, fine. I'll go," I said to the invisible power busy with more promising requests.

Three days later, my airplane landed in California in what's known as a door-to-door, which meant an escorted trip directly from one institution to the next. My new home was an all-female beach house in Newport Beach, which was designed as two living quarters on separate floors and offices extending off the downstairs unit. *Quite an upgrade,* I thought, while a twenty-something staffer named Taylor with a killer tan walked me upstairs to show me around.

"Sorry, no one's here to meet you. They're at the gym but should be back in about 20 minutes," she said, pushing the door open and pointing with her finger.. "That one's yours." I nodded at a nicely made twin bed against the wall with a smile. Until I noticed the Louis Vuitton luggage stacked on the opposite side of the room and decided immediately that I hated whoever my new roommate was. I tossed my ancient black suitcase and promotional duffel bag as far under the bed as I could stuff them before leaving to fill out more intake papers.

Right away, things were different when I noticed my housemates, all nine, averaging in age from late teens to mid-twenties. I felt a reminiscent urge to try and "be cool" like I used to do in high school when we introduced ourselves.

"I'm Krystal, with a 'K,' I got here yesterday," said a blonde with bloodshot swollen eyes who apparently had been crying for the last 24 hours. Next came Mikayla, 20, from some beach town in New Jersey who looked ready to punch someone's lights out.

"Liska," said the girl near Mikayla, "but I don't live here anymore." Telling me she moved up to sober living the week before. "Some of us come over and hang out."

"Oh, that's great," I said, exchanging smiles.

Barbara, a little too perky for me, was from Dallas, but the fancy schmancy Dallas known as Highland Park, a world away from what I knew. She was roommates with Haley, the youngest in the house who dressed in all black and held a taxidermized fox in her arms.

"Want to pet it?" Haley asked me; it was surprisingly soft.

I said hello to them all one by one, forgetting everyone's name the second they said it because formalities made us all feel uncomfortable until the administrators left the room.

"It's too bad you didn't get here last week when Carrie was here. She was a mom, probably about your age. We loved her," said Haley.

"Oh my *God,* Haley, what the fuck, she had a fucking granddaughter," said Mikayla and big laughs on that one.

"Yeah, thanks," I said, "no grandkids here that I'm aware of." After a couple of questions, I told them I had four kids.

"Holy shit, that's a lot," Krystal said. Then somebody asked if they just fell out of my vagina after a certain number, and it was hysterical. Ice broken.

Unlike a traditional inpatient rehab, we had more freedom and responsibilities, including cooking and cleaning. It was the little things I noticed first that already separated this experience from all the others. Besides the obvious lack of an institutional smell, I sat on couches meant for a home and walked on actual carpet as opposed to the commercial kind you'd find in office buildings. Shampoos and razors in the showers, cigarettes on the table, caffeinated drinks on the counter—all of it out in the open instead of in contraband bins to sign out by request only.

But the greatest sight was stacks of books, most of them belonging to my roommate, Sloan, who I'd grow to love dearly, because other institutions banned all reading material unrelated to recovery. A tinge of pleasure fluttered through me, quickly followed my own internal reprimand. *You're not here to have a good time, Emily.*

Saturday began with a weekly deep clean of the house followed by an inspection before our weekend outing. Each of us had a designated chore, and I caught myself enjoying the toilet scrubbing and Windex wiping free from the interruptions of, *Mom? Hey Mom, Mommy!* But Krystal wasn't having it when Mia decided at the last second she needed a 30-minute shower before she swept the floors one morning. Soon enough, I heard the unmistakable sounds of an argument in the making.

"I don't care!" Mia bellowed from the locked bathroom door. Then came the stiff silence when she casually entered the living room with wet hair, the muttering under her breath, the aggressive use of cleaning supplies. We were a typical dysfunctional family.

"If you have something to say, then fucking say it but don't do your muttering," said Krystal across the room to Mia who thought for a solid minute before responding.

"Like, nobody mops like that. You're just spreading it around, like, don't you ever clean?" Mia asked, and my jaw dropped at the direction this was going.

"Okay, first? You took a thirty-minute fucking *shower,* Mia," and Krystal pointed out precisely what time it was, when our counselor was coming to inspect, and everything left to do.

"Not my problem," was Mia's response. I thought to myself, *How long is this going to last? Is it like this every time?* Because we were stuck with each other, for better or for worse. I'm not saying it's the best solution, but it mirrored family life. And I knew the last place I wanted to be was rehabbing with first-time wine moms writing letters home filled with lies about "Mommy Camp" and bumming puffs off Virginia Slims from one another. Because this was conflict. The real deal. What goes on behind closed doors.

And it was coming out.

Eventually, things got settled and ten of us loaded into our white passenger van like a gang of misfits headed to the most wonderful place on earth, Target. We hit the aisles like a dream where we had the whole place to ourselves, unaware that actual everyday life was happening right in front of us. Clueless about how to grocery shop for one, I bought spaghetti noodles, lunch meat, bread, a few apples and mayonnaise to last me a week, then browsed through makeup and sales racks, treating myself to a sweatshirt before meeting up with the others to race our carts back to the van.

"My tail," Haley said. "Guys, my tail." I looked over to see the panic on her face after realizing it was missing. My parenting skills kicked in as a couple of us volunteered to go back and look for it with her. True, that was a first for me, but similar to scouring aisles for a dropped binkie or Paw Patrol figure.

"Got it!" someone shouted from the front of the store. And there it was, the fluffy fox tail, waving in the air to the relief of all of us.

I'll admit, there were moments over the following weeks when I wondered what the hell I was doing there. Meaning, how was any of this helpful? Then again, who's to know the difference between a turning point and an ordinary event? So-called wastes of time turned out to be the most invaluable for me, like how to go to gas stations and not sneak inside for wine or how to shop for groceries and avoid temptations. I relearned how to do simple things I'd never practiced in other places: how to share, how to graciously lose an argument, how to take criticism, how to apologize, how to own your opinion, and how to express your feelings. Instructions, worksheets, and therapy had become useless when tucked safely away inside institutions. Unless we actually got the chance to try and practice these things with women I grew to trust, I'd be right back where I started.

I kept going back to recent advice I'd been told—*be willing to try something different*—and got in bed one night with an almost childlike realization I could be anyone I wanted out in a place so far from home as if the strings that used to tie me into unreasonable beliefs and expectations couldn't reach me. It was the feeling of a beginning, of discovering the possibility I might still have some good left in me.

As I drifted off to sleep, I remembered a few days before when we rented kayaks and paddled out beyond the set boundaries, unsupervised on a perfect afternoon.

"Let's get in," I said with a gleeful look in my eyes, and some of us snuck soundlessly over the edge into the cool water. I took off my bathing suit top. We all did, feeling a light brush of temporary freedom and innocence again. Our pasts were nowhere in sight. None of us had problems, only joy, and I caught myself momentarily without an age attached to me, swimming in an unburdened body I'd long forgotten.

What if some of us missed our chance at self-discovery in the earlier years? In our days of being young women, when the plan was there was no plan, we wanted a television version of motherhood and marriage, but we wanted a lot of other things out of life, too. It never felt wrong like it did now. I let guilt attach itself to fun, thinking if I wasn't sacrificing my time or serving someone else's needs, it meant I was selfish and wasteful, irresponsible, or lazy. Maybe it was the absence of history or the weightlessness of letting go, but I remembered what fun was. And the guilt kept its distance.

But at some point, a sliver of our past comes and finds us. It reminds us all of unfinished business and takes off like a pissed-off thoroughbred kicking up dust on a warpath. We weren't there on vacation. For Mikayla, it was the car crash that killed her best friend. For Ruby, it was the schoolteacher who preyed on her. For Krystal, it was the pimp, a miscarriage, the gunshots. And the face-picking new girl with a shoplifting habit, still a mystery to us. The unimaginable raged beneath our surface, curling us up on the floor and waiting for us to unravel . . . and it's coming for all of us no matter how fast we paddle.

"It's nothing, but I need to talk about this grief I have," I told Kim, the therapist, one afternoon during our appointment. After all, there's work to do. "I've . . . you know, processed it before or whatever, but God . . ." I trailed off without finishing my sentence because I could already feel the tears coming. "I don't want to cry about it."

"Okay, it sounds like there's a lot of pain there, Emily," Kim noticed. I looked across at the fashionable blonde who looked more like a swimsuit model than a professional counselor and sat on the cusp between *I really don't want to unpack this shit* and letting it all tumble out.

"It's pretty stupid," was how I started, then I walked myself backward in time a few treatment centers and explained to Kim what happened on a five-minute phone call with Pete, three years prior. He was giving me updates about their lives at home, as had become our routine when he mentioned his vasectomy so casually that I almost missed it.

Wait, you did what?

"So you two didn't discuss this beforehand?" Kim asked.

"I mean, we'd make casual jokes like, 'haha, four and no more,' but we didn't have an official discussion about it, no."

"How'd that make you feel?" she asked, and I told her the truth. Because down at the core of my existence, a sudden death washed over me. I stood in front of a phone in a room full of passersby at a rehab like I'd been punched with an expiration stamp next to the morning's date. My husband stole my motherhood. That's how I felt, and in swept a primitive, unbearable grief. I wasn't ready to deal with it then, and I wasn't exactly ready to deal with it sitting there with Kim. *Am I allowed to feel like this? To be angry? To feel betrayed?* My emotions morphed into mathematical equations each time women or counselors gave me common sense explanations from a husband's point of view. How, by the looks of things, I already had my hands full with plenty of kids. I can't handle the ones I've got, right?

But you're not listening, I wanted to say. *Stop talking like I'm a child. Please.*

"I don't want it to be over," I said quietly. "I never knew it was the last time. The way my body changes with a baby inside of it, the way a newborn feels up against my neck, how fast it all goes." I paused and wept into my palms. "Every day, they need me less." I'd never said those truths out loud, fearing if I did, I'd start to disappear too soon.

"Oh, Emily. You're such a loving mother; I can't begin to imagine what you're feeling right now," Kim said. "You're right, it sounds like grief, but I think you're feeling other things, too."

I looked up at her and mouthed the word "thanks," unable to stop the flood of tears. I knew it would happen this way, remembering the times I told myself, *don't start crying about it now because it'll be days before you stop.*

My husband was a good man, and a lot of emotions unrelated to him poured out of me. Grief pressed its weight against my throat, but as the two of us sat together, I felt a sense of respect coming toward me. And I finally got the chance to tell someone about the simultaneous terror of being constantly needed and watching the same neediness slip away. I was a woman who'd lost herself. I funneled my entire purpose into one place, leaving the rest hollow. I wanted to brush it off again like I always did, but Kim's attention proved that my experience and emotions were real. That I was real. And it felt like relief to get it out, to say it all, and breathe a little deeper.

The next month, my family flew in for a weekend visit. As they arrived, my roommates poked their heads around the corner of the house and peered through the front window to watch me crouch on the sidewalk with outstretched arms for the little boy sprinting in front of his sisters toward me. We almost toppled over. Stella was close behind, followed by the others, and in seconds, I was once again surrounded by the heart of my existence, wrapping my arms around Rebecca and Shelby. I hugged my mother and thanked her like I always did. When my eyes met Pete's, a thousand words passed between us. *Here I am. I love you. How'd we get here? Don't leave me,* and we held onto each other in the chaos of the moment.

I remembered a time when the whole world seemed to fade around us when Pete captured my attention and we talked for hours as if time and everything in it were meaningless. The two of us multiplied into six, and now it was hard to focus as one of them got too close to the busy traffic.

"Spenser!" I shouted. "Come here, honey. Everybody, let me show you the house before we go to lunch."

"Can we meet your new friends?" asked Stella, and I nodded yes. I was beaming from the inside while I watched the interactions between my family and friends. Not surprisingly, Mikayla and Krystal won the hearts of my girls when we swam at the beach later that afternoon. For two days, I hopped the fence between rehab resident and vacation mom, back and forth, never quite feeling completely unburdened from the sense that I was disappointing somebody.

The caretaker was back in full form, and if I saw that woman today, I'd tell her to stop being so annoying. My family and my housemates survived just fine without me, but suddenly, I stood at the center of it all for a very simple reason—I did it the best. I was The Mother. Call it my ego, a need for control, an obvious example of self-centeredness or a little bit of all three, and sure, no argument. But it would be wrong to ignore the genetic inheritance pumping through my bloodstream, ingrained inside my cells. And on that truth, I balanced on a pin tip.

"I'm really looking forward to tonight," Pete said on their last day. "It's been so long since we've been alone together." He was right. Not only was I free from curfew, but I'd also been granted an overnight pass and didn't need to be back at the house until 10 am the following day.

"So am I," I told him. "Just to sleep in your arms again. I mean, until I get restless because I think you're stealing my air." I joked about how I told him once when our faces were too close he stole all the oxygen from my space. We spent another day in the sun, busy with the kids in souvenir shops and eating burgers on restaurant patios. We all were exhausted when we returned to the hotel. I helped my mom bathe the little ones and get them ready for bed, then went with Pete to our room down the hall to take my own long, hot shower.

Soon, my phone pinged to signal a text message from Shelby that read: *Can you come to our room? Spenser and Stella are having a hard time falling asleep. They really want you. We miss you. A lot.*

Then another one came: *Please, Mom* and I responded, "I'll try."

What was I supposed to do? The good mother goes to her children when they need her, but a good wife stays. A voice in the back of my head representing an age-old Christian lady scolded me that the husband comes first. I wanted to make everyone happy, but again found myself in a situation where we were all hurting, and I had to choose.

"Honey," I said quietly to Pete. "I need to go over to the kids' room. Shelby's having a hard time." He sighed and rolled his eyes. "I'll be back soon, I promise." I was aware I let him down. I quietly closed the hotel room door and left him alone with his disappointment.

I let my eyes adjust to the darkened room filled with sounds of sleep, tiptoeing my way over to Shelby's side of the bed she shared with my mother. Everyone was asleep as I lifted the blanket to lie next to my first born, shifting slightly under the sheets. Right away, she was in my arms as our muscles moved into the perfect position we'd known our entire lives together—the way her head rested near my shoulder, how my arm reached up to stroke her long, brown hair.

My finger brushed against her damp cheek, causing my own eyes to well as if on cue.

"I miss you," Shelby said to interrupt the silence. She was 15 years old, but in the dark, she sounded so small. My little girl was so close when it's so easy to believe those days are over.

I traced the outline of her forehead with my fingertips and told her a bedtime story.

"Once upon a time, there was an angel in my tummy," I said. "And let me tell you, from the very start, everyone knew you were special." She sniffled as I kept deep-diving through Shelby's beginning years, weaving in details of unmatched love from so many people.

She was my entire life again lying next to me, still enough to catch my words like they were feathers for her wings. Then I whispered, "You're the best thing that ever happened to me."

"I love you, Mom," she said, and I said it back, knowing the confusion behind such a natural sentiment for a kid in her situation.

Parenting and alcoholism are both entire universes that separately consume a woman and in the middle of it are our children. As the designated problem, moms get the help, but "kids are resilient," they say. They'll adjust. Learn to trust again and turn out fine although we, the mothers, didn't turn out fine from our own alcoholic parents. And I hate the fact I still remember my dad or my mom coming into my bedroom trying to smooth over whatever recent upheaval had me crying in the dark. All of it feels sick and unfair because it is. I didn't know how to help Shelby that night because I never learned how to help myself. What a god-awful feeling to pass on the same root of your pain to your child.

I didn't have the answers.

Except I did. Contrary to the way my mind usually worked, I realized that for the last couple of days, I'd given Shelby and her siblings exactly want they wanted, to see me happy and alcohol-free. The thought came so suddenly, I could have bolted upright in bed, believing it was almost too good to be true. Maybe it wasn't one or the other—helping myself or helping them—and more about helping myself *for* them. Maybe I was already starting to do the right things even though it hurt like hell.

"Thank you," I whispered to the darkened room. What I knew about my little epiphany was only that it didn't come from me, and the vague understanding was enough. I pulled the covers up to Shelby's chin, kissed the top of her head, and then snuck out the door to Pete's warm embrace.

Reality met me the next morning with a flurry of activity despite our night-before attempt to have things packed and ready to go for the family's flight home to Texas and my curfew. Traffic that morning was awful as our rental car crept along, adding more stress as the flight time got closer. We drove in the opposite direction of the airport because my rehab house was on the other side of town, and it slowly became clear they were going to miss their flight. I had an idea.

"Pull over," I said from the back seat, squeezed between two kids. "Right up here. Pull over, and I can walk the rest of the way." Our eyes met in the rearview mirror, and I saw the sadness linger in his eyes.

"What? Mom, no. You can't," said Shelby.

"We're not just going to leave you!" said Becca, as tears welled up in her eyes. "Right, Daddy?" To a second grader, it's scary to get dumped on a sidewalk full of strangers. But Pete and I knew it was the only way to guarantee they'd make the flight.

Goodbye had come too soon. Panicked hands reached for me as I unbuckled the seatbelt and grabbed my overstuffed backpack, trying to figure out how I could do this in seconds while double-parked on a busy street. I bent awkwardly to embrace each person who deserved my undivided attention one last time because it wasn't my family or the kids as we say it. It was one precious human with their unique relationship with me, six times over, on the brink of another separation that tore at a particular connection between two hearts. Shelby gets a turn. My mother gets a turn. Stella gets a turn. Rebecca gets a turn. Spenser gets a turn. Pete gets a turn, all with eye contact and a special sentiment. We know they want another round, but I have to push them away. Blow kisses. It's never enough for any of us.

In a blink, it was over. I swirled around with my arm in the air to watch my world tuck itself neatly between two cars, fold into the left lane flow toward the highway to disappear from my sight and make their way back to my other life in Texas. I turned, already missing them, and started walking with a giant following behind me. *You could have done better, you could have been more,* it said, ignoring the fact I'd never get it perfectly right. Deep down, I wanted to be everything, yet in front of me I was nothing, a nobody, a stranger with nothing but an overnight bag slung over my shoulder and confidence in my stride. God, it felt good as I pretended to be an independent woman who could do whatever she wanted. Well, I mean, within reason. I was 39 and booking it to make curfew and my therapy session.

"What dreams do you have for your life when you go home? What do you want to pursue? What's your passion?" my counselor asked me later that day. The question seemed to fall out of nowhere and land with a thud at my feet. I had no idea how to answer it. I forgot I was even allowed to dream at all.

"I don't know," I said truthfully.

"Okay, well, what if I asked you, 'Who were you before all of *this*?' How would you answer that?" she asked, and I still didn't have a good answer.

"All I know is I showed up here as three things: a wife, a mother, and a drunk," I said. I didn't know what to say next, so she asked me to search for something I was good at that I could start doing again for myself.

"I guess I could go back and finish graduate school. I think I'm almost finished," I thought out loud. But in the back of my mind, it already sounded like a lot of work, time, and money. Kim stared at me with intent until finally she shook her head.

"No, that's not it. I just don't see it in you, not right now. Something's there, but not that," she said confidently. That's how Kim was, always seeing something going on inside me that I could never notice.

"Well, I like quilts," I said on a whim. "Maybe I'll make quilts and sell them or give them away." Sure, I liked to sew them, but the process drove me nuts. She laughed.

"No. Nice try, but no," she said, and I threw out a couple of more half-hearted ideas until a surge of lightning hit me and I knew. The almost forgotten dream was so precious I didn't know if I had the guts to say it out loud fearing it, too, would get Kim's axe.

"Okay, well," I hesitantly started to say, then took a deep breath. "I've always wanted to write a book." As much as I tried to hide it, the corners of my mouth began to tug upward ever-so-slightly. My hand reached up to cover the smile.

Everything about her demeanor changed. Her eyes lit up as she leaned in closer like she was about to tell me a secret but then she leaned back and gave her hands one solid clap.

"Emily, that's it! It's the book." And then in a softer voice she said, "That's your baby."

I gasped when she said it, then a burn behind my eyes signaled a cry from deep inside me rising to the surface to say, *yes, finally, I've been understood.* Until that day, I blew through Kleenex repeatedly, gutted by all the endings and miss-outs in motherhood and marriage, in life in general, crying about how much I ruined and what a mess I'd become. Then suddenly, someone grabs my attention, changes my view, and I'm weeping at what I discover—something beautiful nestled into what so many of us know as that dark, empty space. I found a young lady I neglected a long time ago. And maybe the beginning I never got.

I was still on the pink cloud of joy when we all headed to our weekly therapeutic jam band session. Audrey, who graduated up to sober living, hitched a ride and decided to vape in the back seat, blowing enough smoke out of her whale lungs to fog out all the windows. *Really, Audrey?* Layla overreacted into a coughing fit triggered by the asthma she didn't have, so we had to pull over and ended up late to the office. Oddly enough, Wes, who led our group, wasn't there yet. No staff was around except for the tech who drove us, so we went inside to our usual room, sat down in a wide circle of chairs and waited over twenty minutes. Then without saying a word to us, a dozen people filed in and stood behind our chairs with a few others walking to the front of the room.

Someone's in serious trouble, was what I thought, panning the room for the guiltiest face.

"We have some news to tell you," said a man I didn't know, and those of us from the house sat frozen. "We received news last night about a friend and former resident who moved up to our sober living program, Liska. She passed away last night from an overdose." And the room erupted.

Her closest friends sprang from their chairs or flung to the ground crying. I sat in my chair shocked and covered my face because we just saw her. She was just here. I pictured her face so clearly sitting in the second row of the van, then in this room. How can someone be sitting next to us one minute, then gone in the next? It felt incomprehensible, even as the following days were filled with blank stares and discussions about Liska, many of which didn't include me.

"It was her fucking ex," Mikayla said. "That's who she was with, I'm sure of it, and he was using again."

"We tried to tell her, but she wouldn't listen," Krystal chimed in. I had little to say. We were all angry at the same fucking disease, the push and pull with grief as I heard them talk about how Liska was on her way to great things. I'm sure she was. I learned more about Liska after she died, more so when her mother arrived at the house, walking in with arms wide open to offer hugs, and I thought to myself, *Where's your anger?*

Losing a child under any circumstance was so incomprehensibly horrible to me. Anger was the first emotion that came to my mind.

"If you all wouldn't mind, I'd like us to paint some rocks for Liska," she said. "Then we can leave some here and I'll take some home with me . . . as a tribute."

I wanted to raise my hand and tell her, *I'm sorry, I think I'll pass, I really shouldn't be here,* and quietly excuse myself. Watching the bottles of bright acrylic paints spread out across the table, her rocks the same as the ones in my front yard, Liska's mom had paint-stained brushes like I did. It made me wonder if we both had years-old vibrant stones placed in our gardens by little hands. We did the same things; my daughter wasn't much younger than hers, and I wanted to scream. *Where or how do I fit in with what's in front of me?* It was selfish, yes, but not enough to forget the bigger picture as I grabbed a rock and a brush.

Afterward, a group of us walked across the street to the beach for a fireside memorial where her mother shared memories of the daughter she loved so much. I couldn't ignore that I was her age, suddenly feeling like I stood out sitting with my newfound friends. As she spoke, I related to the way a mother lovingly talks about her child, how the eyes light up from the inside, the shoulders slightly cave instinctively as if to make a cradle. She smiled as she spoke. It lit up images of my own kids across the night's sky.

But I also related to the addict daughter she mourned. The girl who was dead by complete accident, a victim of a split-second thoughtless decision that left behind lifetimes of heartbreak. Because on countless occasions, that could have been me. It struck me, sitting in the dark, and I broke in two, straight down the middle. Lightning through a tree, a path of a road divided, I knew the child and the mother, but what goes between?

Who was this Emily who wanted to go home and who was also terrified of leaving?

I've never been good at goodbyes. I was the kid who got sad that a trip was over before it even started, the real sentimental type. As my time at the house wound down, I wanted to magically erase the distance between exactly where I was and the home where I was headed in Texas just to avoid an ending. I wanted to carve my initials into a wooden post on the porch to tell the women who'd come after me, *I was here. Don't erase me.*

On the airplane, I sat in my window seat for the four-hour flight and focused on the responsibilities waiting for me. Underneath all the preparation we do for the final launch out of treatment, no one really knows what will happen. We want guarantees but our little worlds are filled with unpredictability. My days of delusional expectations were long gone, but I still felt empowered. A thousand miles away, five missing parts of me anxiously awaited the return of the mother and wife they'd always known, except it wasn't entirely clear who they'd get.

Things would have to change, and that's difficult for everybody. I thought to myself, *Why can't there be another way? If only I could do it for them and do all the work myself.* That was my biggest fear. *I'm starting to like myself. I'm taking charge of my actions, let me do my thing,* I kept telling myself. The closer I got to Texas, the more my nerves returned, but I carried a sense of purpose with me that flitted like a fragile moth. We were the same, up in the air, off on a new adventure and searching for light, and a subtle reminder to stay away from my dark places.

CHAPTER EIGHTEEN

Summer 2016

I was ten when I skipped through the porch screen door, my great-grandma, Stella, close behind, to find Fern downstairs in her kitchen baking bread.

"I was wondering when you'd be down," she said, wiping her hands on her apron.

"Are we going anywhere today?" I asked, realizing that my grandma's answer of *a drive* didn't have a destination. My family would arrive later in the week that summer, giving me ample time to explore the overstuffed cabinets and closets. Fern still had a ringer washer in the root cellar even though it was the mid-1980s, but since I got my finger stuck in it the previous summer, I was limited to hanging wet sheets on the clothesline strung across the backyard. While we were outside, the two of us inspected her garden, looking for ripe tomatoes and cucumbers for dinner that night. Hands down, the walk to the post office with Stella was my favorite activity. Anywhere I went with those ladies made me feel like a small-town VIP since everyone knew them, including the postmaster who greeted us as I whizzed past him to unlock the code for box 94. Just a bunch of junk, they always said, unless of course, a handwritten letter made its way into the mail pile.

On our way back to the house, walking a little slower up the hill, my mouth undoubtedly chatted nonstop. Maybe that was the reason Stella was a woman of few words. How big the world can be without a single worry or fear on one's mind. The Mississippi River across the highway to my left, the VFW hall that smelled like a musty bake sale to my right, it was the ultimate boredom—the kind that inspires porch swing conversations over ice cold lemonade or snuggling on the couch for another episode of Jeopardy. I carried nothing but a stack of mail and my endless imagination toward the same pink house on Main Street where my mom lived when she was ten years old.

"You know, this used to be my bedroom," she told me more than once on visits. "Can you believe four of us shared this little room?" I responded with an interest that lacked a real connection, like a story I wasn't attached to. Our moms couldn't possibly have been young once.

But now, thirty years later, my own daughter Rebecca was the ten-year-old. I was in the driver's seat pulling up to my childhood home, Becca being the first one out to greet her grandma.

"Nana!" she squealed as the back door opened off the garage and my mother emerged, arms opened wide to catch the first hug racing toward her.

"Well, hi, my precious angels," my mom said with a laugh in her voice.

One by one, she got her hugs from all four grandkids, saving the last one for me. Then we walked into the kitchen, kids darting off in different directions.

"Are you doing okay?" she asked me, which is usually the question people ask when they assume you're not. She put a hand on my shoulder to study my face and zero in on my eyes. *Another one waiting for me to nose-dive . . . lovely,* I thought as I nodded and smiled. I looked around trying to decide where to sit, because it determined how long I planned to stay. Kitchen meant a few minutes; family room was more of a commitment.

"Yeah, I'm okay," I said, taking a seat at the kitchen table. "Well, doing the best I can."

"I saw Kari, your old sponsor, at a meeting the other day," she said. "Are you hungry? Let me see if I have anything." She fished out a box of Nabisco crackers and some raw almonds and offered to fry me an egg. The poor woman, always coaxing me, spending all these years living with the idea that I could die any day. I ate the egg.

Afterward, I wandered toward the back of the house to avoid more conversation. The kids were playing in the bedroom to my left and without a thought I said, "Did you guys know this used to be my bedroom?"

"Yes, Mom," someone muttered without a hint of fascination, even when I told them the crazy ways I rearranged the furniture and the different colors I painted on the walls.

"All right, guys, I'm leaving. Have fun with Nana. And be good please," I said on my way out. I told my mom I'd be back in about an hour after the AA meeting.

"No rush," she said. "If you want to go to lunch with some of the ladies afterward, I'm fine with it."

"I don't want to go to lunch, but thanks," I said.

"Okay, I was just thinking if you spent some time with some of the women . . ."

"Mom, please don't. I've already been down that road," I told her, grabbing my keys and purse off the counter and hollering goodbye toward the rest of the kids.

We did the usual goodbye, sauntering out to the driveway to say one last bit of nothing special. I turned to Becca and gave her a squeeze, oblivious to how comfortable and safe she looked in the house that filled me with an unpredictable angst. She was a version of me from a different time, standing next to her grandma with plans to bake cookies and water the garden while I was gone.

"Thanks, Mom," I told her, and kept the rest to myself.

Because, my God, was I wreck that day. Nothing new to report but the same old shit as always. I came back from California and blew it after a year. Wine in the closet. Let's not bore each other with the details. Driving to the same meeting that day where I'd been going for over a dozen years, I thought about all the things I wanted to say but couldn't, like, *AA isn't working for me, Mom, not anymore, not right now. I don't want to talk about God, I don't want to keep doing the same version of all of this.*

What can I say? I came home from California filled with optimism about the future. The familiar smell of my house, the feel of its furniture and upstairs chatter bouncing between walls filled me with the comforts of home. When I ran my finger across dusty window blinds or rested my head on my pillow at night, the obsession of alcohol or self-loathing didn't come to mind. I wasn't bored or unhappy. A little prickly at times, I often say, so I stuck to the basics. The domestics, school activities, AA meetings. In the evenings, I sat at the new computer Pete bought me, staring at its screen late at night typing a flurry of words until my mind went blank. Speechless, as if machinery short-circuited inside of me, replacing vocabulary with flashes of memories I'd rather not think about. I told myself, *it's in the past, you're safe now, move on, Emily,* continuing to bat at scenes for a few months when they appeared at streetlights, on sidewalks, in dreams or when I entered a room.

It's a family process to settle back into normal life with a problem that needs addressing. We, the floundering caretakers, left home expected to shed the alcoholism and returned with expectations to be the same mom and wife, minus the drinking. And in certain cases, it worked. For others, myself included, we weren't the social drinker who crossed the line into a problem. If it ever looked that way, our apologies. We drank to breathe, and it turned on us. Uncontainable. In the end we weren't drinking because we liked the effect; maybe we didn't know what else to do. Or have the means to figure it all out. We were storms coming home in daylight to see the true extent of our destruction. It wasn't broken tree limbs or shattered windows, either.

We're talking years of clean-up from all the damage and in the middle of it, being handed the old terms and conditions that snipped off the parts of ourselves that had once tried to grow in the first place.

"Maybe you should go back to meetings." My mom nudged. "I know it worked for you before," she told me.

To her, the answer was so obvious. Not only did the program work since the first time she stepped in the door back in 1990, but regarding beliefs and traditions in my family, AA held equal importance to the church. As if by being in either place, I gained better access to holy goodness and blessings, just by sitting down and going through the motions. To even insinuate I wanted to branch out and explore something different? It's like joining the circus or running off to a unicorn farm. Those who care about us want us to change, then when we do it's uncomfortable for them. But I wasn't rejecting the program or the 12 steps, I was simply looking for another way to keep trying.

"Emily! I haven't seen you in a while," said a longtime AA acquaintance when I sat down for the noon meeting on the day my mom watched the kids. "You doing okay?"

"Hi! Yeah, just busy with summer stuff," I said, and she nodded while I settled in and sipped my bland coffee from a Styrofoam cup.

"Summer stuff," she repeated quietly to herself.

There was nothing significant about the meeting as the same cast of characters got chosen to read the literature and share on the topic. The group included old Ron, who needed to clear the phlegm out of his throat a dozen times while he spoke, and Bill, who'd been telling the same story about getting sober for the last fifty-two years. I'd been taught to keep what I like and leave the rest, that expectations were my number one offender, and that the problem was me.

I slouched because it was my fault I expected more until the closing reading of an excerpt from the Big Book when my eyes unglazed as if I heard the words for the first time instead of a thousand. *Our book is meant to be suggestive only. We realize we know only a little,* and then further on, *Abandon yourself to God as you understand God.*

I gathered my things and left immediately.

As I drove to my mother's to pick up the kids, my head was spinning. What a strange experience to truly hear something you've been saying for years, like song lyrics we sing to our favorite song. The message delivered was simple—*we don't know*—and it washed over me like a cleansing breeze through my rolled-down windows. No matter how hard a person pounds a book on a table, it still won't hold all the answers. Stop correcting and telling me what to do. When I was little, God was small like me. I didn't understand it, but at the moment, it felt like I'd been given permission to be exactly where I was, unknowing of it all. And I kept it to myself.

Was it divine intervention? Honestly, if divine forces were to intervene, I'd much rather the powers go toward more pressing issues.

I still fought with a need to escape. The smell of wine and the images attached to it made me wretch and gag, but I still drank it. They called it PTSD. Trust me, I'm well aware that others hurt and suffered worse than I ever did and for more respectable reasons. I still struggle with the diagnosis, knowing what happened in my family and how most of it eventually ended. Rona, my grandpa, was captured and sent to a German prison camp during WWII. After being rescued, he returned home to Fern in poor health, never fully recovering despite having six more kids, including my mother in about seven years. But those are the things boiled down into events with dates and medals, written in margins of bibles to pass on for the next generation. It's one thing to talk about what we know; how rarely do we share how we feel.

My parents fell into that category. When they met in college, I wonder if my dad told my mom on a date that his father was also a

POW in WWII because I always thought the odds were so rare. Between both of my parents existed centuries of soldiers who fought in almost every major war. Longer still is the list of farmers on homesteads across the Great Plains, and again it's about the struggle for survival that stretches far beyond one person. My mom and dad were young and in love when talks of another war came around, sending them through the motions of what seemed like the right thing to do. My dad enlisted like his dad did. They got engaged like her mom did, simply a sign of the times unless a crisis struck. While he was overseas, my mom received a phone call.

"Mary Ellen? There's been an accident. You need to come home," the family friend began. And as the tragedy unfolded, she learned that her 17-year-old sister drowned at a camp. The grief was overwhelming. Unbearable to the point that after her funeral, no one could talk about Lynette. Her death turned my mother upside down, and months later, when my dad returned, my guess is he was pretty lopsided himself from his own experience. But neither of them talked about it. Maybe they didn't want to, or maybe they didn't know how, somehow sticking it out with the bonding glue of booze. All things considered, my mom and dad were the post-WWII babies of parents who never said a word about war or death or why Mother is crying at the sink.

It's part of my history, a tumbling of troubles without resolution for the frontline veterans returning to farms or towns and the women who lived with them, yet no excuse for my behavior. However, the brightly colored threads of a loaded silence and a need for self-medicating the mind weaved like veins through our family tree down to its roots. We were part of big German and Irish families with lots of kids, countless weddings over generations and with so many relatives, only some of which got hooked along the way. I got it twice, thus the silent alcoholic, a woman still, and what a pain it is to find us on a genealogy map.

Because by the time someone can see us, we're barely recognizable.

What's it like to get to that point? A person might ask. For starters, my newest bottom was different, but we say that every time, don't we? Everyone who's loved an addict has their breaking point, no matter how much love is in the heart. It's self-preservation, a need for survival, that causes our loved ones to step away. The people who cared the most about me, Pete and my children, weren't angry; they were just done. I understood the distance and almost welcomed it, thinking somehow it was better for them that way until the sheer weight of it woke me up.

I sat outside one afternoon as summer came to a close and took a puff off the cigarette I pretended to sneak without the kids knowing. Of course, they knew; they watched everything I did. It was Thursday, school started on Monday with Shelby's senior year and Spenser going to kindergarten. Another circle of this thing—kids going places, and me going nowhere. *Where did the time go?* Because I could easily look up and see Shelby as the kindergartener and me sitting at the same dead end as I was that very day.

Death sat so close to me I felt its breath blow across me in the stagnant humidity. Its presence no longer bothered me. What scared me was not knowing how it would surface. *What do you want from me? When's it going to be?* I felt like asking. Would the death be mine or someone else's, like one of my children? Would I be the cause? Was that my destiny? To rot away somewhere alone? Or was I already dead, and this was hell right here? I couldn't do it. It was as if I had no choice except I had to choose. Zero options, but pick one, goddammit. Drop me in a pool of water and let me sink, although I don't. I didn't have time.

Then, just like all the other times, I confessed it all to Pete. He followed it up by calling places willing to admit me. One might find the urge to say, *Emily, you're already in financial mayhem. You've put your kids through enough. Can't you stay home and get it together by this point?* And, disappointingly, I'd reply, *No, actually, I can't.*

Rehab Seven had a bed for me, ready that night, but I panicked. This wasn't part of my plan. School started Monday and as insignificant as it sounded, I wanted to be there for *them.* Four kids and Stella was the only one I took to her first day of kindergarten because I'd been in rehabs. I didn't want to miss Shelby's last first day or a chance to see Spenser off to his kindergarten classroom. I am, after all, a mother. I begged for a weekend at home and reluctantly my husband and the facility allowed it. But it wasn't easy.

It's one thing to sneak off to drink thinking nobody was watching, but it was something different knowing Pete was aware of it all.

"Where are you going?" he asked me when I got up from the couch toward our bedroom. It was Saturday afternoon. I turned toward him, not wanting to lie.

"To our room for a sec," I said, but he looked so sad.

"Are you going to drink?" he asked, not in a hostile tone but in one where he wanted me to let him in.

"Honey, please don't ask me that," I said softly, because I didn't want to hurt him. He asked again and I said a quiet yes. It was the first time in our marriage Pete and I exchanged an acknowledgment of the monster inside me that tore between us. I felt exposed, Pete was sad, and both of us knew I had zero control to stop myself. There's supposed to be a clear villain here, a bad guy against a good guy, good versus evil the way most stories go, but not that way for us.

The truth is it's only simple when it's generic. Humans and relationships are complicated. We grieved for each other, felt guilty and angry for the kids and none of it had to do with love. We spent the weekend that way, bittersweet companions in the hell they call addiction.

"I don't know why you love me," I said for the thousandth time.

"Honey, I've never stopped loving you, okay? We're going to get through this. It's going to happen," he said, as if it were a promise.

"Okay." I pulled an empty smile to my surface.

On Monday morning, the backpacks were ready, and the lunches were packed. I took one last look around my house, swallowing the waves of tears ready to spill over the picture of normalcy I was trying to paint for those kids. We got in the car, my husband driving, and headed to the school a couple of blocks away.

Focus on the kids, is what I kept telling myself. *God, just get me through this without crying.* Hallway after hallway, at every turn, there was a flood of smiling parents with their best-dressed kids. The excitement was bubbling around me like Christmas morning. I, however, was in a private hell, already feeling the effects of my last drink of wine begin to wear off. I was dizzy, fluctuating between hot and cold with spots in my vision. I looked as sick as I felt so I kept my head down, wearing a fake smile as I looked down at the tops of little heads with fresh haircuts. Fifth grade hall then third grade hall, each girl getting a kiss and a hug while I choked back a lifetime of regrets. I wanted to stay and watch their excitement when friends walked into the classroom, see them nervously find their seat.

Midway down the kindergarten hallway, Spenser confidently let go of my hand and walked into his class. I said goodbye with a little wave and barely caught his attention. It relieved me to see him ease into the room, but I didn't want to let him go. A part of me wanted him to race back toward me with tears in his eyes for a hug from his mother, again and again, but he was fine. So grown up about it. I hung around too long, leaving myself with only seconds until a self-inflicted emotional bomb would explode.

I grabbed Pete's hand as we forced our way through crowds of excitement until we were out the door, where I could break down into his shoulder and finally breathe. The task was done. My life was over.

A bag was already in the trunk of the car. At 3 pm school would get out, but I'd be gone. Pete would be the one to pick them up and tell them where their mother was, and it'd be weeks until we saw each other again.

"You have to promise me you'll do whatever they ask," he said in the gravel parking lot. We stood next to the car, stalling for a minute before we had to separate our lives again. I finished a cigarette and tossed it on the ground, kicking rocks with my shoe to cover it.

"Honey," he said, "we need you."

"I know," I told him. "And I know I've got to do whatever it takes, but what will they want? Do I get no say? What if what they ask is for me to go to sober living for a year? What then?" I thought about how an unlimited willingness was such huge thing to ask of a mother and a wife.

"Can you keep an open mind?" Pete asked, and I promised I would. We told each other I love you a dozen times, but it still wasn't enough when we walked up the steps and opened the doors to what we hoped was the final last time.

To this day, my stomach sinks, remembering the miserable state of not wanting to die and not wanting to live, of longing to feel alive again, yet afraid to feel anything. Another detox unit, another sterile, crisp-sheeted bed to crawl into, roll over, weep and pray for the minutes to fly past me. I wanted a clock or a watch, always wondering what time it was and what the kids were doing. I thought about their faces when they got home from school. I wanted to vomit.

"You okay over there?" came a voice from under the covers in the bed a foot away from me. *Fuck you,* I thought. I didn't want to talk.

"No," I said accidentally, a mechanical response as if my body remembered we're supposed to be honest in places like this and switched over without my permission. The stupid squeak of a word, same as a stupid first sip, and I tried to hold off for another minute, two minutes, three, until loneliness burst out of me. I couldn't stop myself from spilling highlights of my entire life story to this poor stranger, possibly putting her to sleep halfway through.

She just lay there, no response other than to tell me at the end of it all, "Christ, lady. It's gonna be okay."

"No it's not," I said.

"You just got here," she said into her pillow, clearly annoyed. "Give it time."

"What's your name?" I asked like it was an accusation. It was Ingrid. "Well, Ingrid, this isn't my first rodeo."

"Not mine either. Now shut up," she said, and oddly enough, it comforted me. I knew we'd be friends.

Had someone walked into the room and told me, *This here's your problem, you sabotage yourself just to end up in these places and feel like you belong somewhere,* I'd be tempted to believe them. I got what so many of us don't even know we want—a private place to escape the world and find my people, drop the ropes, and come undone. It's too bad it came at such high costs. AA is known to be the last house on the block, but I've been on that street, and the neighborhood had changed. My homegroup had a Facebook page for god's sake.

Inpatient offered a different kind of privacy, although not everyone enjoys it. I went through three young roommates in two weeks, two went back home after calling and complaining, and one tried to run away.

"Why are you so pissed off today?" I asked Ingrid one morning.

"It's the subs, goddamn, I feel like shit," she said. *Suboxone, that's right,* I started to remember as Nancy, another friend, plunked down in a chair next to us.

"What's wrong with you?" Ingrid asked her.

"This is a waste of my time, no seriously, *my money,*" Nancy said. "Why does everyone want me to talk about my fucking mother?"

"Who knows," I said casually. After an awkward silence I asked her, "What's the deal? Did something happen with your mom?" She actually growled at me.

"Yep, you got me, Emily, we just buried her," Nancy told me.

Well, shit, I thought, looking over at Ingrid rolling her eyes at me for opening my mouth in the first place. No one said anything. Ingrid, a mortgage broker from South Carolina with a heroin problem, Nancy with her Oxy's working as a psychotherapist at a prison back east and me, shaking my head at the situation.

"I'm so sorry your mom died," I said while I poked my shoe in the dirt.

"That . . . that's great, thanks," Nancy said.

"Real fucking genius," Ingrid muttered, and I let out a sigh.

For no reason at all, we started snickering. I don't know about the other two, but I genuinely tried to stifle it, which we all know makes it worse. And in minutes we were laughing and coughing from cigarette smoke in the god-awful humid heat. My sides hurt. Time to go inside. It was Friday and my family was visiting the next day.

I casually waited for the family to arrive shortly after lunch, making sure to look my best. Parents and spouses walked through the front door to meet their family member with looks of apprehension, whispering greetings like they were in a library or possibly at a wake. I actually heard my family before I saw them.

"Spenser, no!" said a young girl's voice.

"Wait your turn, there's a line," said Pete.

"Hi, everybody!" I said when they came around the corner, giving hugs and taking a head count to realize Shelby was missing, opting to stay home. "I'm so glad to see you," I said, watching them soak in the scenery of where Mom had been living these past few weeks.

"You look great," Pete said, holding me in an embrace as Stella looked around for the snacks.

"Hey Mom? Can I get a cookie?" she asked, and in no time, we hovered around a table eating cookies and sneaking into the back of the cafeteria for fountain drinks of juice. Long gone were my expectations that the kids would be on their best behavior or that I needed to cram multiple days of love and affection into a matter of minutes. They got bored now, and it didn't hurt my feelings when they wanted to leave before the time limit.

Rebecca and Stella took turns walking around a little pond with me in the blazing late summer heat, each of them feeling extraordinarily important with every stride for having their mother to themselves. How appallingly simple it was what they wanted, attention, affection, value, time, versus my self-destructive insistence that I do the impossible and rewrite the past so I could be everything and then some. Why are we killing ourselves if it isn't even what they want? The motherhood question of *what am I doing to them?* had become a question of *what am I doing to myself?* Because there, surrounded by misfits where I fit in, it seemed foolish to try so hard to be the opposite of the me I was just starting to enjoy.

Spenser sat next to me on the sidewalk playing in a bed of landscaping stones. He was in a rock-collecting phase, picking out certain ones to stuff in his pockets for me to discover when I did his laundry.

"Mom, I have to keep this one, can I? It's a potato rock," he said, holding up an average brown, sort of potato-shaped rock. "It's very special."

"Sure, but just one, okay?" Thankfully, he agreed. "How is kindergarten? Do you like your teacher?" I asked him. And of course, he loved her. All the kids adored their kindergarten teachers. He didn't seem all that interested in my questions. Instead, he rambled on for ten minutes about playing dinosaurs at recess and a dream he had with a blue monster who stole all the cereal. The whole time he talked with his little lisp, drool glistening on his chin the more animated and faster he spoke, and I stared at him feeling arrows of shame and despair slice through me, splitting my attention with the thought of *God, why? Why did it take so long, and why did my innocent kids have to suffer? They deserved so much better.* I knew the sound of dominoes falling across a mother's mind and picked up the potato rock.

"You know what, Spenser?" I finally said. "I really miss you."

He stopped mid-sentence, turning to me with his adorable face. His whole demeanor shifted into a look of complete confusion. If he wasn't so innocent, the poor guy seemed astonished his mother could say something so dumb.

"Mom," he said emphatically, "I'm right here."

I froze. Speechless. That was it, the burning bush, my bright light moment came down to a handful of words exchanged with my five-year-old that would stick with me forever. No strings attached. To Spenser, I was just his mom sitting next to him listening to his stories.

"You're absolutely right, Spenser. Thanks for reminding me," I said, snapping into the present. A solid hit between the eyes with a long-forgotten notion that forgiveness, at its purest, kept no record of wrongdoing. Still, it boggled my mind, thinking if I asked God again to forgive me, he'd look at me with the same confused face as Spenser's and say, "Emily, I have no idea what you're talking about." Humans, however, aren't God. We're going to remember, but I saw the space inside of forgiveness where our past mistakes were stored in a memorial, a remembrance of the past.

During the years in these places and programs, not once had I sat through a lecture or group discussion on self-forgiveness. It sounded like the easy way out. Moms like me deserve punishment, don't we? Once the story of our past gets out and people see us enjoying life and having fun again, will they be happy for us? It's not easy, is it? The whole forgive-and-forget plan. Sometimes, the best we can do is choose one or the other, but other times, we don't get a choice. I'd never forget. We can't. But at that moment, I felt the beginning of it. Change can come so quickly it's easy to mistrust it. Other times, like that moment, we innately understand we're incapable of returning to who we were before. I held hands with a depth of pain and always would, but its grip felt different once the threat of death was over.

I started to come alive again that day.

Before my bags were packed and it was time to go, I talked out loud for the first time about what happened that spring night when I was 19 years old. I didn't want to, and it would not change anything, but it was the one thing left I'd never done. Rape was a common topic, another tragic way for institutionalized women to form connections and feel understood, and I wanted no part of it. Was that my pride? My ego? Maybe, but I also didn't want to give the experience one second of my breath, like eventually, maybe, it might suffocate itself to death.

"I had no idea I was still this emotional," I told them, hands shaking. "It's . . . rage." I refused offers of tissues or a hug. I didn't hear the feedback, or maybe I did, and it just didn't sink in enough to remember. Ingrid was already gone, kicked out for losing her temper too many times. She relapsed the same week after finding out the neighbor taking care of her daughter refused to give her back. It didn't help the situation when she discovered her former drug dealer took her Volvo while she'd been gone and returned it with bullet holes, but she went back to the exact same chaos she tried to escape. I understood my friend, even if I hated it.

"You wanted to see me?" I asked the man in charge of setting up my aftercare plan as he sat behind a desk on my last day. I'd been there three times already, and each time, he showed me local sober living houses I was encouraged to commit to for a year. This appointment was no different.

"Based on your history, Emily, it's clear why we all have concerns about you going home," he said. I told him I understood his point, loud and clear. I kept thinking about my conversation with Pete in the parking lot on Day One, saying I'd be willing to do whatever they asked me to do.

"Look, I hear you. In a perfect world, sure, but have you looked at the cost to stay at these houses? We can't afford it and there's no money for childcare either. Plus, the residents must be gone until after five o'clock because it's required to have a job. Sir, I already have a job. I'm a mother," I said. The man was making me mad.

"You'd need an actual job. It's the smartest thing for you to do," he said.

"I'm not doing it," I said.

"I'll have to put that in your paperwork," he told me, like a threat made to a child.

My assigned counselor was less than thrilled, her parting words an omen that caught me off guard like an unexpected slap.

"I don't feel good about you," she said. My mouth hung open at the audacity. She'd done her job for long enough to know who'd make it and who'd more than likely relapse again.

"Wow, that's nice to hear," I said sarcastically, shaking my head.

"I hope I'm wrong, but I think you're making big mistakes, Emily," she said. I didn't find it necessary to defend myself as I left her office and said a few more goodbyes. I certainly wasn't waving flags of confidence. I'd done enough reentries to know there were no guarantees, especially knowing that homecoming meant resuming family roles and responsibilities within the space of my fragile sobriety. And all at the crime scene surrounded by my victims.

Each day when I walked into my bedroom, Stella followed me with Spenser and Becca close behind her. I put clothes away, turned around, and they followed me down the hall like little ducklings. When I opened the garage door to throw away a trash bag, the whole family showed up instantly, then acted like it was a coincidence. I couldn't make a move without someone watching me. I knew why; they didn't trust me out of their sight, but still it pissed me off. Then came the questions, like every other time I was new in sobriety.

"What did you do today? Where did you go?" the kids asked me after school and if I was out of sight for more than five minutes.

"Hi, what's happening?" Pete asked when he called at least a dozen times a day.

After two weeks, I started to notice just how agitated I actually was. I needed space. I needed something that was all mine that no one could touch or take away from me. Something else besides wife, mother, and someone trying not to be a drunk.

"Dinner!" I hollered through the house.

The witching hour, as I called it, arrived again with kids digging deep into their sparkling personalities to bring out the very worst they could find. Pull a hair from my head and that was the string I was hanging from when Pete walked in the door and announced he wasn't hungry because of his late lunch. I still loved that all six of us had dinners together, with a system in place to talk one at a time and share about our days. Interruptions and minor bickering aside, I took a deep breath to acknowledge the drink I didn't need.

Later, I stood at the sink scrubbing a glass dish with caked-on tuna casserole, kids scurrying around in the same after-dinner burst of energy that used to drive my parents crazy.

"Guys, guys! It's too much," I tried to say as a warning to all of us, but the words did no good. Put the same meal on a different table and my dad would have hollered from the TV room, "Hey! Knock it off!" And maybe even further in time and place, it was Rona giving Fern a kiss on the cheek, whispering *don't wait up,* to the sound of six pairs of busy little feet on his way out the door to the tavern.

So what's it going to be? Me, standing within mere centimeters of a tripwire poised to blow up the whole damn house with one wrong step, and what? *Don't start a fight. Don't cause a scene or scare the kids, just keep it in,* I thought to myself. It seemed easier, and yet, no. The feeling of concrete in my chest and my head about to explode reminded me silence isn't as simple as we'd like to pretend it is. Just a short while ago, I would have found a quiet way to drink, then spend the rest of the evening keeping a nonchalant distance from everyone. Thinking about that woman . . . it was me but not me now. The whole thing scared me. I needed to get out of the house.

What I wanted that night was similar relief, but I sought it out with visions of a chair and conversation.

"I need to go to a meeting," I blurted out, then more gently said to Pete, "Is that okay with you?"

"Tonight? But you already went to a meeting," he said.

"I know I did, but I just need a break for an hour," I said, assuming I looked like a cornered feral cat by the way he stared at me.

"What?" I asked.

"I don't think it's a good idea. Why don't you just call someone? Why do you have to *leave*?" he asked.

"It's a meeting. I'm doing the thing I'm supposed to do when I feel like this," I said. We stared at each other and had a wordless conversation, until eventually he asked if he could breathalyze me when I got home.

"*Sure*," I said, seething. And I left.

"Call me on your way home!" he hollered as I walked out the door.

The sun was setting on the highway for my twenty-minute drive as I rolled down the windows and turned up the radio to drown out my horribly loud singing. Why was I crying? I wanted to be angry, that was it. *Fuck you*, I said. Then I said it again, fcstcring on that intoxicating power of a pissed off state of mind. Can I make a confession? I talk to myself in the car, which isn't all that unheard of, but I do it with the sense that there are two of me living in the same body. So with the wind whipping through my hair, Eminem lyrics going way too fast for me to keep up with, and angry tears streaming down my face, I heard the words *you earned this*.

"I earned this?" And it was me telling myself, *Just stop. Yeah, dummy, you did.* Picture the pent-up irritation and resentment toward my family after all the lies and let-downs, ultimate disasters I put them through. What right did I have to expect my family to trust me? Why would anyone in their right mind trust me when I always let them down? I used to say that I cried when I was angry but, at that moment, I cried because I was in pain. I lost the buffer to blur my view.

And that's the thing. I've never been a runner in the actual sense of the word, but if we're talking about how miserable a person looks pushing through the last mile of a marathon, uphill, then sure, I was a runner; from what, I never really knew. That night, I woke up but not from a prince's kiss in some fairy tale or from God who suddenly decided to wash the nightmare clean. Like a haunting, I had an awareness that the past was catching up to me, in the car on the run from myself. One day at a time is bullshit when we're given these tiny moments to make a choice. If I didn't do something drastic, history would suck me back in.

I went to the AA meeting, came directly home afterward and used a breathalyzer to prove I didn't drink. It felt like what I imagined was the beginning of dignity or self-respect.

Hush, little baby, I had to. It all sounds so wrongly poetic, but starting over is dramatic.

CHAPTER NINETEEN

2020–

Was it over? Not all of it, but the worst of it? There, parked at the school twenty minutes early with the engine turned off, so quiet and calm, as I felt the sun coming in through my windshield. It'd been on my mind, peeping out from the covers.

I'd been stalling. Dawdling around the last few months, moments actually, like they were my dying breaths. Not just a last chance, but a last chance to get it RIGHT, to nail it like a perfect ten. It was this sobriety, where to quit was to stop, and to stop was to die. Only when I wrote it down did I see the humor in it. I'm such an enthusiast overreactor, I thought to myself, referring to one of the many names I'd been given from some psych test. I liked the term. It made me smile how results from a mental evaluation sounded like requirements for cheerleader tryouts. Still, I felt a tug at the back of my neck, as if to say *watch out,* and I was scared. Not of the usual doldrums that repeatedly got attention, but of the minuscule things I didn't yet know existed.

I wasn't used to all the empty space after everyone was gone for the day. The sudden stillness of my house made me think the whole world was out doing something important. Opening the window blinds to let in the sunlight, I wrote *I hate dusting* with my finger through a layer of dust and sat on the couch, lost on where to start.

As a so-called homemaker who hated cooking and cleaning, I wandered from room to room unwilling to commit to a task.

I decided not to do any of it.

The first months of sobriety were difficult, no matter how many times I'd done it. That's the physical nature of the beast we call addiction, where alcohol called the shots. Afterward, I strapped myself into recovery mode knowing it was far from over and thought of everything else that had to go. All the secrets and lies, my obsession with sneaking, hiding and buying wine, then the full-time performance of pretending I was doing just fine. The ongoing list of another life, one where addiction made me capable of anything headed in the wrong direction, felt powerful and apologetic at the same time. *Exhausting,* I thought, remembering, and checked the time. I walked across the parking lot to stand with the other parents in front of the school. At precisely 3:37 pm, Pharrell's "Happy" blasted from the loudspeaker above us, the front doors opened, and a swarm of kids barreled out, some of them wearing backpacks that skimmed the back of their knees. I found three smiling faces headed my way. Whatever kind of day I'd been having, it immediately improved.

"Mom, please, *please,* can we go to the playground today?" Stella asked the second she reached me, pushing Spenser aside while he showed me his day's workload. "Just for a little while? All my friends are going." Her hands were clasped in prayer for a miracle since we'd been twice already that week. I got distracted, though, and couldn't think of an excuse on the spot.

"Fine." I surrendered, and she took off running. "Just for a few minutes!" I added, watching Spenser tag along behind her. I turned to Becca, who wanted to go home, too, and promised we wouldn't stay long as the two of us walked around the school to the playground together.

"How was your day?" I asked her.

"Boring," she said, then told me about schoolwork and the boys' insufferable body odor now that the weather was getting warmer.

"Did you have a good day?" she asked, changing topics.

"I sure did," I said. "Just the usual." I smiled. Her long hair was pulled back in a bun on top of her head, making it easy for me to see her face soften as she gave me a nod. Becca, like her siblings, found comfort in the routine I followed every day while they were at school. They liked the security of knowing I left the house at a specific time and went to a meeting at noon, came home for lunch and most importantly, I'd be waiting at school to greet them at the end of their day. Monday through Friday, it rarely changed. Pete, at the office five days a week for nine or ten hours a day, was in his own familiar routine.

I heard my phone ring from inside my bag while I scanned for a place to sit down, motioning Becca to go play.

"Hey, Mom, what's up?" I said.

"Oh! Where are you?" I briefly filled her in. "Well, I'm actually calling about Daisy," she said, referring to her beloved dog with a sigh. "Something's not right, I've never seen her sick like this."

Daisy used to be mine—a bulldog puppy Shelby and I got when we lived in an apartment—who'd grown into a well-loved member of our family.

"Oh, God. I hope it's nothing major, Mom. I'm so sorry. Keep me posted," I said, and she promised she would before hanging up.

Stella dashed past me with a pack of girls in tow engaged in a game of boys and girls chasing each other. As I watched them play, part of me envisioned Daisy, infuriatingly stubborn at times with a personality suitable for a carnival act, running along with her in one of her wild frenzies after a backyard escape. *Daisy.* All the history attached to that dog. After my second divorce, the impractical, irrational decision of buying a puppy for Shelby and it was one of the most joyous and liberating events I'd had in years. The freedom of choice. Her squishy face and pudgy little body romping around on a picnic blanket next to barefooted Shelby with her hair in pigtails was engraved in the golden glow of memories from my first time in sobriety.

But I didn't think it through or didn't know how to handle the weight of it all. When everything fell apart, the apartment, my job, finances, sobriety, poor Daisy fell with it, like I'd stupidly bought a present for myself but couldn't afford it.

Fortunately, my mother could, but the weight was still with me.

"Ten minutes!" I hollered to Stella, the next time she ran past me. The kids were a welcome distraction as I watched Spenser disappear into a tunnel slide. I called it my bookend year with him as a kindergartner on one end and Shelby as a senior in high school on the other. It was a new phase of motherhood, reminding me how fast the time goes by, even though half an hour at the playground could feel like forever. I felt the four o'clock fatigue creeping in.

Most of my energy went toward the nonstop focus of reprogramming into a sober person. Every day, I wrestled with the need to be responsible, earn back trust, and hold a steady line in a life that normally pulled me under or overwhelmed me. Still, I couldn't help it, I wanted something more for myself, picturing the idea squeezed between the pressure of the time and space of a family. If I could do anything, what would it be? What sounded exciting? It felt wrong, like another fight with selfishness, trying to prioritize myself inside a mother-brain that scolded me for even being on the list. I heard the murmur of rational attempts to inject heroics with the airplane analogy, picturing myself putting my own oxygen mask on first so I can save the kids, when actually, we were all desperate for air. Even my mom was caught in it, breathless in her own way, where the threat of death and loss was always nearby. A sick daughter, a sick dog. And a history that whispered a tragedy was close by.

But not everything needed to be shared with the people in my life. Telling someone I felt different with this sobriety, for example, was a terrible idea. Entertaining the thought I'd never drink again was equally awful but quietly, I did both. Not to panic. The thought of a drink caused the bile to rise in my stomach with immediate scenes of my own funeral. All day long, every breath I took focused on staying right where I was, alive, and each night I'd lie awake counting those breaths until I could fall asleep. Somewhere deeply hidden was the dark idea that no matter what, if things got bad enough, painful enough, tragic enough, alcohol could save me. It was a muscle memory inside me, *In case of emergency, break glass. Drink.* And everything centered on destroying the thought so I could survive. More than a sobriety date, August 22 radiated with a terrifying hope, a kind where the longer I stayed sober, the more it rumbled beneath me.

"Can you pick up my dry cleaning tomorrow?" Pete mentioned casually after dinner one night as I walked into our bathroom. He had started the shower for Spenser, nineties hip hop pumping through his portable speaker as I set down a stack of clean towels.

"Shit," I said under my breath. "I forgot again, sorry. I'll get it tomorrow, promise," I said. "By the way, Stella asked about a sleepover on Friday, but I told her no. She's got a soccer game."

"What team is she playing?" he asked. Spenser bolted through the bedroom already undressed, tossed his pajamas on our bed and started a funny dance in front of the bathroom mirror. "Hey Pup! Water's ready." Pete opened the shower door.

"Are these clean?" I took a sniff and picked clothes off the floor, then mentioned a random team, "Bumblebees."

"No, we played them already," he said, then turned toward the shower, "Yes, Spenser, you have to use soap." I shrugged my shoulders.

"I can't remember," I said, my voice suddenly drowned out by Stella's hysterical laughter seeing her brother pressing his bottom cheeks against the shower glass. My subtle hand signal to Pete told him to cut the music, overloaded by his impromptu song in his opera voice about Moons Over My Hammy, our favorite Denny's breakfast.

"Honey, seriously?" I said to him, trying to stay calm, then I turned to the kids. "All right, c'mon guys."

Afterward, like most nights, we all got in my bed lined up like a package of hotdogs to watch a recorded episode of *Arthur* on PBS. All four kids in pajamas somehow tucked around me with their wet hair in perfect stillness, my body began to relax from the soothing fragrance of clean and tired children.

It looked so normal. Meaning *average*, as in, no big deal or not that special compared to other families. We fell somewhere inside the enormity of the middle, between exemplary and unsatisfactory. Anybody walking through our front door would agree they saw the same thing. Our family of six moved forward each day filling up the calendar with volleyball and soccer games, appointments and drill team practices. I kept up with all of it, along with my own routine, watching my feet take one step then another, making sure I looked away each day when we drove past places like the grocery store where I stole the wine or my stay at the discreet redbrick building disguising a mental hospital. Those sights were too much, too soon for me.

And then, the page flipped over to a new month of empty squares waiting for us to do it all over again.

Undoubtedly, my history stayed on everyone's mind. They all remembered what I'd put them through. My sobriety date didn't come with a Best Mom Ever badge, nor should it. Memories were everywhere, in any direction for miles, and I watched the kids like weather maps to forecast what they needed. What did they remember? Did it bother them to see the Mother's Day display covered with wine bottles, or shirts and mugs with jokes about moms drinking? I didn't know what to expect and was afraid to ask questions, fearing I'd bring up something they'd forgotten.

It was different with Pete, who remembered everything. He was a walking encyclopedia of data who seemed to have a second brain exclusively for sports knowledge and amazingly had something in common with every person he met. He remembered more about my life than I did. It unnerved me how he carried a catalog of my memories.

"Hey Mom, remember when you died?" Spenser asked me one day after an ambulance drove by, buckled in his booster in the back seat of the car. I turned down the music.

"What honey?" I must have heard him wrong. His little voice asked the question again, *"Remember when you died?"* So simple the way he said it, cocking his head forward when he spoke. The punch in my gut. I froze, the slight pause between two seconds, and flashed to what I imagined must have been running through his memory. The sight of me falling hard to the floor of the kitchen out of nowhere; a three-year-old watching Mommy's body shaking in spasms, but she won't get up. Him screaming. Running with his sisters out the front door wailing, "My mommy's dying!" A rush of neighbors he didn't know and the ambulance at our house that took his mom away.

Quickly, I told him, "Yes, I remember what you're talking about, but I never died, Spenser. It was called a seizure, remember?"

"No, you died." He said it with a matter-of-factness to emphasize, *I was there, Mom. I saw you.*

Four o'clock in busy traffic, unsure of what to say and goddammit. *Do we have to talk about this* was my first thought. *I'm a different mom now, that was years ago,* I wanted to tell him. Spenser didn't want the generic answer parents reach for when a question strikes a nerve. *Mommy's all better and you have nothing to worry about* wasn't going to work.

"Honey, listen, okay? I'm being serious. I am so, so sorry that happened and you had to see me like that. I know it was super scary," I said with my eyes on the road, waiting for him to respond, but he didn't. "When somebody dies, their heart stops and their brain stop and so does every other part of their body, so it's dead, dead. Like forever. It's just a body of nothing. And the person goes off, you know, to heaven, and it's so wonderful."

You sound ridiculous, I told myself.

"Here's the important part. What you saw happen to me was

something different called a seizure, and it happened in my brain. It got all mixed up and confused, maybe like a robot when its wires get crossed and weird stuff happens. I think you can even see it happen with special cameras but I'm not sure," I said, realizing I might have gone too far with that last part.

I checked the rearview mirror and saw him looking out the window and told him, "That's what it was and why the ambulance came. To help me and get my brain back on track. But it's better now, okay?"

He was quiet, thinking over what I said. "Is it going to happen again?" he asked.

"No, honey, *God, no.* It's not," I told him confidently. "I'm all healthy. You won't ever have to see your mom like that again, okay?"

We finally made eye contact through the rearview mirror, and I flashed him a big smile. Relief passed across his face and a smile beamed back at me.

"Okay, Mom," he said, and went back to gazing out the window. "But I still don't like ambulances."

"That's perfectly fine."

My grip loosened on the steering wheel when we pulled onto our street, but I had no idea what to think of our talk. No mother wants to screw up and say the wrong thing.

I was 42 years old that day, a mother almost half my life and still, as I scrolled through filed stacks of information in my head to answer simple questions from a five-year-old, I came up blank. I needed someone else to assess, suggest, or instruct how to do it, then point out my mistakes. I pulled into the driveway wondering, *Did I pass the assignment? Do I get the stamp of approval? Did I do something wrong?* I still yearned for a pat on head as assurance.

"I'm gonna race you!" Spenser hollered before unbuckling and bursting out of the car. I took off after him following his trail of laughter into the house and tried to leave the rest behind.

Eventually, I walked outside to back porch, sat down and took a deep breath. The far-off stare on my face resulted from thinking everything or thinking nothing. I couldn't tell the difference. For some reason, I believed if I sat still enough, then a single thread could make its way to my ears, and I'd hear it. Or if I focused hard enough, I'd see a line of understanding. I looked across the suburban skyline of our HOA color-approved rooftops and wondered, *Now what?*

It's hard to do things differently when I felt like everything different had already been done. *What am I supposed to do with all of this?* I thought to myself. *Who would want to sit and listen to me unpack all this?* Nonsense questions swam in my head until suddenly, I started to wonder who I was asking. Myself? You? God? As a self-reminder, I used to sit outside my old apartment a dozen lifetimes ago and talk to God in the branches of trees, thinking I'd gone crazy. I was a genuine believer until it got impossible to squeeze myself into the same answers I'd been getting since sixth grade Sunday school. Regardless, I sensed something, like an old friend was close by.

"We don't have much to say, do we?" My whisper sliced a narrow gap toward someone I used to know, and after a moment I sighed. "And it feels like you left me."

Because it seemed like there was an understanding between us. I was tired of trying to follow rules and feeling like I had to clean up my act before I even mentioned the word "God." Like times I spent an hour dolling up my feet before I dared to get a pedicure at a nail salon. I couldn't tell you what caused me to blurt out, "I have to fire you, God." Only that restarts and fresh starts never worked. I wanted to *start.* Just the two of us, somewhere quiet enough where we could hear one another. "Is that possible?" I whispered, slightly bracing myself in the silence for a giant hole to open up in the yard and send me straight to hell. But nothing came.

I kept waiting, sitting long enough for the silence to bend its sharp edges and my anxious posture to relax into the chair. A breeze swayed high in the branches of our neighbor's tree. Its limbs stretched over our wooden fence, like arms reaching out for a handshake. It'd been twenty years since the nights alone on my apartment patio, little Shelby fast asleep, watching for leafy branches to wave in the wind and send me a sign. I closed my eyes, feeling the fresh air brush across my face, and a calm came over me. *Hello,* I heard it say. I smiled thinking, *Hello, it's nice to meet you again,* then I went inside. It was time to start making dinner.

Still, it felt like I found a starting point. By accident or not, I pictured myself stumbling on a half-buried tent stake, the metal kind my dad would hammer into the ground for our 1970s Coleman canvas tent, poles like aluminum scaffolding, so it didn't collapse on our campsite. Possibly a leftover from his Army days and if you're one of the fortunate who remembers, those iron bad boys might take the strength of two adults to pry one back out of the dirt.

So, one could say I discovered exactly what I needed—a sturdy anchor tethering me to a spot marked *start here.* The simplicity drew me in, not once feeling a need for elaborate descriptions of God, only to say every one of us were idiots by comparison. Images were meaningless as I started on a new path, unencumbered by directions or destinations. It was the only thing I trusted. However, just because it made sense didn't mean those who loved me would agree with it.

Years ago when I lived in Utah, I'd hang out with my friend Melanie, another Texas transplant. While we sat around drinking Dr. Peppers and reminiscing about the Lonestar state, I'd occasionally ask her about those secret things they did in her church. Melanie gave me quite an education. To a point.

"Come on, is it really that big of a secret?" I asked about a particular rumor I'd heard.

"No, not *secret,* Emily," she corrected me. "It's *sacred.* That's the word they tell us to use—sacred—so it sounds more . . . religious." I never forgot how clever I thought that was. Parts of my recovery were sacred enough to remain private, too fragile yet for public viewing.

That night, I grabbed a box of crackers and my little notebook and got in bed early to write some things down. *Am I too late?* The pen hovered over the question's enormity. *It's like the kids grew up and I missed the whole thing. I hate feeling like time goes too fast.* I stopped and thought about all the things I tossed aside with the attitude, *I'll deal with it later,* as if there'd come a time when life would slow down enough for me to catch up. And now, getting crumbs on the sheets, I realized later had arrived. Suddenly, someday was now.

Sobriety came with its own pressures. It was a balancing act between my peculiar strategies to changes I needed to make and a family that relied on the conventional, systematic approach. Even the kids knew how it worked, often reciting a quote for a laugh. Another epic fail at cooking a pot roast, *Keep coming back, it works if you work it.* Road trips guaranteed one mutual meltdown after ten hours in the car and someone muttering the serenity prayer. But like a lot of things in our culture, there was an unspoken right way of doing things . . . a concept that "more" kept someone safe, even recovered them. The kids knew that part, too.

Thus, I got more involved. A preemptive block of pleasing and appeasing was partly what it was. I loved my friends but wanted something from a different universe, beyond a recovery group or housework and caretaking. As important as it was for me to cut loose from old habits, I needed a beacon leading me somewhere new.

I thought about the anchor, even saying out loud, "Show me what I'm supposed to see," and slowly, I followed forgotten loves, renewing my passion for art and music, poetry and good books. I made space a few nights after family dinners to slip off to a coffee shop and write in journals while Pete took over at home while I tried to find a balance.

"Hey, I'm home," I said, peeking my head out the back door one night and seeing Pete still smoking a cigar. "How'd it go with the kids?"

"Fine," he said, sounding annoyed as I sat down next to him, still holding the car keys. "How was your night?" he asked me.

"So great, honey. I wrote some crappy poems and looked up song lyrics, stuff like that, but it was good to get out. Thanks again, by the way." Pete didn't say much other than he was happy to hear it went well. "Are you coming inside soon?" I asked him.

"Yeah, in a little while." I sighed from another short answer. *What had I done now?* I wondered, afraid to ask. Pete kept watching the show on the screen. I sat there, a third wheel, and decided to go inside.

"Oh, I almost forgot," I said. "Some ladies invited me for coffee Saturday morning, so I told them I could go. It's at Sarah's house, somewhere in Plano before the women's meeting, but I'll skip that." He looked at me, confused. "Is that okay?"

"On a Saturday?" He turned and looked at me, shaking his head with disapproval. "No, not really. Weekends should be for family, don't you think? You do enough meetings during the week. And I want time with my wife."

"Sure, but it's a one-time thing," I explained, "And I thought you'd be happy since it's women. You're the one who said I should try to find some sober women friends."

"Look, don't turn this around on me. Go if you want to, but don't blame me. I'll figure it out," he huffed.

"No, that's not what I'm saying—"

"Is it such a bad thing that we want you around?" he asked me, "What's so wrong with a husband wanting to spend time with his wife?" Tears welled up in my eyes at his words, and I stopped speaking. My sobriety came first, but only when it wasn't too disruptive. My body folded again. I had enough of crying over it and said everything I could that night, but for once, I didn't beg.

How do we know we made it? That we're finally where things will be okay, and it's enough? And at what point are we allowed to lift our face off the floor without the fear of it all pushing us back under? When can I exhale the tightness in my chest? The questions looked like trick candy, so enticing the way they swirled around me in technicolor until I started wondering why I still needed permission. It exhausted me.

It was late, an hour until midnight when my mom called, and I assumed she had a quick question until I heard her voice.

"I'm at the emergency vet. It's not good, Emily. Daisy's in pain," she said. "I need . . . we're going to put her to sleep." It sounded like she'd been crying for hours.

"What? Oh my god, Mom. I'm so sorry. Are you alone?" I peppered her with questions before I slowed down. "What do you need?" I asked her, getting the usual answer.

"Nothing, nothing. I just wanted to call and tell you. I know it's late," but I interrupted.

"Mom, stop, it's okay. And anyway, you're just as important as everyone else in this family," I said. "I can be there in ten minutes. Do you want me to come and meet you there?"

"You know, yes," she said after a long pause, and I was on my way. I told Pete what was happening before leaving.

He bolted out of his chair. "Yeah, go. She needs you," he said without hesitation. And I was gone.

After giving a quiet knock on the exam room door, I walked in and Daisy slowly lifted her head from the table, my mother's arm wrapped lovingly around her loyal friend as she looked at me with red, swollen eyes.

"Emily."

"Hi, Mom," I said, sliding an extra chair over to sit next to her. I rubbed her back in gentle circles while we put a hand on our furry friend to gently soothe her.

She and I were quiet in our thoughts, as if communicating telepathically what words spoken out loud could never encapsulate the experience of Daisy herself, or what it felt like to sit there and wait. We watched her, resting our cheeks on her soft fur and thinking of how to say goodbye. I mentioned all the happiness she gave us and how we'd always remember her.

"I'm sorry, Daisy," my mother softly said. "You were a *good* dog, a *good* girl." Which was true despite Daisy's tendency to poop in forbidden places or terrify strangers with an overzealous greeting. We loved every ridiculous, affectionate thing about that dog. It's what made her a good dog. It's what made her Daisy.

I grabbed more tissues from the counter and handed one to my mother. How long had we been there? A strangeness settled into the room after saying our goodbyes, one where we watched the door and waited for a lifeless dog. The two of us whispered back and forth, *Is she breathing? I can't tell. Should I get the vet? He said he'd come back. What if they forgot we're in here? I doubt it. Go listen to her chest. Fine.* We didn't want to wake her. Deep down, I thought the whole clinic could at least stop to give a moment of silence and honor the dead. Instead, there was a knock on the door, a conversation with the vet, and a nightshift technician leaving the room with a dead dog wrapped in a sheet.

Years before, my mom called me after her mother, Fern, died when I lived in North Carolina. Losing a loved one is always difficult, but the depth of sorrow I heard in my mom's voice was a grief much different than our night together at the vet clinic. The phone line filtered out the frayed nerves of a sleep-deprived postpartum daughter desperately trying not to drink that day, but still, I wanted so badly to squeeze out a sliver of myself and give it to her. Shelby was eleven years old, Becca and Stella were four and two, and Spenser only a few weeks old. Pete was back to working long hours, and again, I tried to hold the whole thing together while struggling privately in alcoholism's relentless vice grip.

I couldn't carry my mother's grief; I could barely carry my newborn son.

And now, I felt the painful clarity of knowing she never asked me to carry a single thing. Beyond the polished conversations about alcohol use disorders are the quiet places many of us don't want to talk about. They're the ones where I still remember the immeasurable shame I felt on certain days when I longingly watched the phone in my hand ring with the tender word "Mom" signaling my incoming caller, and I did not answer.

But now, she and I walked together to the parking lot to embrace and talked for a while before I headed home, driving under streetlights and getting lost in my thoughts. Staring out my windshield, I pictured my mother crying and suddenly noticed the absence of my usual nauseating guilt. I realized for the first time in ages, I wasn't the source of her sadness, the reason for her tears. If anything, I was her support and strength.

I gave her something good, this tiny message came out of nowhere, a light on my darkened drive. Somehow, in all the uncomfortable confusion, I knew I was headed in the right direction. But more than that, so was Daisy herself. I wasn't fixated on how I dumped off on someone else, more that she was loved, and we got to say goodbye. This time, when it was hard, I stayed.

It's funny how I wanted recognition for decent behavior, wishing I'd see a thumbs-up in a childlike way. I was accustomed to someone else offering me an assessment, and I'd take it from there rather than listen to my gut. My need for control, what it really was, reminded me of a different exchange with my mother. Before a holiday celebration at her house, my stubborn attitude and micromanaging eventually caused her to explode on me, "Emily! Can't you just be an *observer* for once?"

The idea, now, meant doing nothing when life seemed to scream at me for action.

I began to learn a foreign language, listening to its linguistics and separating it from other voices. All the talking. I'd miss the snapping sound that sent an insatiable urge to get out of my skin, rage or bawl my eyes out, hide somewhere or run from the panic, but instead, I was learning pausing, breathing. Working on it, I already knew "this too shall pass," but it didn't help at the moment. All those obscenities of polished advice to call someone, count my gratitudes, downward fucking dog. *This is when I drink. In case of emergency.* There it was. But somehow, I softly reminded myself that no, we weren't doing that today.

It was raining the night I drove to my favorite coffee shop, deciding on the way to do an assignment related to recovery before starting my other projects. *Just get it over with,* I thought, thinking more about reading some old poetry of mine I found and little essays I was writing happy to be free from obligations at home for a couple of hours.

"There you are," said my favorite barista with a friendly smile on her face. "I was wondering if you'd make it out tonight."

I said hello, deciding to wait before I ordered a coffee, and glanced toward my usual corner. The empty chair next to a man using my space like a portable office almost made me want to head for the door. Such a territorial creature of habit, but I plunked down anyway, pulling a notebook out of my canvas bag with a bright yellow rehab logo emblazoned on one side.

I'll be finished in less than an hour, I thought, and methodically started to write out the harms I'd done since the last time I'd done one of those lists. At first, only a few things came to mind. Sheets of paper for different people, all the pages written in my sloppy handwriting. It wasn't the first time to know what I'd done. We talk about those things all the time with other alcoholics. Still, I kept writing until all of it was out, then decided to go home early.

The minute I stepped out the back door to our backyard, a thick heat wrapped around air-conditioned goosebumps. Pete sat in his usual spot puffing a cigar on a late night when the humid temperature outside still lingered at 92 degrees. I loved it.

"Nice to see you out here," he said with a twinkle in his eyes. "I thought you were headed to bed."

"No, not yet," I sighed, sitting next to him in a folding chair, waving off a puff of smoke. "Hey, guess what? God talked to me in my car today," I said, grinning. It seemed like a good conversation starter.

"Really? Not sure it works that way," he said lightheartedly, shaking his head, "but maybe." Pete shrugged. "What did he say?"

I changed my mind; I didn't want to tell him.

"Never mind," I said. It felt combative between us, and maybe it came from me. A triggered reaction set off in my nervous system that didn't pertain to Pete personally, or maybe it was a sense he'd be critical about what I had to say, I didn't know. It didn't feel safe to talk about God, not the way it used to, but I stayed outside, both of us sitting in the quiet for a while.

I had something else on my mind.

"So, actually," I said, slowly breaking the silence. "There's another thing I wanted to talk about."

Instantly, he was looking at me with alarm.

"What's wrong?" he asked me.

"Nothing's wrong. I don't know," I started to say. "I mean, yes. I do know. But it's nothing bad."

Pete looked ready to pounce before I could finish my sentence.

"What happened? Did you get hurt out there? Is it about drinking?" He fired questions off, one after another, before I could respond.

"God, I hate it when you do that," I was finally able to reply.

"Emily, you have to be honest, tell me," he said. "Did you buy alcohol? Is it something else? A guy? What is it?"

Stop doing this to me! I wanted to scream. His accusations and suspicions backing me against a wall were the main reason I shut down our first conversation. Over a year had passed since my last drink. For the first time, I was genuinely changing in a positive direction, moving forward in more ways than just sobriety, and I wasn't going back. Pete needed to loosen his grip, and it seemed like the harder I pulled on it, the tighter it got.

"You're going to lose me," I said with a calm certainty. When he didn't understand what I meant, I asked him, "Why do you think I'm sitting out here? For *this*?"

"How am I supposed to know what's going on if you won't talk to me?" Pete asked.

"I want to talk to you but every time I do, you find a flaw. It's never right, and I sit here listening to what I should have done, or you correct me. Honestly, it's like you're the parent and I'm your stupid kid."

"I never think like that! All I ever want to do is help you, honey."

"Maybe I'm just sharing and don't require help. I'm so sick of everyone thinking I need to be fixed."

I sighed and said, "Listen. There were empty little cartons of wine in one of the bins I opened out in the garage. That's what I wanted to say." My words were calm but sliced. "From when, I don't know, but it freaked me out to see them. Makes me fucking sick, actually. And I want to be absolutely honest about these things with you."

"So what did you do?"

"Nothing! I'm screwed no matter what I do."

"What do you mean?" he asked.

"I can't just say what happened, how I somehow found wine after all this time, and think for one second that you'd actually believe me. This happened before, you know," I said, looking at him. "I understand, it's hard, and I even thought about putting them in a garbage bag and trashing them without saying a word about it. But what if you found it? You'd probably send me off again. What if one of the kids took out the garbage and for whatever reason they accidentally saw it in there? I mean, shit, what if they found it and kept it a secret? It's too much. I can't live like this for the rest of my life. I can't do it."

We didn't speak. It was just the two of us, sitting with our backs to a brick house where the kids were fast asleep, our whole life right on the other side of a wall.

Pete didn't know what to say or what I needed to hear, and neither did I. It's easy to forget we're on the same side. That somebody else is hurting just like we are. And the somebody happens to be your best friend.

Slow down, I thought. Change is foreign territory, uncomfortable and scary even when it's for the good. If we were going forward, we had to go together, and I wasn't going to drag him.

"I love you," I whispered.

"Emily, I love you too," he said. We stared at each other like we hadn't seen the other's face in such a long time. Me, a prickly cactus that wanted affection, vulnerability I guess, but Pete always knew the way through my thick skin. I saw him, too, underneath the need to save me, to love me enough for the both of us. I reached my hand out and he squeezed it, our fingers intertwining. *Hold on,* it said. Of course. It's what we always did.

I was back at the coffee shop not long after, a steaming cup of Earl Grey tea in my right hand too hot to drink and a dainty Le Pen with pink ink in my left. Looking at the legal pad in my lap, I scanned my handwritten timeline, wondering if I missed something. And still I didn't see the connection. But the more I settled in and let the sounds of muffled conversations fade into the background, vivid memories started popping up in my head. The things I did, my traumatic behavior and the cold-hearted words I spoke to the ones I cared about the most made my stomach turn with emotions. But this time, I felt it from *them.* As if somehow, I switched places and landed across the table staring right at myself. What a horror to sit in on my children's view. I might as well have had a plate of meatloaf and mashed potatoes in front of me.

The truth was I asked the same questions as everybody else did. *What was wrong with me? How could any mother do that to her own children? How could any decent human keep drinking after all the hurt they caused? What the hell was I thinking?*

We got caught up in all the repetition, didn't we? Everyone, me included, stared at the same thing from every imaginable angle for a solution; the way a person moves around a puzzle to get a different view, turning a piece around in their fingers, so sure it will fit perfectly. It was obviously my alcohol abuse. All of us thought, *eliminate Emily's drinking and the problems go away,* which made sense, to a point.

Only then did I see it. Like a bird perched on the ceiling, I looked down and saw strings of addiction that began when I was a child, sneaking food to comfort me. Later, an adolescent overweight, stuffing myself to fill a need that went unanswered, then a teenager and young adult with eating disorders and self-abuse like cutting that required medical intervention. It kept going—co-dependency, distorted eating relapses, self-harm, abusive relationships, but alcohol was the beast that took me down and ruled them all, my last stop, the one that really tried to kill me.

"Sorry to interrupt, but did you want to order something to go? We're about to lock up."

My friend's voice was like a rubber band snap across my wrist. I looked up to a coffee shop closing.

"Oh my gosh, I completely lost track of time," I said, apologizing. "No, thanks for offering, I'm good. You go ahead, I'm leaving right now." I quickly started packing up my things. In the rush, I felt my heart start to pound, knowing what it meant.

Swallow, keep breathing, swallow again, I told myself in a race against time to the car.

Most likely, we've all experienced a cry that suddenly sneaks up and fills the back of our throat, water welling up behind the eyes, a burning in the nose. The urge hit me hard as I stepped out into night. Looking upward, I tried to blink it away, saying, "Nope, we're not going there, I can't do it," over and over. The empty lot was still wet from the rain, glistening from the glow of nearby streetlights and twice I had to leap across puddles before reaching the old dusty Ford Expedition. Frantically, I fumbled through my shit for my keys, then leapt inside, flinging my bags into the back seat with the rest of the mess I called the kids'.

I sat behind my steering wheel and pulled on my cardigan, wrapping my arms around myself. Stubbornness and anger would not pull me through that night, but the car hid me from the outside world like a traveling sanctuary.

I wasn't afraid of crying. My fear was, once a single drop broke loose, the unstoppable flood would never end. But then a new thought came to me. Why not cry? I was right on the edge of it, the irrational notion that would be the death of me felt so real. It was hard to explain how scared I was of emotions or how they showed up all together in a tangled knot of chaos, but time was rushing past me, running in circles outside. I'd been in that spot too many times. *For God's sake, Emily, do something!*

I covered my face and bawled. The flood came like I knew it would, but the fears attached to it vanished right away, replaced by an uncontrollable cry. With concrete weight in my lungs and electricity charging beneath my skin, the sob shook through me until it sounded like a little girl's whimper. I saw nothing in my mind's eye, and then everything.

Versions of myself at different ages during certain times, from a little child to a woman three years ago who I despised, looked directly at me with pleading eyes, and it broke me. I tucked my head into my oversized sweatshirt, wanting to hide myself from sights that this time, I forced myself to see.

The truth is hard. It takes an effort on our part to simply know what it is and remember that once, we were the little girls. I can still see one of them running barefoot across the yard with grass stains on her yellow dress. She rode a plastic hippopotamus with bright blue handles fast enough to burn holes through her little sneakers, and the first fish she ever caught was off a dock in Minnesota, standing next to her daddy. Her name was Emily. I'd cried a million times, over a million things. But I never cried for *her.* How many versions were there, stuck inside, relieved to finally be seen? I could hardly bear it, punching my fist against the seat, fighting my way through it because no one else could do it for me. But I refused to calm the panic and forced my way through it because no one else was going to do it. My body, clenched tight, began to rock back and forth in a natural rhythm.

"It's okay," I whispered, out of breath as the tears subsided. "It's okay, it's okay, you're okay now." It's something a mother says to her own children. I opened my eyes feeling like I'd crawled out of a hole and sat up with a new, firm spine. I grew tall enough to see I wasn't a child but a woman, a coward who found courage by herself.

We are masters at pretending. Dear mothers like me, let's pretend for a second that everyone knew our secrets and none of it mattered. Imagine we woke up in the morning, and it all had been a dream. We got exactly what we wanted with our kids pressed close, resting on our chests in their jammies. We were safe, rested, and settled. I used to wish for a miracle, going over it all the time and thinking if I hung on a little longer with enough faith, it would come. If I did more and went out of my way for other people's happiness, then one day, everything would change. But it wasn't real. Somewhere, I learned that if we said the hidden ugly parts out loud, then the toughest part was over. Sanctified. Mission complete; move on to the next. When in reality, I got it out and discovered the magic trick was fake.

All the cards were out on the table, and now what? To question or oppose a lifetime of information was to open the possibility of eradicating parts of my identity. And I had a choice. Do I play it safe and stay, pruning myself in the impossible quest to fit the mold of current standards? Or do I take a risk and venture out toward an uncharted place beyond American dreams that were never meant for me?

As I drove home, my anxiety withered into a quiet sadness. Maybe it was defeat, the kind where no one really wins in the end, but still, I survived. Against the calming hum of my engine, I stared down the highway at the obscure ending of a war. My mind quieted enough to notice a sudden clearness break through my thoughts. It startled me at first, like some strange phenomenon where life's cacophony hit one harmonious note, and I happened to hear it before it was gone. Unmistakably, I heard "It's time," and couldn't grasp the meaning of any of it, only how wonderfully small I felt in the aftermath. I crawled out of the foxhole I'd been living in and looked out the window at an endless open sky.

Sometimes we change and realize for the first time we are finally ourselves simply because we fit in our skin. Only then did I realize that willingness and an open mind might not lead to where everyone else is going. That truth wasn't absolute, but a canvas of facts pinned like stars into a story infinitely bigger than my own. I didn't really know who I was, mostly who I wasn't, but at that moment those things mattered little to me.

In reality, we are all failing on some level, hooked on something, because pain and suffering are part of this marvelous, heartbreaking life experience. It turns us into seekers looking for our own answers, but no one knows for certain what's going on beyond the grasp of our human understanding. Not until I shifted my view and saw the deepest of love and the lengths I'd go to save it did I grasp how it felt to lose it, the anguish of its absence. To endure the depths of emotional despair meant that I had the same endurance to embrace the greatest joy. That was the beauty of it—to look at all of it, take it in, and realize, I was whole and unafraid. I could do it. I was ready. And it was time.

CHAPTER TWENTY

Finally

A burst of laughter erupted across the living room where the six of us lounged against each other on the massive couch that we bought for this very purpose. I glanced up curious and peered over my readers, entertained on an otherwise lazy Sunday afternoon.

"What's so funny?" I asked, listening as Stella retold a comical story from some family adventure. Her giggling sisters chimed in with details until the laughter was contagious.

"Hang on a sec," I interrupted, "when was that?" I didn't remember any of it.

We paused as a collective look to passed between us until Pete summed it up saying, "Oh."

"Yeah, you weren't there, Mom," Stella confirmed.

"I think you were at rehab," Becca mentioned over her shoulder, causing Spenser to perk up and ask if it was the one with the good cookies.

"Classic," I muttered, a smile tugging on my cheeks, as I picked at colored cloth scraps in my lap. Yes, I was making a quilt.

We'd grown accustomed to occasional run-ins with my past absences, of darker times when Mom was still drinking. The casual acknowledgments were signs of progress, however slow, moving us forward from the fragile feel of sobriety when nervous glances watched my every move and braced for my reactions. The idea we could talk about unspeakable things and nothing bad would happen was new enough to still felt awkward, even dangerous sometimes.

It was an alcoholic home gone sober beyond addiction's eviction, with each person on a separate learning curve, and not everyone wanted to be there. We had spectacular fun with great conversations and on any one of those days, a torrent of sloppy emotions could tumble out between us in a mess of confusion. *What now?* I wondered under the load of responsibility. *Is it puberty hormones and normal stress I'm dealing with, or did I actually ruin the kids?*

And yet, *this* was better.

Middle school and high school replaced the elementary days, trading daily monotony for teenagers toying with independence and Shelby in college nearby. I was Mom, Mother, Mommy searching stages and counting hashmarks on football fields to find my own child in a sea of identical uniforms or disguised in character for a play. Like every parent, we looked for the tiny insignificant clues, a particular tilt of the head or the angle of a footstep, that pointed to the one we've known since birth. I let out a sigh each time I found them. To watch them shine in their own unique talents was everything I ever wanted.

Darkened auditoriums to stadium bleachers under the lights, it amazed me to simply be alive in the experience. Each time I reached out my open palm on the cusp of teary-eyed relief, Pete's loving hand always found it, interlocking with my fingers to hold me in assurance.

I could end the story there.

A quick mention that I never drank again and leave it. Considering it, my pen hovered over the pages, the years, and my gaze drifted out the window to think it over. So much time and energy to get this far, we all could use a happily ever after. Maybe a beach scene like those family photos we took with the kids all dressed in white. A message of hope, a dash of serenity, and my mother's favorite word—gratitude. Because I, too, wanted the satisfaction of knowing it all worked out in the end. Truthfully, it had. It just wasn't what I expected.

Maybe it was a sense of safeness settling my nervous system enough to notice a glitch. I was in the kitchen, 2017, the first time it felt like something was off with my brain. Not mentally but the physical perception of misaligned gears or a mouse caught in a maze. I couldn't reach the words I wanted; they couldn't find their way out of my mouth.

Not a mood or emotion, but the physical feeling of gears gone off track in my head had remained for months after my psychiatrist insisted it was depression and gave a curt comment about brain damage. A neurology appointment that evolved into years of evaluations and another story I never knew existed. Medical doctors gave run-around answers through the lens of my health history and saw a mental patient, then sent me back to psych for another spin on diagnosis wheel. The shuffle of anxiety, mood, and attention disorders was so commonplace that I zoned out listening to my neuropsychiatrist until a particular term came out his mouth.

"Post Traumatic Stress Disorder?" I scoffed. Of all the labeled disorders attached to me that came and went, none topped my embarrassment for PTSD. I was the kid who wrote pen pal letters during the Persian Gulf War because it was too sad to think about the soldier who would not get a letter on mail day.

"What trauma are you talking about anyway?" I pressed, an agitation inside of me even after he patiently explained the conclusive results before moving on to other diagnostics. My scores confirmed significant impairments in memory and cognition.

Pete and I talked a lot about how things changed, often with the tone of two lighthearted romantics. Small things like turning the dining room into a cozy parlor filled with antiques where we sat together saying things like, "Well the tests came back. Apparently, I'm smart, moody, and dumb as a rock. So how was your day?"

Making fun of ourselves and our circumstances felt refreshing amidst our mutual confusion about current situations and also the facts around what happened *back then*. Finally, we decided to get organized and write down a list of events. Pete dashed off for paper and a pen then hopped onto the bed next to me drawing lines across a legal pad in a chart for places I'd been next to the date and columns to mark whether the institution was for psychiatric, detox, or rehab purposes. Despite what both of us remembered, the task took longer than expected.

"Is that the one where a nurse cut up your bras with craft scissors? Took the wires and fasteners out?" he asked me.

"No, that one was later." I grimaced in his direction. But I wasn't sure. "I think it was the place where Spenser literally *ate* an entire pack of gum on your trip to visit me, then threw up pink vomit all over the back seat of the car." A little snicker slipped out after I said it. Pete put his head in his hands and started laughing.

"What an absolute shitshow," he said, and wrote a dramatic checkmark. We scrolled our phones for old calendars and photographs to reference places and once finished, I wasn't sure what to say.

I lived in institutions a total of twenty times. The number astounded me. Eighteen different places, two that saw my lovely face twice, but it didn't seem real. From the comfort of home, how did I feel about it now? How did Pete feel? What would any person feel after reading about that woman? No one asked me what it was like because we're a culture that's not equipped for those conversations. Most people wouldn't know what to say, and even more wouldn't want to talk to me at all. Certain topics made me squirm, too, so it wasn't always as personal as it sometimes felt.

But sometimes it was.

Those trite comments from family of, "Em, get over it, all that's in the past. Move on," in response to things I tried to share about my life like they did. I wasn't living in the past, and even so, I didn't find it off-limits. Over time, the words stung me. No matter how much work I put in going forward, there'd be some who would always hold me captive to an image that didn't resemble the woman in front of them, and likely never had.

So much of it was out of my control. It still is.

People *can* change, and not everyone will accept it. Regarding addiction, dependence, alcohol abuse—all of it bleeds the patience from the ones in our proximity. Progress is not a quick, straight shot. We don't see the climactic reveal after sitting through commercials, and it's a hard day of disappointment to realize a changed person still has flaws like everybody else.

No big surprise, my quilt-making days didn't last. Too much math for someone who measures once and cuts twice, but I hadn't given up yet on the book.

I needed to research and check my facts, it was back to the attic, dragging out dust-covered storage bins from a time we now called "the blue period," as a nod to Picasso's era of blue-toned depressive artwork. Thousands of papers tossed in a mess of thick binders, worksheets, assignments, photocopied PowerPoint lectures no one ever wants to read.

Sitting alone on the floor, I lifted a lid for the first time and started reading. Instantly, the partition between the past and the present became nothing more than a paper-thin membrane I easily broke with a nauseated thud in the pit of my stomach. My familiar handwriting pulled both ends, leaning me in closer to see all I'd forgotten and what I remembered. The facts caught my throat in its grip until a blue whisper escaped. *Oh my God, it's true. It really happened.*

It never occurred to me that fifteen out of those twenty times happened in only six years. I doubt I'd believe it if it wasn't right there in front of me, officially signed and dated by someone in charge. I've never spoken about how it affected me. If someone asked today, I'm afraid I wouldn't find the words. Severed connections from meaningful people left me with a lifetime to wonder *what happened to Nancy? What about Neal, did he make it? Is Janet alive?* It's the hope we all survive haunts me the most because the fact is we don't. I know I shouldn't be alive.

Looking back can be a dangerous endeavor. There's no map or warning for what we'll find. Sometimes the truth can turn us into liars. Answers will only bring more questions. And still we do it, hardly noticing our faulty memories or hindsight's false impression that our lives or someone else's could have turned out better, worse, or gone in another direction.

I was there once with the rest of the crowd believing it's never too late when sometimes it is. We can be anything we want to be, but it's not that way for everyone. The truth showed up and it didn't care how I felt reading another report from a brain MRI or lab work. Some things can't be repaired.

We're used to taking sides and want simple solutions. There's not enough time in our schedules to care about every complicated backstory or the frank impossibility we're on the best side every time. It's too unsettling to look at contradicting aspects of one person, deciding to separate the man as either a military war hero or a child abuser, but not both. The woman was either a devout community volunteer or an angry online bigot, but it's hard to accept both sides of your great-aunt, Susan.

I didn't want to participate when I saw myself doing it. I hated how it felt trying to filter parts of me through the racket of bandwagons rolling through town. I left the entire scene and let out a yawning stretch. No more splitting the narrative of myself between good or bad, right or wrong, a selfish drunk or a loving mother, when the truth had always been I am both sides and much more. I'd rather be whole as myself, whatever it looked like, and show my kids what it meant to be human. I had better things to do with my time.

Somewhere in between, the book I'd romanticized came to life like a cold glass of water tossed in my face. My naïve twelve-month project turned into six years of failing, quitting, bawling, and restarting. The kids kept bustling in and out the door as pages got written and all of us got older. Maybe a little wiser.

I thought I could figure out a reason why it all happened, to crack a code hidden in the details. If I could put it all together in a ribboned bouquet, then I'd have an explanation to deliver. But it turned out my map pins were dart holes missing the point. None of us can hang a universe by our single string and dammit, I tried. I'm the one who ended up with a flower garden by the door, finding reverence for the artist of it all.

There's a part of me that's gone and she's never coming back. I wanted it all to work out and it turns out it did. Life didn't get easier and slow down, but it's me who did those things, free from the burden of perfection. Free from authoritative nit-picking, I dug deeper inside myself for a different view. I hung what I found in a quiet room's window at home and let it be. I traced what I saw between the sunshine and shadows with the slow tip of my finger, following the edges of light so I could write down what happened to me, what happened to us, to so many of us.

The simple idea transformed into a path where Pete and I walk arm-in-arm leading a way out of harmful cycles and patterns for our children to follow. Antique photographs in frames on my wall turned into real men and women connected to me across the generations. It unfolded a reminder that I am simultaneously insignificant and important to something far beyond my comprehension, and it soothed me to know I'm not in charge. The ship won't sink.

The things we hide make us who we are. It's the reason the bigger story matters—not to expose family secrets or make villains and heroes of one another, but to get a sense of what's really going on, what we inherit, and most important of all, what we pass down to our children. The more we bury, the more difficult it is to grow.

I stood outside with goodbyes on my mind hearing God waving

through a breeze, and I pictured Eliza Jane sitting shotgun in her covered wagon on a trail going west. There's no documented reason why they turned around in the mountains of Colorado and headed back for the open plains of Nebraska to start a farm. But I thought I could feel the roots of it. There's always the push to go further. To do more, achieve greater, and I will not submit myself to it any longer. It's not a gold rush. We can manifest whatever destiny we choose.

My world was small and right in front of me. I had my family and a life filled with creative endeavors spread throughout the house. I didn't need to know the ending, because nothing was over.

And goodbyes have never been easy for me, anyway.

ACKNOWLEDGMENTS

To Kristen McGuiness, my editor, publisher, and friend—thank you for seeing something in me and this story from that first draft I sent. Even when kids shouted in the background of our calls, or life handed out a temporary crisis, you never let go of my hand. It means everything to me.

To Jamie, Lauren, and the entire Rise team who turned this book into reality—I still can't believe it. All your time and hard work make me weep with gratitude.

To Pete—thank God I don't have to sum it all up here. Thank you for being the greatest dad and man I've ever known, for being goofy and stubborn and patient and hilarious. Thank you for supporting my wild idea to write a book and the years it took to do it. This process required long talks about things we'd rather forget, but it gave us so much more.

To Mom—thank you for getting sober and loving me through it all.

To my kids—in a way, this book became a love story written for you. Thank you for second chances and uncomfortable conversations. I'm so proud of your courage and the unique, beautiful people you are. It's who you are.

I'm forever grateful for the women who mothered my children in my absence. Kaitlyn, Angela, Mom, Brooke, Mary, Maritza, Lindsay, Tammye, and others, thank you with all of my heart.

Kimiko Miller, who saw a woman in me beyond the title of this book and inspired me to go find her.

My dad who visits me in spirit.

Additionally, I'd like to acknowledge my thanks to the following:

Alateen, Al-Anon, Alcoholics Anonymous, Valley Hope, Fellowship Hall, Holly Hill, La Hacienda, Balboa Horizons, Pavillon, Carrollton Springs, Sunspire, Baylor Hospital of Dallas, Presbyterian Hospital of Dallas, Richardson Methodist Hospital, Garland Hospital, Green Oaks, and other institutions for extending my life one day at a time.

Anna David for sharing her knowledge and experience about the writing world.
Gary Bourland, the best therapist I ever had. And I've had a lot.
Dr. Douglas Smrekar, you were the father figure I needed and never forgot. I think of you all the time.
Krystal, Mikayla, Arielle, Ingrid, Nancy, wherever you are, I love you.
Terry and Debbie Davis
Dave and Mary Schmidt
My brothers
My aunts, uncles, and cousins. Even Danny.
My loving God who knows it all.
The military men and women who serve our country with dignity and honor, and the families who love them.

And finally, Mary Fern and Stella, both writers and readers, who led me to untold stories. What I wouldn't give for another day in their house on Main Street. I know I'm not alone.

ABOUT THE AUTHOR

EMILY REDONDO is a writer, bookworm, and proud mother of four whose articles on recovery and motherhood have been featured by *Love What Matters*, *Genius Recovery*, and *Legacy Launchpad*. Her interests include gardening, camping, collecting antique curiosities, and tinkering with her latest DIY project in her workshop. She lives with her husband, Pete, and their lively household in McKinney, Texas.